To my friend - Bill King

The only way to say thanks for
the trouble to arrange
a get together for us -
with love and friendship -

Harry

Jan. 1991

Steamboats and the Cotton Economy
River Trade in the Yazoo-Mississippi Delta

Steamboats
and the Cotton Economy
River Trade in the Yazoo-Mississippi Delta

Harry P. Owens

UNIVERSITY PRESS OF MISSISSIPPI
Jackson and London

The author gratefully acknowledges the support provided by the following:

To the United States Army Corps of Engineers, Vicksburg District, for permission to use the material he gathered for research, and for material presented to them in his historic preservation reports, 1976–78.

To the Mississippi Department of Archives & History and the Mississippi Historical Society for permission to publish excerpts from his article, "Steamboat Landings on the Yazoo and Tallahatchie Rivers (1875–1882)," in the *Journal of Mississippi History,* vol. 47 (November 1985):266-283.

To the Old Court House Museum, Vicksburg, Mississippi, the Memphis and Shelby County Public Library and Information Center, Memphis, Tennessee, and the Murphy Library, The University of Wisconsin at La Crosse and the Missouri Historical Society for permission to publish steamboat photographs.

93   92   91   90   4   3   2   1

The paper in this book meets the guidelines for permanence and durability of the Committee on Production Guidelines for Book Longevity of the Council on Library Resources.

Library of Congress Cataloging-in-Publication Data

Owens, Harry P.
    Steamboats and the cotton economy : river trade in the Yazoo
-Mississippi delta / Harry P. Owens.
        p.   cm.
    ISBN 0-87805-436-7 : $30.00
        1. Steamboats—Mississippi—Yazoo River—Delta—History.
    2. Inland water transportation—Mississippi—Yazoo River—Delta-
    -History.   3. Cotton trade—Mississippi—Yazoo River—Delta-
    -History.   4. Yazoo River Region (Miss.)—Commerce—History.
    I. Title.
HE566.P3084   1990
386'.22436—dc20
                                                              90-33067
                                                              CIP

British Library Cataloguing in Publication data available

The history of steamboats on the Yazoo River system
is dedicated to the memory of Captain Sherman H. Parisot
and all who steamed under the Mystic P.

Contents

Illustrations   ix

Preface   xi

1 / The Only Way   3

2 / Coming of Age   20

3 / Rendezvous   37

4 / The Yazoo Fleet at War   53

5 / A New Beginning: The P. Line   69

6 / Parisot Fights Another War   84

7 / P. Line Family and Fortunes   99

8 / Yazoo Boats   114

9 / Of Wrecks and Rivers   131

10 / The Long Decline   145

Appendix A: Steamboats   167

Appendix B: Wreck Heaps on the Rivers   183

Appendix C: Yazoo-Tallahatchie River Landings   189

Appendix D: Commercial Statistics   203

Notes   209

Bibliography   235

Index   243

Illustrations

MAPS

1 / The Yazoo River System 6

2 / Railroads in the Yazoo River System, ca. 1905 146

FIGURES

1 / River Trade by Major Commodity, 1890–1928 151

2 / Rafted Logs and All On-Board Freight, 1890–1929 153

3 / Cotton and Cottonseed, 1890–1929 154

4 / Lumber and Staves, 1890–1929 156

5 / Grain, Provisions, and Miscellaneous, 1890–1921 157

Preface

The Yazoo River is unique. There is no other like it. Muddy waters flow relatively slowly through a meander channel that was once the bed for what we now know as the Ohio River. The Coldwater, Tallahatchie, and Yazoo rivers, actually one river and the mainstem of the entire system, form the eastern border of the fertile Yazoo–Mississippi River Delta. Smaller streams and myriad bayous and shallow waterways drain into the Yazoo River from the central Delta. Water from more than thirteen thousand square miles of the drainage area flows into the mainstem river. An early econometric study concluded that a properly developed national water and road transportation system could have been as effective in providing a commercial network as the nineteenth-century railroad system.[1] The Delta waterways offer a chance to test that hypothesis on a small scale, for it may have been that Yazoo steamboatmen of the nineteenth century almost succeeded in developing such a system.

Several years ago the United States Army Corps of Engineers, Vicksburg District, began an environmental impact study before starting work on the Yazoo River channel. Professor Robert M. Thorne of the Center for Archaeological Research at the University of Mississippi, as the principal investigator, asked me to do the archival research for the historical period. Steamboat wrecks and river landings had a high but not exclusive priority. After this introduction to archaeology and historic preservation, I continued research on the history of steamboats on the Yazoo River system.

I intended to gather information so that this study would become part of the historic preservation process. Providing names, dimensions, and descriptions of almost six hundred boats was only part of that process. Efforts to publish with the intent of preserving the archaeological past require presentation of considerable data and specific information. Sometimes the sheer number of steamboat names and dimensions makes it impossible to see the rivers for the smokestacks, boilers, and paddle wheels. I believe that the inclusion of so much detail contributes not only to the preservation process but also to describing the century-long history of Yazoo steamboating.

Discovering and evaluating the role of steamboats in the everyday social fabric of the Delta was equally important. The vital economic function of the river transportation system was a third major theme, and one that was made easier by the data bank preserved and published in the *Annual Report of the Chief of Engineers* from 1890 through 1928. A final theme that was unanticipated, at least in its scope, but that presented an intriguing challenge, involved the entrepreneurs who developed the transportation system. This study is also the biography of one such businessman, Sherman H. Parisot, and a case study of his business, the P. Line. Too often, nostalgia and romanticism flavor steamboat history so that southern steamboat captains and owners have not been viewed as entrepreneurs who helped develop the region's economy. It is time to recognize that rivermen were also businessmen.

Several caveats are in order. Different dictionaries indicate that *sidewheel* may be one word, a hyphenated word, or even two words. It is time to end such pedantry and to decree that *sidewheel, sidewheeler, sternwheel,* and *sternwheeler* are acceptable usages. For readers who may be unaccustomed to steamboat history, the alphabetical list of boats in Appendix A is based on the first letter of the first word or the first initial of a name. This list of steamboats should not be considered as definitive. Undoubtedly, other boats used the waterways, but their names were not in the available records. I will always be happy to learn of other boats.

No historian completes a book without incurring a debt of gratitude to all who provided help and offered suggestions—especially ones who corrected an error or improved an awkward phrase. I owe special thanks to Robert M. Thorne of the University of Mississippi and to Shelia Lewis of the U.S. Army Corps of Engineers Vicksburg District Office for leading me to the richness and variety found in combining history and archaeology. History Department chairmen Frederick Laurenzo and Robert Haws have offered encouragement and given me support for too many years while completing this work. My thanks to Gerald Walton, not only for reading the manuscript, but also for convincing me to stop work on it and to submit it to the University Press of Mississippi. Several people at the University Press of Mississippi have been invaluable. My sincere thanks to the Press's readers who offered positive criticisms and recommendations, to Trudie Calvert for her remarkable ability to spot inconsistencies, and to JoAnne Prichard for her patience. To my wife Mary Lou and our children Rebecca and Charles: thanks for putting up with my impatient disposition when I let steamboats and the Yazoo River become a consuming passion that too often invaded our home.

Harry P. Owens
University of Mississippi

Steamboats and the Cotton Economy
River Trade in the Yazoo-Mississippi Delta

1 / *The Only Way*

The small, 110-ton, sidewheel steamer *Missouri* left her home
port of New Orleans and steamed to Natchez, "Under the
Hill," in February 1830. The *Missouri*'s captain contacted the
cotton factors Broadwells, Fulton and Company, who placed an
advertisement in the local newspaper announcing that the
Missouri would leave on February 17 or 18 for Hannan's Bluff,
which was later named Manchester, and still later Yazoo City. The
advertisement urged those who wished to attend the sale of lots in
Manchester to contact the steamer's agent. On a cool day in late
February, the captain of the *Missouri* gave the orders and the
fireman opened the firebox doors and threw in wood to raise
steam. When the engineer saw the steam gauge rise to the mark,
the *Missouri* backed from the Natchez landing. With bell ringing
and smoke billowing, the steamer turned up the Mississippi River
to the Yazoo country. Businessmen, farmers, and speculators
aboard the *Missouri* undoubtedly talked at length about the pros-
pects for business as they entered the Yazoo River and steamed
toward the new town that would soon be known as Yazoo City.[1]

The *Missouri* was not of great historical significance. She probably was not the first boat on the Yazoo River, nor was she the only
steamer to take buyers to Manchester. The *Walter Scott* commanded by Captain W. B. Culver soon began operating as a "regular coasting trader" between New Orleans and Manchester.
Captain James Shirley of the *Talma* and several other captains used
their boats to remove the Choctaw Indians from their ancestral
lands and returned with speculators. The voyage of the *Missouri*
was just an early incident in the history of steamboats on the
Yazoo River.[2]

More than a hundred years after the *Missouri* steamed into the Yazoo, employees of the Federal Writers Project, under the Works Progress Administration, interviewed "old-timers" and recorded their recollections. An elderly gentleman in Humphreys County, recalling the steamboats, lamented the passing of a way of life by observing that "there remains today little evidence of the old steamboat landings." He capsuled a hundred years of Yazoo steamboat history by saying that except for the hulls of a few wrecks, one would hardly know that the river and steamboats provided *"the only way to the outside world."* 3

Steamboats, whether sidewheel, sternwheel, cotton boat, or elegant packet, provided the connecting link between the sparsely settled, insulated, and isolated areas of the Yazoo and Tallahatchie river bottoms and the outside world. The steamboats brought excitement and perhaps luxury to farmers and townspeople; they brought newspapers, letters, and packages; captains, pilots, and clerks provided the latest news (or gossip) from nearby landings and from the far distant cities of New Orleans and St. Louis. But primarily, the boats served the herculean task of moving bales of cotton and rafts of timber to distant markets and returning with boxes and barrels of foodstuffs, luxury goods, and the thousands of prosaic items needed for everyday life in the rich cotton lands of the Yazoo Delta. The reverberating "puffing" from the tall chimneys, the distinctive whistle, the loud clanging bell announced "steamboat's coming!"

Neither the first nor the last steamboat can be named with certainty. The scarcity of records precludes such precision. The first steamer probably entered the Yazoo River in the mid-1820s. Construction of the *Fort Adams*, whose name was associated with the early history of the Natchez District between the Yazoo River and the thirty-first parallel, was built at Bruinsburg, Mississippi, in 1825 and the finishing touches were added at New Orleans. She was one of the earliest reported boats to steam in the Vicksburg–New Orleans trade, and she was soon joined by the *Helen McGregor* and the *Lawrence*. Perhaps the *Fort Adams* or the *Lawrence* entered the Yazoo River in search of cotton from one of the earliest plantations on the lower Yazoo. The last steamer, except for the Corps of Engineers dredge boats, ceased operations in 1934. One or two small steamers may have remained on the river until World War II. Between the first and the last unknown boats, about six hundred steam-powered boats plied the waters of the extensive Yazoo River system.[4]

The Yazoo is the mainstem of a river system that drains more than 13,400 square miles of rich agricultural lands and provides a thousand miles of navigable waterways during high-water stages. Indeed, the Yazoo River has been described as the "great highway" of the Yazoo Delta.[5] The Yazoo, Tallahatchie, and Coldwater rivers, actually one river with tributaries, form the mainstem river, which flows along the eastern border of the Delta. The Coldwater River rises in northwest Mississippi and had a tenuous connection with the Mississippi River during flood stage by way of Moon Lake and Yazoo Pass. Meandering to the southeast, the Coldwater joins the Little Tallahatchie River, which rises in northeast Mississippi, to form the Tallahatchie proper. This river flows generally southward through a narrow and twisting channel until it is joined by the Yalobusha near Greenwood, Mississippi. The Yalobusha, flowing from the east, provided a water route to Grenada and even to Graysport during high water. The converging Yalobusha and Tallahatchie rivers become the Yazoo, which flows in a meandering arc toward the southwest. The Yazoo River, divided by Honey Island between Greenwood and Yazoo City, forms the west bank of the island, with Tchula Lake, a navigable stream until the late nineteenth century, borders the island on the east. Coming together at the foot of Honey Island, the Yazoo River continues past Yazoo City on its way to the Mississippi River. About thirty-five miles downstream from Yazoo City a series of smaller streams beginning with the Big Sunflower River flow into the lower Yazoo from the center of the Mississippi Delta. Quiver River and Bogue Phalia flow into the Big Sunflower deep in the Delta. The Big and the Little Sunflower rivers are interconnected with Deer Creek and Steele's Bayou by a morass of small creeks and bayous. Steele's Bayou, the southernmost stream flowing from the Delta into the Yazoo, enters the mainstream about nineteen miles from the old mouth of the Yazoo River. The Yazoo, with waters drained from northern portions of the state and from the central Delta, flowed into the Mississippi River approximately nine miles above Vicksburg. During the twentieth century, a diversion canal was opened, which relocated the mouth of the Yazoo to Vicksburg.[6]

The lands bordering the river system could not be settled by

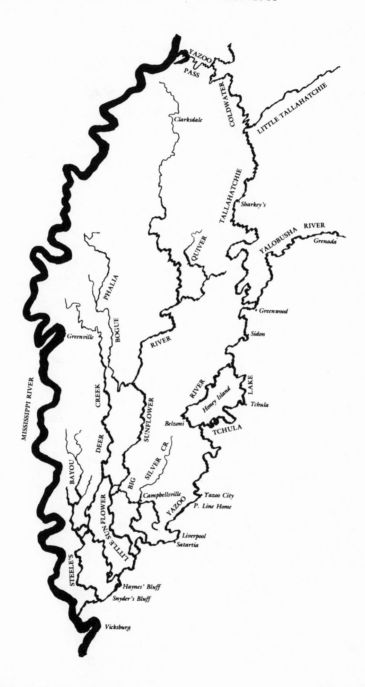

Map 1. *The Yazoo River System*

American farmers until the original inhabitants, the Choctaws, were removed. The Treaty of Fort Adams (1801) created the southern border for the Choctaw Nation near the mouth of the Yazoo River. The northern border, crossing the Coldwater River and separating the Choctaws from their neighbors, the Chickasaws, was established by the English and later recognized by the Americans. The major navigable portion of the Yazoo River system lay within Choctaw lands. The incessant demand for land by Americans in the Old Southwest caused Andrew Jackson and Congress to decide to move the Choctaws to lands west of the Mississippi River.

Two treaties between the United States and the Choctaw Nation opened the Yazoo lands for settlement. The Choctaws surrendered their lands on the lower half of the Yazoo River by the Treaty of Doaks Stand in 1820. The northern boundary of the cession crossed the Yazoo River a few miles above the present town of Belzoni and eventually became the Leflore-Humphreys county line. The United States government surveyed the lands bordering the lower Yazoo River, and when the surveys were completed, offered the lands for sale. Beginning in 1826, land-hungry farmers, speculators, and planters began to buy land along the Yazoo River. Manchester, later Yazoo City, was a result of the land speculation in the cession of Doaks Stand.[7]

Before all the lands were sold, and long before the rich farmlands were developed, settlers demanded that the Choctaws be resettled west of the Mississippi River. The removal of the Choctaw Indians from their ancestral homelands was completed by the Treaty of Dancing Rabbit Creek in 1830. Lands along the Yazoo, Tallahatchie, and Coldwater rivers were surveyed and offered for sale during that decade.[8]

Steamboats plying the Yazoo River in the mid-1820s began to transport passengers and agricultural produce to and from the rich Yazoo Delta. The Choctaws were among the earliest passengers. Five steamboats, *Walter Scott, Brandywine, Reindeer, Talma,* and *Cleopatra,* transported Choctaws from the Yazoo River to Indian Territory. These and other boats not only removed the Indians but brought buyers to the new lands. During the three decades before the Civil War, almost all of the land bordering the rivers was sold. Land titles may have passed through several names before the settler moved onto the land and began the hard work of clearing it.

The promise of great wealth in cotton gave a strong impetus to rapid expansion, and as farms and plantations developed along the river, planters demanded the services provided by steamers. Each farm, plantation, or town established a landing site on the river. The relatively late development of the Delta is indicated by an 1857 steamboat directory, which listed 51 landings on the Yazoo River between its mouth and Yazoo City and 81 landings between that river town and Greenwood. Two decades later, more than 250 landings fronted the Yazoo River between its mouth and Greenwood.9

Steamboat landings were not elaborate. They needed only to be reasonably accessible to both the farmer and the steamboat. A steamboat captain required little more than a clear and safe approach to a gently shelving bank to enable him to nudge up to the shore and lower his stage or gangplank to receive freight or passengers. The farmer needed only a riverbank that was convenient and accessible to his home and barns. The location of landings naturally changed with the water level of the river. During high-water stages a landing might have been a considerable distance from the normal meander channel. Strathmore, the home of Eli Staton on the Tallahatchie River, was a picturesque landing in the late nineteenth century. A tree-shaded lawn offered a pleasant view from the house, which was about four hundred feet from the riverbank. The barns, cotton gin, quarters, and commissary were back of the house. At McLemore's Landing on the Yazoo, the house, cotton gin, commissary, stable, and quarters were only a few yards from the water's edge.10

The steamboat landings became important identifying features of river transportation. Distances were reckoned between landings. Unusual events, especially steamboat wrecks, were reported as occurring "above," or "below," or "near" a particular landing. Steamboat pilots used the names of landings to identify hazards such as sandbars or snags. The names selected, or commonly used, reflect a variety of interests. Most of the landings bore the owner's name, although some landowners gave their farm or plantation or landing more elaborate names.

Some landings bore Indian names such as Chickasaw, Choctaw, Tokeba, Koalunsa, or Inchucka. Indeed, Yazoo, Tchula, Tallahatchie, and Yalobusha are Indian words. Local terrain features provide explanations for such names as Pebble Bluff, Sandy Ridge,

Shell Mound, Riverside, or Island Side. Winter Quarters and an 1870s landing named Freedman's Bureau are indicative of place names representing usage. Distinguishing features such as a particularly large tree or a grove of trees gave rise to landings named Elmwood, Ashwood, Beach Grove, Holly Bend, Oakwood, Glen Oak, and Double Oak. Eagle Bend and Eagle Lake landings may have indicated the onetime prevalence of the now endangered eagle. Wilderness Landing sounds forbidding, but Rough and Ready suggests adventure.

Some names reflected the experiences or hopes of the owner. A. R. Wilson named his landing Hard Times, and Dr. and Mrs. J. H. Lucas, who lost all their property except one small farm soon after the Civil War, named their homestead Last Resort. The names of Hope On, Good Hope, and New Hope reflect a more optimistic outlook. Sherman Parisot went even further and named one of his plantations Success. Golden and Money landings did not reflect the owner's greed but were family names. Lodi, Hidi, Blue Sack, and Over Cup elude ready explanation.

Several planters selected more sophisticated names for their plantations. A sample would include Excelsior, Eureka, Callao, Eldorado, Llanada, Pala Alto, and Alterra. Gandercleugh, Loch Lomand, and Strathmore suggest family origins in the British Isles. Twilight and Silent Shade sound restful and singularly attractive when compared to the noisy steamboats and hot Delta sun. Almost four hundred named landings dotted the Yazoo and Tallahatchie riverbanks by 1880.[11]

Landowners relied on steamboats to bring the supplies they needed to operate their farms. They depended on the steamers to transport their cotton and farm produce to distant markets, and the packets provided transportation when farmers needed to go to the nearest river town or to distant cities. Increasing numbers of steamboats entered the Yazoo waters during the antebellum period in response to the expanding population of farmers, planters, and townspeople.

Almost 250 steamboats operated on the Yazoo River system before the Civil War. All of the known steamers were sidewheel boats except for twenty-two small sternwheel steamers. The sidewheel steamer was not as efficient as the sternwheel boat, but until technical problems were overcome, the wheels remained on the side. The arrangement of the machinery dictated the location of the paddle wheels. The boilers were usually in the forward third of the boat, and the engines, or cylinders, were located in the after third. The cylinders, one to a side, turned the great paddle wheels situated about one-third of the way from the stern. When the wheels were located on the stern, the hull tended to "bow" or "hogback" because of the heavy weight on the stern. This problem of "hogging" was not overcome until the 1850s, when the bow and stern were tied together by chains running above the boiler deck. These chains, often metal rods fastened with turnbuckles, were known as "hog chains." Sternwheel boats operating in the antebellum period were "workhorses" of the river. They were small, shallow-draft boats, which often lacked the prestige associated with sidewheel steamers. Most of the Yazoo River steamers were built according to established designs in boatyards along the Ohio River.[12]

Documentation exists for 172 of the 250 antebellum steamers. Almost three-fourths of these 172 boats were built at boatyards along the Ohio River. Boatyards at the four ports of Cincinnati, Ohio, Louisville, Kentucky, New Albany, Indiana, and Pittsburgh, Pennsylvania, built 129 steamers that served the Yazoo system. Another 17 boats were built in small yards along the Ohio River. Only 26 of the known boats were built in yards along the Mississippi River. New Orleans boatbuilders contributed only 1 boat. No documentation exists to indicate that any boat was built on the Yazoo River system before the Civil War.[13]

Because so many of the Yazoo steamers were built in yards along the Ohio River, they conformed to standard construction patterns. Hull designs of Yazoo boats were practically uniform except for size. These boats were generally described as "low-water boats" and usually measured less than 250 tons. Tonnage measurement for the antebellum boats when computed by the boatbuilders was known as the "carpenter's measurement." The law required that steamers be inspected each year, and the tonnage computed by the inspectors was recorded on the annual certificate of registration. The carpenter's and inspector's measurements often differed. The first Congress of the United States established the procedure for measuring tonnage, and because this system remained consistent throughout the antebellum period, tonnage figures for boats offer a reasonable way to compare sizes. Congress changed the method of measuring tonnage four times after the Civil War, however, limiting the accuracy of comparing tonnage statistics for the postwar period.[14]

The antebellum Yazoo boats varied in size from the 16-ton *Richmond* to the 435-ton *T. P. Leathers*. A few larger boats entered the mouth of the Yazoo, but because they were not active farther upstream, they have not been counted as Yazoo boats. Tonnage measurements for 198 Yazoo boats indicate 51 boats of less than 100 tons and 115 measuring more than 100 but less than 250 tons. Only 32 boats were more than 250 tons, and one of these, the *T. P. Leathers*, measured more than 400 tons.

The smallest of the known boats, the sidewheel steamer *Richmond*, was built in 1833 at New Richmond, Indiana, and she served the Yazoo system from January through June 1836. Before the problem of hogbacking was solved, two small sternwheel boats plied the Yazoo River. Of these, the *Dove*, was on the Yazoo in the "early part of the season" in 1843 and sank on the White River near Elmo, Arkansas, in June, and the *Paul Pry*, which was built in Cincinnati in 1838, sank one mile above the mouth of the Big Sunflower on the Yazoo River in 1842. Another small boat served the Deer Creek trade, and although she was noted by the *Vicksburg Whig* when she reached that port city, the writer described her only as the "miniature steamer *Sportsman*."[15]

If boats of less than 100 tons were small for the Yazoo system, medium-sized boats ranged between 100 and 250 tons. Those over 250 tons might be considered the larger Yazoo boats. Mississippi River steamers were described differently. Boats of the "larger class" on the Mississippi included those of 500 tons or more; those of less than 250 tons were considered "low-water boats." Among Yazoo boats of medium tonnage were the sidewheelers *General Stokes* and *W. P. Swiney*, both of which served the Yazoo system during the 1850s. Captain J. C. Brown brought the *General Stokes* to the Yazoo trade in May 1853, and she was soon referred to as the Vicksburg-Tillatoba packet. At the beginning of the fall cotton season, Captain Brown advertised his boat as a "Vicksburg, Satartia, Yazoo City, Tchula, Greenwood, Leflore, Locopolis, and Tillatoba Packet." The *General Stokes*, measured by the inspectors at 140 40/95 tons, had ten staterooms with two berths each and was licensed to transport fifty deck passengers. Despite her large deck passenger capacity, she had only eighteen life preservers and one lifeboat. The *W. P. Swiney*, measuring 199 57/95 tons, was built in Louisville, Kentucky, in 1853. Her captain, F. P. Pleasants, registered his home port as Vicksburg and was licensed to run from New Orleans to the "head of navigation on the Yazoo River." The *W. P. Swiney* maintained accommodations for more passengers than the *Stokes* and received higher praise from local patrons. She had twenty-two staterooms with two or three berths in each and forty-five movable berths. For safety the *Swiney* carried one hundred life preservers, one lifeboat, one yawl, and two floats. No evidence exists to indicate that these safety features were ever needed. After serving the normal four-year life span for steamers, the *W. P. Swiney* was quietly abandoned in 1857.[16]

Mississippi River steamers of the larger class may have been found in the lower reaches of the Yazoo River, but they would not have operated in the middle reaches around Yazoo City without having been noticed by the newspapers. The largest boat reported by name at Yazoo City was the *T. P. Leathers*. Captain Caleb P. Bennett took the *Leathers* into the Yazoo trade in early 1854 and made occasional trips to Yazoo City during that season. The sidewheel steamer, named for Captain Thomas P. Leathers of the Mississippi River steamer *Natchez*, maintained twenty-nine staterooms with a capacity for fifty-six cabin and thirty deck passengers. She was built in Memphis, Tennessee, and was licensed to run in the New Orleans–Memphis trade.[17]

Although the Yazoo boats varied in tonnage as well as in passenger accommodations, builders constructed the hulls according to the "rule of thumb" that was used in boatyards along the Ohio River. Hull construction became more or less standard by 1840, but significant changes occurred when the sternwheel became the standard arrangement in the 1850s and again when towboats were developed after 1870. Hull design and construction techniques for the wood hulls of mid-nineteenth-century steamers were practically uniform except for variations in length, breadth, and depth. Few boatbuilders ever used models, drawings, or detailed specifications. A potential owner merely named and described the waterway he intended to use, and the builder proceeded to construct a hull proportioned for those waters. Construction required no more sophisticated techniques than those possessed by a master carpenter.[18]

Boats on the Yazoo River system were usually described as low-water boats, with a high ratio between depth of hull and cargo capacity. The hulls were flat-bottomed without keels but with keelsons. The bow was steeply raked to facilitate docking at river landings and for pushing through sandbars. The bow and stern were slightly sheer, and the sides were almost perpendicular to the bottom. The hull contained a series of cross and longitudinal braces and arches which were sometimes planked to form bulwarks. By 1850, standard sizes of three-by-six- or four-by-five-inch white oak timbers were used in the hull. Hull planking was usually two-inch oak, and the main deck was usually made of one-and-a-quarter-inch pine. Superstructure and cabins were made of lighter woods such as poplar or cedar, and on the upper decks the cabin walls were often quarter-inch planks.[19]

The available records indicate that most of the antebellum Yazoo boats contained three decks: the main, the boiler, and the hurricane. The latter supported the pilothouse. Some of the larger boats on the Yazoo may have had a texas, but these were more common on the larger Mississippi River steamers. The hull was referred to as the "bottom" or "hold," and because of the shallow depth and cross braces, it offered little room for cargo storage. Most cargo was carried on the main deck.

The main deck was the largest deck because it extended beyond the hull to encompass each wheelhouse of a sidewheel steamer. The extension beyond the hull was known as the guards and served the structural purpose of supporting the sidewheels. The guards were partially supported by extended deck timbers and partially by stanchions or chains extended from the second or boiler deck. The width of the main deck was determined by the combined width of the two sidewheels and the hull. Few dimensions for length, width, and depth exist for the antebellum Yazoo boats. The hull of the *Stella* was twenty-eight feet wide, and each wheel was seven feet wide, making the main deck forty-two feet wide. In 1860 the main deck of the *Yazoo* was forty-eight feet from "out to out." Her hull was thirty-two feet wide, indicating that the sidewheels were about eight feet wide. The low-water boats of the Yazoo probably had wheels that varied from four to eight feet in width. Mississippi River steamers of the larger class, especially those that were on the Yazoo River during the Civil War, had sidewheels that were fourteen to eighteen feet wide. The main deck housed the boilers, cylinders, auxiliary engines, pumps, fuel storage area, and sidewheels and served as the major cargo deck.

When loaded with bales of cotton, the main deck often touched the water.[20]

The boiler deck, so named because it was above the boilers, was not as wide as the main deck. The height of the boiler deck from the main deck varied but was probably ten to twelve feet on most of the Yazoo boats. The boiler deck was slightly wider than the hull proper but not as wide as the guards, and it supported the main cabin and staterooms. The main cabin, running longitudinally, contained several areas that served different purposes. The forward section often contained an office for the clerks, as well as the bar and men's cabin. The central part was the dining area or was used for dances. The ladies' cabin was usually aft of the sidewheels. A row of staterooms with one, two, or three berths flanked the central dining area on each side of the boat. Doors from the staterooms opened to the main cabin on the inside or to a promenade deck on the outside.[21]

Unlike the floating palaces of the Mississippi River, the Yazoo boats were seldom described in detail. When a new boat reached Yazoo City or Greenwood, the local newspaper commented on its outstanding qualities, particularly if the captain or clerk brought the latest newspapers from New Orleans or Memphis or provided entertainment. These comments usually referred to speed, cargo capacity, or general appearance, but they rarely commented on the passenger accommodations except in the most general terms. Captain P. C. Wallis, a Yazoo captain, entered his new boat the *S. S. Prentiss* as a Vicksburg–Yazoo City packet in 1853, soon after she had been completed in Cincinnati. The editor of the *Yazoo Democrat* inspected the boat and proclaimed its generally excellent appointments and size, and he must have been impressed with the staterooms for he commented favorably on the "spring mattresses and life preservers." Similarly, the writer for the *Vicksburg Whig* noted unusual features aboard the *Dew Drop* when he wrote about the "large staterooms" which were furnished "with all the toilet conveniences." Two years later, after a thorough "repairing and reornamentation," the *Dew Drop* was reported as being "unsurpassed in the taste, elegance and comfort of all her appointments." Her captain, Sherman H. Parisot, earned recognition for his "genial urbanity" and for an "accommodating spirit." His boat, acknowledged as a "universal favorite with the shipping and traveling community," was touted as the "most elegant boat in the trade." Such glowing praise for the *Dew Drop* suggests gleaming white linen on the main cabin tables, with chairs neatly placed and flatware meticulously arranged.[22]

The ceiling of the main cabin was often higher than that of the staterooms, and the additional wall space contained windows, or transoms, which provided light and air for the main cabin. Some of the smaller Yazoo boats, especially after 1850, had a texas on the hurricane deck with cabin space for the officers.

Although comfortable staterooms and gleaming appointments provided an air of elegance, the power and purpose of the steamers was concentrated on the main deck. Boilers, two engines referred to as cylinders, with a series of shafts, valves, and pipes, provided the power to move freight and passengers rapidly along the Yazoo River system. Most of the Yazoo steamers had two or three boilers; a small boat such as the *Dove* may have had only one. Larger boats on the Mississippi had six or even eight boilers. The boilers were located in the forward third of the boat. On the early boats the firebox end faced forward so as to force the draft with the natural air flow. By the mid-nineteenth century, when steam pumps were used to force steam into chimneys, the fire doors were relocated to face aft. The boilers were made of staggered one-quarter-inch wrought iron plates which were riveted and bolted together. The ends of the boilers were cast iron, and the firebox rested on a cast-iron ashpit, which was partially surrounded by firebrick. The firebox grating in Yazoo boats was about three-quarters of an inch thick and about four feet long. The two chimneys on the forward end of the boilers passed through the boiler deck but in front of the cabins. Some of the larger Mississippi River steamers had chimneys that reached ninety feet above the main deck. The smaller Yazoo boats had chimneys that were fifty to sixty feet above the waterline. The sound produced when steam was forced into the chimneys to increase the draft can only be imagined.[23]

The sounds on board steamboats often shattered the quiet Delta days. In addition to the puffing of the chimneys, the bell and steamboat whistle added to the din. Large bells cast specifically for steamers were used by captains to make signals to passing boats and to landings. In 1852 Congress required steamboat inspectors to establish rules of the river, and the inspectors ordered that the steam whistle be used instead of a bell to signal approaching and passing boats. Understandably, captains and pilots developed distinctive methods of using the steamboat whistle.[24]

The two cylinders provided a rhythmic hissing sound as steam escaped at the end of a stroke. The cylinders were located on each side of the boat between the boilers and sidewheels, slightly more than a third of the boat from the stern. The heavy cylinders with brass valves, pressure gauges, and reversing apparatus were bolted to the heavy hull timbers. The cylinder's piston was connected to the sidewheel by the pitman, a squared timber reinforced with metal strips. The pitman was, in turn, fastened to the crank and forged iron shaft of the sidewheels. The cranks were positioned at right angles to each other to maintain a steady power flow. In addition to the two cylinders, boats after 1850 often had one or more small "doctor" engines, which with a short stroke of less than a foot were used to pump water to the boilers, to pump water from the hull, to serve as firefighting pumps, and to operate a steam capstan.[25]

The sounds of steam flowing steadily from boilers to cylinders, with bells ringing, whistles blowing, and captains, engineers, pilots, and deckhands shouting accompanied brightly gleaming or weathered gray boats to landings along the Yazoo River system. The cry "steamboat's coming" announced that the outside world had reached isolated landings. Business began as soon as the steamer's stage touched the landing.

Steamboating on the Yazoo River system was in many ways a microcosm of the Mississippi River trade. The first steamboat reached New Orleans in 1811, and during the next two decades steamboatmen established the procedures that remained in use through the antebellum years. When steamers entered the Yazoo system in the 1820s, they brought Mississippi River practices to the Yazoo. The Mississippi River was divided into "trades," or stretches of river that became the "home waters" or normal trade areas for a boat. St. Louis to New Orleans was the longest trade, but only the larger boats advertised a scheduled run between these ports. The river was further divided as the New Orleans–Memphis trade or the St. Louis–Memphis trade. These subdivisions were divided into New Orleans to Vicksburg or Memphis to Vicksburg. These were divided yet again into shorter distances: Vicksburg to the Bends (Greenville) or Natchez to Vicksburg. The tributaries of the Mississippi were often described as separate trades such as the Red River trade, the Arkansas trade, or the Yazoo trade.

During the early decades of steamboating on the Yazoo, the trade extended from New Orleans to Manchester. As the upriver population increased, the trade became known as the New Orleans–Greenwood trade. Just as on the Mississippi, the Yazoo trades were subdivided. After 1845, the major trades were Vicksburg–Greenwood, Vicksburg–Yazoo City, or Vicksburg–Tillatoba. After the Civil War, the Yazoo was divided into trades between major towns. Yazoo City–Belzoni was one of the most active; Greenwood–Tchula, Tchula–Yazoo City, and Yazoo City–Sartartia were other subdivisions. Vicksburg quickly became the major port for the Yazoo system, and Green Sharkey's Gate or Sharkey's Landing on the Tallahatchie River was accepted as the normal head of navigation. The tributaries formed separate trades: Sunflower trade, Deer Creek trade, and the Yalobusha trade from Greenwood to Grenada.[26]

The trades, whether on the Mississippi or Yazoo, were simply informal designations of a route between landings. Captains would, and often did, take their boats into any trade in search of cargoes and passengers. The depth of the water was the determining factor. Large boats of five hundred or more tons were confined to the deep water of the Mississippi or lower Yazoo. During high-water stages even boats of the larger class entered the Yazoo trade. As the water level dropped, they left the river system. At normal water stages, low-water boats dominated the Yazoo system. The captains of the large boats on the Mississippi River called these low-water boats the "mosquito fleet," because they flitted ahead of the larger steamers and into the shallow tributaries in search of cargoes. Captains of the small boats had no hesitation in going to New Orleans if that city were the destination of their cargo. But more often, they secured cotton in a small trade and then trans-shipped it on one of the larger boats. Most of the Yazoo River steamers were considered part of the mosquito fleet.

Itinerant steamers from the Mississippi River mosquito fleet characterized steamboating on the Yazoo before 1850. Most of the steamers entered the Yazoo in the cotton season, which lasted from November through March. Only a few steamers remained through the summer months. Although seven steamers were reported on the Yazoo River during the five summer months from April through August 1835, only four made more than one trip. During the early cotton season of the same year, thirteen boats regularly entered the Yazoo. Newspaper reports for 1838 are more complete, indicating that twenty-one boats steamed up the Yazoo in January, but only eight boats entered the river system in April. Thirty-two boats served the river system in the calendar year 1838, but only eight were reported as making more than five trips. These eight could be considered to be the regular Yazoo fleet, for some of them also served during the summer months. The *Patrick Henry* was the most active of these regular steamers, according to the Vicksburg newspaper. Captain A. O. Powell of the *Patrick Henry* made one or two trips each week between Vicksburg and Yazoo City during the cotton season. The 301-ton *Bunker Hill* entered the Yazoo trade in 1836 and remained active on the rivers until 1840. She was the largest of the regular traders during 1838 and was exceeded only by the *Oronoko* of 367 tons, which entered the Yazoo trade only once during the year and would not be considered a regular Yazoo boat. Twenty-four of the thirty-two boats in 1838 could be classified as itinerant mosquito fleet steamers. Most of these boats entered the Yazoo system for one or two trips during the cotton season and then followed cargoes and profits to other trades. Twelve boats, ranging from the large *Oronoko* to the 94-ton *Albert Gallatin*, made only one recorded trip into the Yazoo. Most of the boats that entered the Yazoo during the busiest times of the cotton season and then left for other waters were the mosquitoes for the Mississippi River. But the regular Yazoo boats also competed with a mosquito fleet.27

The boats of the Yazoo mosquito fleet were usually small, shallow-draft steamers that ran in the Yalobusha, Tallahatchie, and Coldwater rivers and the small streams draining the central Delta. The *Harry Bluff*, a shallow-draft sidewheel steamer of unknown tonnage, made several trips to Grenada in 1838. The *Big Black* made three trips to Grenada on the Yalobusha, and the *Erin* and *Hannibal* plied Tchula Lake. The shallow-draft steamer *Enterprise* was built in Cincinnati in 1844 and entered the Yazoo trade. Steaming from Greenwood in February 1845, she ran in the Yalobusha River during the remainder of the cotton season. The next year, the *Enterprise* advertised for the Vicksburg–Yazoo City trade and served in that capacity until she was sold to the United States Army. The Yazoo mosquito fleet was indistinguishable from the regular traders except that the smaller boats were more often found on the shallow tributaries.28

The first two decades of Yazoo steamboat history, 1830 to 1850, were dominated by the low-water sidewheel steamers of the Mississippi River mosquito fleet. During these years, the number of boats on the Yazoo increased as the harvest season got under way in the late fall until nine or ten steamers reached Yazoo City almost any week during the peak of the cotton season, and nineteen or twenty boats could be found steaming somewhere on the river system during a four-week period in February and March. As the harvest season dwindled, so did the number of boats, until only two or three remained for the summer doldrums.[29] The competition bordered on chaos as boats raced for cotton and captains and clerks bargained for passengers and cargoes. Yazoo steamboating ended a century later, and with historical or even poetic symmetry, towboats steaming in from the Mississippi River dominated the closing decades of river transportation on the Delta waterways. Between the opening and closing decades, locally owned boats with captains, pilots, clerks, and crews who grew up along the Yazoo River system dominated the rivers and provided the only way to the outside world.

2 / Coming of Age

Yazoo steamboating changed during the last decade of the antebellum period. Although subtle at first and interrupted by war, these changes resumed and accelerated in the postwar years. The slight increase in the number of sternwheel steamers following the adaptation of hog chains was evident by 1860, as was the growing number of plantations along Delta waterways. The two most important changes were interrelated and involved replacing the itinerant Mississippi River mosquito fleet with locally owned boats and the coming of age of captains, pilots, and owners who grew up along the Yazoo River system.

The first two decades of Yazoo steamboating were characterized by boats that entered the Yazoo trade for only a short time. For example, newspapers reported fifty-nine steamers on the rivers during the five cotton seasons from 1838 to 1843, but fewer than one-third of these made more than four trips into the Yazoo. During the five seasons beginning in September 1850 and ending in March 1855, forty-two boats served the Yazoo country, but almost half, or twenty boats, made repeated trips up the river each winter and returned season after season. Thirty-six boats steamed on the Yazoo River system during the three seasons before war interrupted normal patterns in river transportation. All but seven of the steamers running during these three years were locally owned and were repeatedly reported on the rivers.[1]

The decreasing number of boats plying the Yazoo River system that were not owned locally were either small tramp steamers or larger Mississippi River boats which ran in the New Orleans to Yazoo City trade. Several boats illustrate the former category. The *Julia*, a sidewheel steamer of 99 tons, was built at Louisville,

Kentucky, in 1848 and made a few trips into the Yazoo. The *Julia* was reported on the Yazoo for only two weeks in 1851 before she left for other waters. As late as 1856 she ran in the New Orleans–Memphis trade but did not reenter the Yazoo before she sank on the Arkansas River.[2] The 79-ton sidewheel steamer *Major Aubrey* usually ran out of New Orleans but entered the Yazoo in 1855. Although she was advertised as a "regular Vicksburg to Greenwood packet," this small boat apparently made only one trip before returning to her home waters.[3] The *Badger State* of 127 tons was usually in the upper Mississippi River trade, but in 1858 she made a trip to the lower Mississippi River. On 22 December 1858, she left Vicksburg bound for the Yazoo country, but she was not again reported on the Delta waterways.[4]

Several of the Mississippi River steamers of medium tonnage engaged in the regular trade between New Orleans and the Yazoo country during the decade before the Civil War. The 376-ton sidewheel steamer *D. S. Stacy* was built in 1852 to run in the New Orleans–Vicksburg–Milliken's Bend trade, but she entered the Yazoo during the peak of the cotton season. She was advertised as a "weekly packet" running in the Greenwood–New Orleans trade during the winter months. By spring she had entered the New Orleans–Quachita River trade and was not again reported on the Yazoo.[5] Captain George W. Carras commanded the *P. C. Wallis* for her New Orleans owner. This sidewheel steamer of 230 tons, costing $30,000, reached Yazoo City on her maiden voyage in March 1855. During the remainder of the cotton season she ran in the Yazoo City–New Orleans trade before she steamed to Mobile, Alabama, where her new owners, Cox, Brainard and Company, put her in the Alabama River trade.[6] The *Bride* of 295 tons ran for only a few weeks in the Yazoo City–New Orleans trade, whereas the *Col. T. H. Judson* of 191 tons maintained a successful trade between New Orleans and the Yazoo country for three years. Her New Orleans owners must have felt pride in the steamer when she was reported in the Vicksburg newspaper as coming out of the Yazoo River "literally wrapped up in cotton."[7] Many other steamers in the Yazoo River trade were licensed to run between New Orleans and the Tallahatchie River. For example, the *Grenada*, measuring 217 tons with twenty-two staterooms, was owned by Captain Michael Gwartney and others of Grenada, Mississippi. She was too large for the Yalobusha River and was sold to Captain Richard

P. Crump of New Orleans after she collided with the *Mammoth Cave* on the Sunflower River in 1852. Even though she subsequently ran in the New Orleans–Quachita trade, she retained her license to run between New Orleans and Yazoo City.[8]

Other Mississippi River steamboats that were not owned locally built a reputation among Yazoo planters. The *Glendy Burke*, a sidewheel steamer of 425 tons, was owned by the Vicksburg firm of Cobb and Nanlove and later by Captain Jacob Bently of Kentucky. The *Glendy Burke*, made famous by a Stephen Foster song, may not have reached Yazoo City; nevertheless, her captain had a keen eye for business because the editor of the *Yazoo Democrat* often reported the latest news as coming from the officers of the *Glendy Burke*. The *Alex Scott*, measuring 466 tons, also advertised in the Yazoo City newspaper, but there is no evidence that the steamer ever entered the Yazoo River system.[9] The *Compromise*, steaming for New Orleans owners, and the *Sallie Robinson*, owned by Captain Dyas Power of Aberdeen, Ohio, ran in the Yazoo River trade for brief periods in 1856–58.[10] Captain Caleb Bennett, owner and master of the *T. P. Leathers*, steamed to Yazoo City in 1854, but this Memphis-built and owned boat was not again reported by the Yazoo City newspapers.[11] One locally owned steamer, the *Lewis Whitman*, was an exception to the general rule. Captain John S. Wallace of Yazoo City had been master and part owner of several Yazoo boats before joining with Captain B. F. Powell, also of Yazoo City, to purchase the *Lewis Whitman*. This 319-ton sidewheel steamer had thirty-nine staterooms and could accommodate fifty deck passengers. Her three boilers were twenty-five feet long and forty-two inches in diameter, and her safety features included 179 feet of fire hose, twenty buckets, one lifeboat, one yawl, two floats, and seventy-eight life preservers. In 1858, she ran between New Orleans and Yazoo City before Wallace and Powell sold her to a buyer in Mobile, Alabama.[12]

Although a boat steaming between Yazoo City and New Orleans was more consistent with the romantic version of steamboat history, the low-water boats regularly running on the Yazoo River system contributed more to the well-being of Delta planters. During the 1850s, owners, captains, and pilots living in Vicksburg or along the river system began to take control of their waterways. Although the process was interrupted by war, several local captains and owners ran more than twenty steamers during the decade. These men and their boats appear regularly in river town announcements of arrivals and departures, illustrating the trend of consolidating Yazoo River traffic among local owners and officers.

Captain William Moore of Vicksburg served as master of the New Orleans–Vicksburg steamer *Hard Times* in 1850 and occasionally took her into the Yazoo River during the cotton season. By mid-decade he was owner and master of the trim sidewheel steamer *Home*. She measured 183 tons and offered eighteen staterooms to passengers between Vicksburg and the "headwaters" of the Yazoo. Captain Moore ran her in the Yazoo River until 1860, when he took her to the Ohio River for repairs and refurbishing and she was turned "up-side down" during a storm. Moore sold her to a New Orleans steamboatman who ran her in the Red River trade, and himself purchased the *Hope* (193 tons) and reentered the Yazoo–Tallahatchie trade.[13]

During an eight-year period, Captain J. C. Brown of Yazoo City owned and operated five steamers in succession. Brown was master and part owner of the *Volant*, with Milton P. Dent as pilot, when she burned near Cardiff Landing on the lower Yazoo in 1853. She was replaced by the *General R. H. Stokes*, which, although licensed to run from New Orleans to Grenada, was almost always reported as running in the Yazoo and Tallahatchie rivers. Brown commanded her for two cotton seasons before he became sole owner of the *John Strader*. This sidewheeler had been measured at 205 tons, but when Brown lengthened her hull, she measured 235 tons as her captain-owner steamed her into the Yazoo trade. After one season on the Yazoo, Captain Brown sent her into the Arkansas River trade and purchased the small, one-boiler *Creole* for the Yazoo River to run with his other small steamer, the *Roebuck* of 164 tons.[14]

None of the known Yazoo captains was associated with as many boats before the Civil War as John S. Wallace. He first appeared as master of the *Belmont* in 1842. When she sank on the Little Tallahatchie River about fifty miles below Panola, he became master of the *Lacon*, which sank at Oxbows on the Tallahatchie in 1846. The next season, Wallace was captain of the *Laurel* but became master and part owner of the *Jeff Davis* in 1850. After two seasons with the *Jeff Davis*, Captain Wallace commanded the *Sarah*. Having established his career on five small Yazoo boats,

Wallace moved to larger steamers. In 1852, he was captain and part owner of the 287-ton sidewheel steamer *Afton*, which he steamed for four seasons between Vicksburg and the Tallahatchie River. Fire destroyed the *Afton* as she steamed downriver from Yazoo City loaded with 2,160 bales of cotton on a Sunday afternoon in late April 1855. Wallace rebounded from the loss of the *Afton* by joining with Captain B. F. Powell of Yazoo City and former captain-owner of the *John Wesley* to purchase the fine steamer *Lewis Whitman*, which they entered in the New Orleans–Yazoo City trade. After selling her to a buyer in Mobile, Wallace purchased the *J[ohn] M. Sharp*, a 218-ton cotton boat, for $22,000. Only a few months before Mississippi left the Union, Captains Wallace and Powell purchased the elegant packet *Yazoo* of 371 tons, which they ran in the New Orleans–Yazoo City trade before the Civil War.15

Joshua Wiley, although slightly different from other local steamboatmen because he maintained his legal residence in New Albany, Indiana, should be recognized as a Yazoo captain. Wiley came to the Yazoo River system in the late 1840s with his steamer *Tallahatchie*, which often ran as a through boat from her namesake river to New Orleans. According to Sherman H. Parisot, Wiley took his steamer far up the Tallahatchie River during one winter season and was trapped by rapidly falling water. Unable to steam downriver, Wiley dismissed his officers and crew and remained aboard with his wife until the boat could be refloated by spring rains. Weeks later, the *Tallahatchie* steamed to Vicksburg, but her troubles were not over. Roustabouts refused to unload the cotton because every time they moved a bale, hibernating snakes stirred to life.16 Because T. G. Ledbetter, later a noted Yazoo River pilot, began his steamboating career as second clerk aboard the *Tallahatchie*, Captain Wiley should be acknowledged for training local young men. The Indiana captain is also recognized for increasing the importance of the Sunflower River system. His second boat, the *Argo*, a small, one-boiler sternwheel steamer measuring 136 x 21 x 4 feet, was regularly reported as a Sunflower River packet during the cotton seasons 1858 through 1861. Wiley was sole owner of the *Argo* and purchased a half interest in the *Fair Play* just before the Civil War began. He lost both boats when they were in service to the Confederate government.17

While Captain Wiley trained the young Ledbetter for Yazoo service in 1848–49, three other young men completed their apprenticeships aboard Yazoo steamers. In 1840, the census taker for Warren County listed Mary A. Dent, a widow with seven children, as a resident of Vicksburg. She would become the matriarch of three generations of steamboat officers. Her two oldest sons, John and Milton P. Dent, were teenagers in 1840, and after beginning work on steamers, they listed their occupations as steamboat clerk and pilot, respectively, in 1850. Milton was a licensed pilot aboard the *Volant* before she burned in 1853. After serving on several Yazoo boats, Milton and John joined with a third Yazoo man, Sherman H. Parisot, in 1860 to purchase a boat. This early business association between Parisot and the Dent brothers developed into a lifetime friendship.[18]

Sherman H. Parisot, the last of the three young apprentices, began his steamboating career in 1846 and remained an influential figure until the twentieth century. During his long life, 1826 to 1917, Parisot contributed more to the history of Yazoo steamboating than any other individual. He owned two boats in 1860 and lost both of them in Confederate service but returned to the Yazoo after the war and built the Parisot Line before he left steamboating in the last decade of the century. Notable for his organizational skills, insistence on reliable service, entrepreneurship, and especially for a sense of style in steamboating, Captain Sherman H. Parisot was unique in Yazoo steamboat history.

John M. Parrisott, a French veteran of the Napoleonic Wars, settled in Benton, Yazoo County, where he operated a hotel that provided food and lodging for land buyers on their way to Manchester. In 1830, Franklin E. Plummer, a Mississippi politician, used the tavern as his headquarters. Plummer publicly praised Parrisott as "the prince of tavern keepers" and rode off before his astonished host could present the bill to his departing guest. The Parrisott family then consisted of the veteran and his wife, two males under five years of age, and one female not then ten years old. One of the young boys was Sherman H., who was born in 1826, the same year the small *Fort Adams* inaugurated her regular runs between Vicksburg and New Orleans. When the census was recorded in 1840, the "Parrasott" family included two more young boys, Henry and Franklin. Apparently they did not survive to be reported in the 1850 census. Sherman's sister Josephine married Fountain Barksdale, a prosperous Yazoo City merchant, in 1842, and his surviving brother, Amandus Augustus, referred to as

"A.A.," became a hotel keeper, merchant, and large landowner at Belzoni after the Civil War. Sherman, known to his childhood friends as "Sherm," would, in time, standardize the spelling of his family name to "Parisot" and change his nickname to "Shum" to avoid the reminder of the Civil War general who twice invaded the Yazoo waterways.[19]

The Parisot family moved to Yazoo City, where the future captain participated in town life and became infatuated with the Yazoo River. He began his steamboating career while a teenager, and in 1847 he was a licensed pilot aboard the *John Wesley*. Four years later, the census recorded Sherman "Parasott" as the pilot aboard the *Lewis Whitman* when she tied up at Yazoo City. Three years later, Parisot piloted the *S. S. Prentiss* on her record-setting run from Vicksburg to Yazoo City.[20]

The 272-ton *S. S. Prentiss* holds the record for the fastest steamboat run from Vicksburg to Yazoo City, a distance of 110 miles, in 1854. Boatbuilders believed that a long boat was a fast boat, and a long boat had a length-to-width ratio of six to one. The *S. S. Prentiss*, built by James Howard in Jeffersonville, Indiana, in 1853, was 180 feet long by 30 feet wide. Two boilers, each measuring 26 feet by 44 inches, provided the steam for the cylinders that powered the sidewheels with a seven-foot stroke. Captain George W. Carras was master and the young Sherman H. Parisot was pilot when the *S. S. Prentiss* made her record run. Her decks were loaded with wood as Parisot backed the steamer from the Vicksburg landing "at precisely 12m." Trouble erupted on the first leg of the run when the pumps overheated, and the boat was stopped for twenty minutes. Parisot averaged only ten miles per hour on the thirty-five miles between Vicksburg and Haynes' Bluff. But the steamer made up time on the run between the mouths of the Little and Big Sunflower, averaging seventeen miles per hour. With bell ringing and smoke billowing from her chimneys, the *Prentiss* averaged nineteen miles per hour between the Big Sunflower and Satartia. The excited editor of the *Yazoo Democrat* announced proudly that the "beautiful passenger packet, *S. S. Prentiss*," reached the Yazoo City landing "at fifty minutes past six o'clock." According to the editor, "this exhibition of speed proves the *Prentiss* to be one of the fastest boats . . . afloat." The *S. S. Prentiss* averaged slightly more than sixteen miles an hour for the 110-mile upstream trip.²¹ After a successful, albeit short, career as a pilot, Parisot soon became captain of his own steamer.

A small 86-ton sternwheel steamer was launched at New Albany, Indiana, in 1856. Named *Ranger* and measuring less than one hundred feet in length, she steamed to Louisville, Kentucky, and sometime later reached Vicksburg. Perhaps Joshua Wiley, the Yazoo captain from New Albany, introduced Parisot to the *Ranger.* Incomplete newspaper records for 1857 leave Parisot's initial interest in the sternwheeler obscured in the murky waters of history, but he probably purchased the *Ranger* in the fall of 1857 because he was advertising his "new" steamer for the Yazoo trade in January. Parisot built a reputation for running on schedule and offering good service to his passengers. On early trips up the Yazoo, the *Ranger* left Vicksburg for Yazoo City at 4:00 P.M. Monday afternoons and left Yazoo City for Greenwood at 8:00 A.M. Tuesday mornings. The upward run went through Tchula Lake, and the down trip, which left Greenwood at 8:00 Wednesday mornings, remained on the Yazoo. During her first cotton season, the *Ranger* came to be known as a "very reliable boat." Running on schedule through the summer months, Parisot gained the approval of commentators who reported that "the little packet *Ranger*, . . . though small, can accommodate a number of passengers and in fine style." The editor of the *Vicksburg Whig* proclaimed that the *Ranger* was "one of the few boats we can recommend . . . as safe and punctual." Service and reliability remained the keystones of Parisot's long career as a Yazoo captain. With an eye for business, Parisot joined Captain J. C. Brown of the *Roebuck* in a joint contract to deliver mail to Yazoo River post offices. His first year as captain and owner was apparently successful because before the next cotton season started, Parisot had a new boat built to his specifications.²²

Leaving Milton Dent in command of the *Ranger*, Parisot boarded the *William Garvin* at Vicksburg and headed for the Ohio River. He contracted with the Marine Railway Company of Cincinnati for a hull designed for the Yazoo River waterways and with the Niles Works for the machinery. Parisot "superintended her construction," and when she was completed except for furnishing, he named her *Dew Drop* and steamed for Vicksburg and the Yazoo trade. The *Dew Drop*'s hull was 150 x 26 x 4.5 feet and measured 184 tons. Her two sidewheels, 6 feet wide with a diameter of 21 feet, made her main deck 38 feet wide, including guards. Two 18-foot-long boilers provided steam for her cylinders as well as doctor engines for water pumps, freight-hoisting machinery, and steam capstan. Parisot designed the *Dew Drop* to carry twelve hundred bales of cotton and seventy-five cabin passengers. After "furnishing her in magnificent style throughout," Parisot steamed the *Dew Drop* to Vicksburg.23

Parisot arrived at the Vicksburg landing only four days before Christmas and introduced the *Dew Drop* to the public. The local press responded enthusiastically. The *Vicksburg Whig* spelled the captain's name as "Parisott" and pronounced the *Dew Drop* "one of the neatest and most unique boats that has ever been built for the trade." The writer said her hull was "beautifully modeled," praised her staterooms as "large and furnished with all the toilet conveniences," and complimented her captain for sparing "neither pains nor expense in making her a first class passenger boat in every respect."24

The cost of the new boat is not known, but Parisot had to sell the *Ranger* to finance the *Dew Drop*. Milton Dent served as master of the small sternwheeler and also acted as Parisot's agent, selling the *Ranger* to Captain Ellison Ledbetter of Jackson, Mississippi, for $5,000 with the provision that the *Ranger* continue on the Yazoo until the *Dew Drop* reached Vicksburg. The old steamer had served Parisot well, but Ledbetter was not so fortunate, for the *Ranger* "burned to a floating crisp on the Pearl River," near Carthage, Mississippi, a few weeks after leaving the Yazoo.25

With Parisot as master and Dent as pilot, the *Dew Drop* entered the Yazoo trade. The captain understood the value of maintaining good public relations, and when the next season began he offered a free excursion aboard the *Dew Drop* to a large number of passengers in Vicksburg, Yazoo City, and Greenwood. Newspapermen were included on the guest list, and a printer for the *Yazoo Democrat* responded with glowing praise for the *Dew Drop*. He reported that the steamer "ploughed the waters with her accustomed ease and speed," and at "almost every landing" new passengers joined the guests "until the main cabin of the *Dew Drop* teemed with happy faces." The return trip from Greenwood "was accomplished with equal safety and undiminished pleasure," while the "whole-souled Capt. Parisot, always sociable and pleasant," presided as the "embodiment of all that's genial." The clerks added to the "general joy," and so did the steward by "dispensing 'dew drops' to those whose tastes led them to his department."[26]

Parisot continued to operate the *Dew Drop* successfully and acquired another boat in early 1860. When Captain Brown's *Roebuck* sank on the Tallahatchie River, Parisot, with John and Milton Dent, purchased the wreck. After raising the *Roebuck* they sent her to New Orleans for repairs, and when she returned to the Yazoo in April, Milton Dent was master. Parisot and Dent ran the *Dew Drop* and *Roebuck* on complementing schedules during the remainder of the cotton season but sold the *Roebuck* to Captain Andrew Jackson Parmale of New Orleans for $6,500 in October. Just as the *Ranger* was sold to buy the *Dew Drop*, Parisot and Dent sold the *Roebuck* to purchase the *Dixie*. This new sidewheel steamer of 106 tons was 130.8 x 24.4 x 4.2 feet and boasted one of the first calliopes heard on the Yazoo waters. Milton Dent was master of the *Dixie*, and Parisot continued in command of the *Dew Drop*. Both boats remained on the rivers to serve the Confederacy. Dent also purchased part interest in the steamer *Atalanta*, which after a short season on the Yazoo returned to the Mississippi River and was not again reported at Yazoo City.[27]

The Yazoo captains, especially Parisot and Dent, built their steamboating careers by offering dependable service, particularly running on schedule. Earlier packets offering passenger accommodations and freight service and cotton boats without passenger accommodations seldom announced a schedule. Exceptions include the *Joan of Arc*, a New Orleans–Yazoo City packet, which in 1841 advertised three trips a month to Yazoo City but gave no day or time. Captain F. A. Waters announced that his *Belle of Ouachita* would leave Yazoo City for Vicksburg at noon on Tuesdays, Thursdays, and Fridays during the 1845 cotton season. Several years later, John S. Wallace, master of the *Jeff Davis*, advertised that the boat would leave Yazoo City at noon on Mondays, Wednesdays, and Fridays bound downstream for Vicksburg. Most boats with announced departure time in the Vicksburg newspapers left that port for the Yazoo country in the late afternoon to arrive at Yazoo City in the early morning. Parisot and Dent, steaming the *Dew Drop* and *Dixie* in a concerted schedule, provided the most dependable service of any antebellum boats. When other steamers were delayed to complete a cargo or by fog, low water, or accident, Parisot's dependability generated business for his Yazoo boats.[28]

As businessmen, steamboat captains and clerks wanted to move cotton, merchandise, and passengers at a profit. Antebellum records provide little information about operating costs. A Mississippi River steamer of 325 tons reported monthly expenses of more than $2,000. The captain, pilots, and mates received $615, and twenty-four crewmen, including engineer, firemen, deckhands, stewards, and cook, earned $1,140. A steamer of this size burned as much as twenty-four cords of wood a day, at a cost of $3 to $4 per cord. Because the cotton trade was highly competitive, freight rates varied with the season, the size of the crop, and the number of boats bidding for it. The charge in 1840 for a bale of cotton shipped to New Orleans from Memphis was $2; the rate from Vicksburg was $1.50, and from Natchez, $1.00.[29]

Expenses for the smaller Yazoo boats were lower. A 150-ton boat operating on the Yazoo and Tallahatchie rivers normally had a captain, a mate, two pilots, an engineer and his assistant, and twelve deckhands. Packets also had a cook and one or more stewards. Fine packets such as the *S. S. Prentiss* or *Dew Drop* would also have one or two young men as clerks. Mississippi River pilots earned $200 a month, but Yazoo pilots were paid $150. Freight rates on the Yazoo system during the antebellum period are virtually unknown, but one may make inferences from a later period. Rates per bale of cotton from Greenwood to Vicksburg were about the same as from Vicksburg to New Orleans. Rates from the Tallahatchie River landings were higher, and from Yazoo City they were correspondingly lower. It cost $3 to send a bale of cotton from Greenwood to New Orleans and $1.50 from Greenwood to Vicksburg in 1881. Whiskey was shipped from Vicksburg to Yazoo City at $1 a barrel, dry barrels cost 25 cents, and sacks went for 15 cents in 1877.[30]

Antebellum cargoes were seldom reported in river town newspapers. The *Creole* was an exception, for she was advertised in 1831 as having a capacity of a thousand bales of cotton. A few years later, the editor of the *Yazoo City Whig* noted that "five small boats," ranging from 63 to 116 tons, steamed on the Yazoo and that each could transport three hundred to six hundred bales. The five small boats that were regularly reported during the fall of 1845 were the *Maid of Osage, Lucy Long, Wabash Valley, Enterprise,* and

Hatchie Eagle. The *Unicorn* was loaded with fifteen hundred bales when she burned on the Yazoo River in 1855. The cotton boat *J. M. Sharp* had a capacity of eighteen hundred bales of cotton, and the *Dew Drop* carried twelve hundred bales. The steamers serving the Yazoo River system before the Civil War transported thousands of bales of cotton from the river country to the market centers at Vicksburg, Memphis, and New Orleans and returned with smaller loads of merchandise.31

Just as steamers provided the only means of moving large cargoes swiftly to outside markets, they also provided the fastest and least expensive means of bringing manufactured goods to farmers and merchants. Only in rare instances when river transportation charges were so expensive did merchants resort to wagon trains. During the early fall of 1854, when the Mississippi River was at a low-water stage, the water rushing from the Yazoo River created such a strong current that boats could not get back into the Yazoo. The sidewheel steamer *W. P. Swiney* unloaded cotton near the mouth of the Yazoo because her captain, F. P. Pleasants, was "fearful that if she gets out she cannot return." The more efficient sternwheel steamer *Ben Lee* had enough power to breast the current. Captain R. Kinman, realizing that his was the only boat capable of going to Vicksburg and returning, raised his freight rates. Merchants in Yazoo City complained that the *Ben Lee* charged such "enormous freight rates" that they could not profitably patronize her. Instead, many merchants found it "cheaper to have their goods brought by wagon." 32

Such exceptional charges were rare, and merchants depended on steamers for their wares. Boats entering the Yazoo during the early cotton season came loaded with barrels and crates containing all kinds of manufactured goods. Captain Joshua Wiley and his young clerk, T. G. Ledbetter, must have observed with both pleasure and impatience as a large shipment for Wolfe and Dwight of Yazoo City was loaded on board the *Tallahatchie* at the Vicksburg landing. A partial list of goods in the shipment included St. Louis flour, Connecticut River shad, coffee, "gunpowder tea," sugar, sperm candles, sperm oil, nails "of all sizes," Procter and Gamble's "best brown soap," and "very superior old bourbon monongahelia [sic] whiskey." The steamer *Mammoth Cave* also brought dried beef, cider, vinegar, hams, lime, and cement to Wolfe and Dwight. The large steamer *St. James* unloaded "33 barrels copper distilled whiskey" for J. V. Caldwell, and the steamer *Sarah* brought "french corsetts," ladies' walking shoes, hats, capes, ginghams, and silks to Nunnally and Company. Gin stands, wagons, buggies, guns, gunpowder, patent medicines, window glass, and "surgical and dental instruments" were for sale in Yazoo City. All came by steamboat.[33]

Steamboating was not an easy life. The cotton season began in the late summer or early fall and reached its peak in the cold winter months of December and January. Trips up the Tallahatchie in January could be cold and wet, with ice and an occasional snow making the decks slippery and dangerous, but the steamers plied the waters for cotton as long as visibility was good. Moonlight made it possible for steamers to make their way slowly at night. But during cloudy or rainy nights, the steamers slowed to a crawl or tied up for a short time. Fog was the most dangerous condition for steaming. Visibility was limited, and in heavy fogs the sounds of approaching boats were muted, creating danger of collision.

Storms could play havoc with boats. Even when tied to a secure landing, boats sometimes suffered damages. Two Mississippi River steamers, *Kentucky* and *Mary T.* along with three Yazoo boats, the *Argo, Dew Drop,* and *Cotton Plant,* were tied to the wharfboat at Vicksburg when winds blew at gale strength in the late afternoon of 6 July 1860. The wharfboat broke loose and carried the *Kentucky, Mary T., Argo,* and *Dew Drop* downstream. The *Cotton Plant* was "lying just below the landing" when a loaded coal barge broke her moorings and drifted heavily toward the steamer. The barge "was driven against her with such force as to almost cut her in two forward of the wheel house." The severely damaged *Cotton Plant* "drifted down a short distance," and as her hull filled with water, she "careened over and sank almost out of sight." In the meantime, the crew of Parisot's *Dew Drop* raised steam and rushed to tow the *Kentucky* out of danger. The *Argo,* with steam up by this time, was spewing sparks, some of which landed on the upper works of the *Dew Drop* and started a small fire. But no serious damage was done before it was put out. As soon as the weather cleared, crews worked to raise the *Cotton Plant.* Within a week, the editor of the *Vicksburg Whig* triumphantly reported that the "*Cotton Plant* was up." The hull was quickly repaired, and by late August the *Cotton Plant* returned to the Yazoo–Sunflower trade.[34]

Bad weather caused temporary delays, but low water could idle the Yazoo boats. Faced with a scarcity of water and cargoes, many Yazoo captains tied up for the summer or used the slack season to repair and refurbish their boats. The few boats that continued to run in the summer faced the difficulties and dangers of low water. The steamer *Afton, Jr.* had a "good load" of cotton but was trapped above the Satartia bar in 1858. With only three and a half feet of water covering the bar, the *Afton, Jr.* was reported as "scuffling unsuccessfully for thirty-six hours" before the deckhands ferried the cotton bales to the nearest shore. When the boat was light enough, the *Afton, Jr.* crossed the bar and the cotton was re-loaded.35

Low water brought more than inconvenience and lost profits. Snags of stumps and sunken logs became especially dangerous when the water level fell. Exposed snags provided little danger except for the unwary, but unknown logs and heavy limbs of fallen trees, safely passed in normal boating conditions, were much closer to the surface in low water and created hidden hazards. The jagged end of a sunken log could break through the thin wooden hulls. Limbs could tear off the planking or damage the wheels. Many boats, after ramming a snag, managed to reach shallow water, where the hull was repaired as quickly as possible. One of the earliest reported wrecks involved the steamer *Veteran.* She ran onto a snag a few miles above Manchester in 1835 but was re-paired, pumped out, cleaned up, and put back in service in less than two weeks. The *Alice Maria* was snagged at the same time but was back in service in only a few days. The *Gladiator* was one of the earliest total losses on the Yazoo. She was in the trade during the cotton season 1837–38 and hit a snag just below Liverpool Landing on the lower Yazoo while on her run from Greenwood to Vicksburg. The *Gladiator* sank and was abandoned in January.36

The extant records indicate that at least twenty-eight ante-bellum steamboats found watery graves in the Yazoo River sys-tem. Many others sank but were raised, repaired, and put back into service. Perhaps other boats, unreported in surviving records, sank in the rivers, but of the twenty-eight reported wrecks, twelve were recorded as "sank," or "abandoned" without further descrip-tion.37 These boats may have hit snags or sandbars so hard that the timbers were damaged beyond repair and the captains beached them. Finding that repairs were impossible, they abandoned the hulls after salvaging as much as possible of the cargo, machinery, and accoutrements. The *W. N. Sherman* sank in Tchula Lake in 1855 but was raised and ran again. Within six weeks, while "boundup" from Vicksburg, she sank in ten feet of water below Satartia. The boat was considered a "total loss" after the cargo was saved. Captain Joseph M. Hendricks's light draft steamer, *U.S. Aid*, sank "just below Tchula" on Tchula Lake. Abandoning the old hull, Hendricks salvaged the machinery and built a new hull for the old boilers and engines. The *Bluff City* was about five years old when she was declared "stranded" and was soon abandoned. The wreck was sold to "Mr. White, the wrecker," for $1,200.[38]

Snags claimed at least eight steamers before the Civil War, but few of these wrecks proved to be total losses. The *Jeff Davis* hit a snag and sank "a short distance below Satartia" in 1850. A few weeks later, she was raised and repaired, then offered for sale. The sidewheel steamer *Muscle No. 2*, while making a trip from Vicksburg to Greenwood, hit a snag and sank "100 yards above the mouth of the Little Sunflower." She sank in fourteen feet of water and was considered a total loss except for the machinery. The *James Jacobs* and the small sternwheel steamer *Wagoner* of just forty-three tons sank on the Yalobusha River below Grenada. Only one steamer was lost because of a collision. The *Mammoth Cave* was rammed by the *Grenada* and sank on the Little Sunflower River in 1852, but she was raised and was again on the Yazoo River for the summer and fall months.[39]

Many of the boats that were snagged were raised and repaired, and others that sank were abandoned because of age and the need for extensive repairs, but boats that burned were total losses except for parts of the machinery that could be salvaged. Only four antebellum boats were reported as having burned: the *Afton*, *Texana*, *Unicorn*, and *Volant*. Captain J. C. Brown, former master of the *Vicksburg*, owned the *Volant* when she caught fire from a "broken jug of wine" and sank "below Cardiff" on the lower Yazoo River. The *Unicorn* was heavily loaded with 1,500 bales of cotton when she burned near Salem Landing about fifteen miles south of Yazoo City. The largest of the antebellum wrecks was the 348-ton *Texana*, formerly the *Franklin Pierce*, which burned near Chickasaw Bayou in 1855. The *Afton* was loaded with 2,160 bales of cotton when fire broke out while she was "about halfway between this place [Vicksburg] and Yazoo City." Captain John S. Wallace beached her on the lower end of Belcher's Bar but was unable to contain the fire. The "boat and cargo were entirely destroyed," but no lives were lost.[40]

The word *Yazoo* is most often translated as "river of death," but the history of the antebellum steamboats on the Yazoo River suggests that the river did not live up to its reputation.[41] The extant records reporting that only 28 of more than 250 steamboats were damaged beyond repair indicate that the river claimed less than 15 percent, while the steamboats had a better than 85 percent survival rate. The Civil War changed that record.

The last cotton season before the Civil War reflected the increased role of locally owned and operated boats. Existing records show that fourteen steamers served the river system between the election of Abraham Lincoln in November 1860 and the Confederate bombardment of Fort Sumter the following April. All but two of the fourteen were locally owned and operated. Captain Charles V. Wells of Sistersville, Virginia, built the 343-ton sidewheel steamer *Planter* for the New Orleans–Yazoo River trade. She entered the Yazoo for one or two trips before her captain took her to Mobile, Alabama. The *Col. T. H. Judson*, which steamed in the New Orleans–Yazoo City trade for three years, was taken out of the trade before the season ended and her owner, Mary Hiern of New Orleans, put her in Confederate service.

Two locally owned boats left the Yazoo before the season ended. Captain E. S. Butler of Vicksburg operated the *Prince*, which had been on the Yazoo for several previous winters, but he replaced her with the *Anna*, which he ran for the remainder of the season. Butler soon sold the *Anna* to Captain John W. Cannon, who owned two other boats steaming in the New Orleans–Vicksburg trade. Cannon sent the *Anna* into the Red River, where she ran between Shreveport and Alexandria as late as 1863. The remaining ten boats served the Yazoo system and the Confederacy.[42]

At the beginning of the last cotton season before war erupted, Captain Parisot, who was regarded as "one of the most competent and favorable known officers in the Yazoo River trade," prepared the *Dew Drop* for a busy season. The steamer, when completed, was "unsurpassed in the taste, elegance and comfort of all her apartments," and her "popular and courteous" captain entered the Yazoo for his last prewar season.[43] Milton P. Dent and his brother John steamed the *Dixie* in concert with the *Dew Drop*.

Recovering from the summertime loss of the *Home*, Captain William Moore entered his boat *Hope* on a regular schedule between Vicksburg and Yazoo City. This "beautiful little boat, of graceful appearance," was such a favorite in Yazoo City that a group of citizens chartered her for the July Fourth celebration in 1860.44 Captain J. C. Reives of Vicksburg commanded the *Charm* during the cotton season, and Joshua Wiley, the Indianian, ran the *Argo* and the *Fair Play* in the Vicksburg–Sunflower River trade. Frank Johnson, master and owner of the *Emma Bett*, was reported on the Sunflower and occasionally as running far up the Tallahatchie River during this last season before war. The little *Cotton Plant* regularly returned to Vicksburg from Deer Creek or the Sunflower waterways, and Captain John Wallace pushed his cotton boat, *J. M. Sharp*, to pick up waiting cargoes on the Yazoo and Sunflower rivers. The large sidewheel steamer *Yazoo*, running with John Wallace and B. F. Powell as joint owners, often completed her load by receiving Sunflower cotton from the *J. M. Sharp*. With a full load, Captain Wallace took the *Yazoo* to Vicksburg and then to New Orleans.45

Mississippi seceded from the Union at the peak of the cotton season, and a month later delegates from the state participated in organizing the Confederate government at Montgomery, Alabama. Before all the cotton was moved out of the Yazoo basin, the boats flew the flag of the Confederacy. Perhaps the captains celebrated, influenced by the euphoria of the moment. Undoubtedly they tried to anticipate the effect that such a momentous event would have on their lives, their trade, and their boats. As they settled into the summer routines in 1861, they could not have envisioned that within twenty-four months all of their boats would be destroyed.

3 / Rendezvous

The *Hope*, whose name reflected Confederate expectations for the future, made her way down the Yazoo carrying the "good news" that "Fort Sumter had been taken" by Confederates. Morale was high the next week when a recently organized military company boarded the *Hope* at Yazoo City bound for Vicksburg. Enthusiasm was evident along the Yazoo and aboard the steamers moving up and down the river system with the latest news. As Captain Reives passed Satartia aboard his steamer *Charm*, he fired a cannon in honor of the home guard drilling on the high ground. But slowly exuberance gave way to concern about rising floodwaters, which had destroyed part of the corn crop and had delayed cotton planting. Indeed, as the summer ended and the harvest season began, Yazoo steamboat commerce did not reflect the normal frenzy of getting the crop to market.[1]

Throughout the cotton season that began in 1861 and ended the following spring, few boats from the Yazoo or even Vicksburg steamed to New Orleans. Indicative of reduced activity, the New Orleans–Coast trader *Lafourche* was the one boat most often reported as steaming between Vicksburg and New Orleans. Fine steamers of the larger class such as the *Natchez, Mary E. Keene*, or *Prince of Wales* stopped at Vicksburg during their runs between Memphis and New Orleans, but they loaded small cargoes at the Mississippi port city. Of the locally owned boats, the *Charm* made only two or three runs to New Orleans during the early fall and was not again reported at the Crescent City. In early December Parisot advertised that the *Dew Drop* would connect with the New Orleans boat *Mary T.* at Vicksburg, but he soon discontinued advertising. During January and February 1862, the *New Orleans*

Picayune rarely mentioned a Vicksburg boat and none from the Yazoo. The extant records suggest that quiet had settled over the Yazoo country. Floods, low crop yields, individual decisions to hold cotton for more certain times, or new markets offered by the Confederate government or the Quartermaster Department may help explain the decline in steamboat activity during the 1861–62 cotton season. As peach trees began to blossom, even in a distant orchard near Shiloh Church in Tennessee, the Yazoo River system began to experience the war at first hand.[2]

Two Union flotillas and three Confederate squadrons met in separate rendezvous between early April and 1 July 1862. Forty-one steamboats flying the Confederate flag, never designated as squadrons but in three distinct groups, converged on the Yazoo River. The ten boats regularly on the Yazoo formed one group bound together, at least in the beginning, because of being on their home waters. As the days passed, twenty-three privately owned Mississippi River steamboats from New Orleans to Memphis varying in size from the eighty-ton *Ben McCulloch* to the eight-hundred-ton *Natchez* sought sanctuary on the Yazoo River. The third group of eight Confederate government boats ranging from the little *St. Mary* of forty tons to the oceangoing steamer *Star of the West* measuring almost twelve hundred tons entered the Yazoo River before the end of June. These forty-one steamboats constituted the Confederate Yazoo Fleet, and they were bound to the Confederacy, if not by official designation, through national loyalty, self-interest, and circumstances.

The Confederate Yazoo Fleet began to gather in April 1862, when David G. Farragut, USN, anchored his West Gulf Squadron at the New Orleans waterfront. Later, when he took the Union flotilla up the Mississippi River to Vicksburg, steamboats that were once part of the lower Mississippi River cotton trade raced for safety. Some of these steamers found temporary refuge in the Louisiana bayous; others went into the Red, Arkansas, White, or Yazoo rivers. Still other boats that had been impressed into Confederate service steamed up the Mississippi River as government transports, supply boats, and makeshift gunboats to meet Commodore Charles Davis's Union flotilla of ironclads and rams, which was preparing to break through the Confederate defenses at Island No. 10 far upstream from Vicksburg. Even before the Yazoo Fleet completed its rendezvous, Confederate authorities, acting under orders of General Leonidas Polk, impressed the *Yazoo* into Confederate service. The *Yazoo* became the first casualty of the Yazoo Fleet when she was destroyed at Island No. 10 in April. As Commodore Davis's Federal flotilla continued down the Mississippi River, Confederate gunboats under the command of Captain James E. Montgomery met them in the Battle of Memphis on 6 June. Only one Confederate gunboat, the *General Earl Van Dorn*, escaped to make her way into the Yazoo River as the last boat to join the Yazoo Fleet. When the *Van Dorn* entered the Yazoo, the Confederate rendezvous was complete.[3]

The last stage of the Union rendezvous began. Charles Davis remained at Memphis with his Mississippi River Squadron for several weeks before sending part of his flotilla into the Arkansas River system. In a separate movement, Lieutenant Colonel Alfred W. Ellet, commanding the rams attached to Davis's flotilla, reached the mouth of the Yazoo River nine miles above the Confederate stronghold at Vicksburg on 24 June 1862.[4] Six days later, Farragut ran his fleet past the Vicksburg batteries and on 1 July joined Davis and Ellet a few miles from Vicksburg. Shelby Foote described this rendezvous as being as though the "upper and nether millstones had come together at last, and now there was not even grist between them."[5]

Forty steamers found sanctuary on the Yazoo River system. The thirty-two privately owned steamers in the Yazoo Fleet were some of the newest and best of the peacetime packets. Although the normal life of a Mississippi River steamboat was about five years, nineteen of the Yazoo boats were only one or two years old or had been thoroughly overhauled for the 1861 cotton season. Three boats were built in 1858, two each year in 1856 and 1857, and three in 1855. The *Capitol*, built in 1854, was the oldest steamer on the rivers. These privately owned steamers, with a total tonnage of more than thirteen thousand tons, may be divided into three categories according to size. Ten boats measuring less than two hundred tons each are considered small boats; seven boats that measured between two hundred and five hundred tons have been designated as large steamers. The remaining thirteen boats, each measured at more than five hundred tons, are regarded as "boats of the larger class," a designation often used for the largest of the Mississippi River steamboats. All of the steamers on the Yazoo River system were sidewheel boats except the three small stern-

The Confederate Yazoo Fleet

NAME	RIG	TONS
Acadia	SW	343
Alonzo Child	SW	493
Argo	StW	99
Arkansas, CSS		
Ben McCulloch	StW	80
Capitol	SW	448
Charm	SW	223
Cotton Plant	SW	180
Cotton Plant	SW	59
Dew Drop	SW	184
Dixie	SW	106
Edward J. Gay	SW	824
Emma Bett	StW	79
Fair Play	SW	162
Ferd Kennett	SW	591
General Earl Van Dorn	SW	524
General Polk	SW	390
Golden Age	SW	250
H. D. Mears	SW	338
Hartford City	SW	150
Hope	SW	193
Ivy	SW	454
J. F. Pargoud	SW	523
J. M. Sharp	SW	229
John Walsh	SW	809
Livingston	SW	680
Magenta	SW	768
Magnolia	SW	824
Mary E. Keene	SW	659
Mobile	SW	282
Natchez (No. 5)	SW	800
Paul Jones	SW	353
Peytona	SW	653
Prince of Wales	SW	572
R. J. Lackland	SW	710
Republic	SW	699
St. Mary	SW	40
Scotland	SW	567
Star of the West	SW	1172
Thirty-Fifth Parallel	SW	419
Yazoo	SW	371

Key: SW = Sidewheel
StW = Sternwheel

DIMENSIONS (FT.) (l x w x d)	APPRAISED VALUE	DISPOSITION
188 x 35 x 7		Scuttled at Greenwood on the Yazoo River
222 x 36 x 6.5	$ 35,000	Scuttled at Snyder's Bluff
136 x 21 x 4		Burned up the Sunflower River
165 x 35 x 18		Exploded on the Mississippi River
100 x 22 x 3.9	42,500	Burned on Tchula Lake
224 x 32 x 6	25,000	Scuttled at Liverpool Landing
		Destroyed on the Big Black River
158 x 31 x 6.5		Burned on the Tallahatchie River
		Scuttled on Lake George
150 x 26 x 4.5	60,000	Burned on Quiver River
130 x 24 x 4.2		Ordered to the Red River
277 x 39 x 8.5	150,000	Destroyed at Greenwood
		Destroyed up the Sunflower River
139 x 27 x 4.7	25,000	Captured on the Mississippi River
238 x 40.5 x 6.5	150,000	Destroyed near Greenwood
182 x 28.3 x 10.7		Exploded at the Liverpool raft
180 x 35 x 8		Burned at the Liverpool raft
180 x 32 x 6.5	75,000	Scuttled at Southworth's Bar
214 x 34 x 5.5		Destroyed up the Sunflower River
		Destroyed near Greenwood
145 x 26 x 4.5		Burned up the Tallahatchie River
191 x 28 x 9		Scuttled at Liverpool
243 x 38 x 8	200,000	Burned near Yazoo City
147 x 29 x 8		Destroyed on the Yalobusha River near Greenwood
275 x 38 x 8		Scuttled at Southworth's Bar
180 x 40 x 9.5		Burned at the Liverpool raft
268 x 40 x 8.5	250,000	Burned above Yazoo City
275 x 40 x 8.5	180,000	Burned above Yazoo City
235 x 38 x 8.5	240,000	Burned at French Bend on the Yazoo River
		Destroyed at the Confederate Navy Yard, Yazoo City
290 x 40 x 10	225,000	Burned near Belzoni on the Yazoo
172 x 34 x 6.5		Destroyed on the Big Black River
268 x 38 x 8.5	150,000	Burned above Yazoo City
248 x 40 x 7		Burned above Yazoo City
275 x 40 x 7	100,000	Scuttled at Southworth's Bar
249 x 40 x 7.5	25,000	Destroyed at the Confederate Navy Yard, Yazoo City
89.6 x 15 x 5		Captured near Yazoo City
225 x 38 x 7.5	60,000	Scuttled at Southworth's Bar
		Scuttled on the Tallahatchie River near Fort Pemberton
	70,000	Burned up the Tallahatchie River
178 x 33.5 x 6.5	75,000	Destroyed at Island No. 10. on the Mississippi River

wheelers, *Argo, Emma Bett,* and *Ben McCulloch.*[6] See table for a list and description of the boats in the Yazoo Fleet.

The ten small boats most often, but not always, steamed on the Sunflower River and the tributaries that penetrated the central Delta. The *Dew Drop* and *Dixie* with the *Argo* and *Emma Bett* occasionally steamed into Bogue Phalia and Quiver River in search of cargoes. Two boats bore the name *Cotton Plant.* The larger one, of 180 tons, formerly named *Flora Temple,* operated around Greenwood and steamed into the Yalobusha and Talla-hatchie rivers; the 59-ton *Cotton Plant* sank on Lake George. The *Hartford City* and *Ben McCulloch* found work around Yazoo City and in Tchula Lake.

Several of the boats measuring between two hundred and five hundred tons and designated as large boats performed outstanding service for the Confederacy. The smallest of this class, *J. M. Sharp,* was a cotton boat without passenger service. She engaged in transport on the Sunflower River and was sunk on the Quiver River but was refloated and later used on the Yalobusha River. The *Acadia,* built by the Howard Ship Yards at Jeffersonville, Indiana, in 1860, was owned by the New Orleans and Bayou Sara Mail Company. Escaping Farragut's advancing flotilla, the *Acadia* entered the Yazoo River, where she literally wore out while transporting provisions and troops on the Sunflower River system. The *Alonzo Child,* once reported as having averaged twenty-nine miles per hour on a four-hundred-mile Missouri River run, was almost six years old when she was scuttled in December 1862.[7] During her year on the Yazoo River, she earned a substantial sum for her owner, Captain David De Haven.

The boats of the larger class included some of the finest boats engaged in the antebellum cotton trade along the lower Missis-sippi River. The *Republic,* although one of the oldest boats, had been considered "quite a floating palace" when in her prime. Mark Twain once served as a cub pilot aboard the *Republic.*[8] Although some of these boats, such as the *R. J. Lackland,* were considered too large to be of use, others that were too old or too worn out, such as the *Scotland* or *John Walsh,* served the Con-federacy by being scuttled to block the Yazoo River channel. The newest boat on the river, *Ferd Kennett,* was built in 1861 and ran in the Memphis–New Orleans trade with a Confederate States mail contract before entering the Yazoo River. Under charter to Confederate authorities, the *Ferd Kennett* remained on the lower Yazoo as a storage boat along with the *Edward J. Gay*.

Although some of the boats were used as prosaic store boats, or plebian transports, five of the boats of the larger class became cotton-clad gunboats. The *Prince of Wales*, built in 1859 at Cincinnati, Ohio, had a reputation as a gamblers' boat when she ran in the Memphis–New Orleans trade before the war.9 The *Magnolia* was "strictly speaking a cotton boat" without passenger accommodations, and she made her record load of 6,536 bales of cotton during her first season on the lower Mississippi River.10 The *Magnolia* was part of the Confederate cotton-clad squadron with the *Magenta*, *Mary E. Keene*, and *Natchez*. The beautiful *Magenta* measured 265 x 40 x 8.5 feet and boasted eight boilers, each 30 feet long. She was built in New Albany, Indiana, in 1860, and ran the New Orleans–Vicksburg trade until forced into the Yazoo. Thomas P. Leathers, the sometimes irascible but always astute businessman who described himself as "an A Number 1 steamboatman," commanded his eight-hundred-ton *Natchez*.11 Built in Cincinnati but completed in New Orleans in 1860, the *Natchez* ran in the New Orleans–Memphis trade. Jefferson Davis, president-elect of the Confederate States, boarded the *Natchez* for the first leg of his trip to the Confederate capital at Montgomery, Alabama. Leathers, once accused as a "Yankee spy," remained a totally unreconstructed rebel. His *Natchez* of the Yazoo Fleet was the fifth boat to bear the name; the sixth *Natchez* lost her race with *Rob't E. Lee*, and two other boats bore the name before Leathers's death in 1896. Leathers hauled down the American flag from the fifth *Natchez* in 1861 and raised it again on the seventh *Natchez* on 4 March 1885, when Grover Cleveland, the first Democrat since Abraham Lincoln's inauguration, moved into the White House.12 While the civilian boats served in a variety of ways, the government boats were first called to defend the Yazoo River.

The eight government boats included the remains of the Confederate River Defense Fleet, the ram *Arkansas*, which was completed on the Yazoo River, and several transports. The River Defense Fleet has been described as consisting of steamboats with guns aboard rather than gunboats. The *General Polk* and the *Ivy* had iron "only on their bows—they looked very much like a cowcatcher." The *Livingston*, built at a cost of $80,000 on the keel of a ferryboat, was constructed more substantially than either the *Polk* or *Ivy*. But she had iron only "as a protection to her machinery." The *General Earl Van Dorn*, originally owned by Captain Ed Montgomery, was fitted with an iron ram and a thin iron casemate. Of all the government boats, the *General Earl Van Dorn* was the only one that resembled a gunboat.[13] Confederate Commander Robert F. Pinkney steamed the *Polk* and *Livingston* into the Yazoo in April, and the *General Earl Van Dorn* reached the river soon after the Battle of Memphis. The *Ivy*, the *Mobile*, and the historic *Star of the West* left New Orleans ahead of Farragut's flotilla and steamed into the Yazoo for safety, while the *St. Mary* served on "patrol duty."[14]

The activities of the Yazoo Fleet formed a dramatic episode in the history of steamboating on the Yazoo waters. Although several major studies of riverine warfare and scores of pages in multi-volume histories of the Civil War describe the activities of the *Arkansas* and the Union expeditions to Chickasaw Bayou, Yazoo Pass, and Steele's Bayou, the civilian steamers are rarely mentioned.[15] The history of these boats is a study of logistics and military use of private property and of self-interest combining with national interest in a striking example of Confederate nationalism.[16]

More than thirty captains sharing limited commerce looked forward to a bleak year. A dozen or so steamers more than met the antebellum transportation needs along the Yazoo River system, and after the Civil War Parisot coordinated as few as eight boats to serve efficiently even in a busy cotton season. In the summer of 1862 most of the steamers lay idle, but such inactivity was not unusual for that slack business season. The approaching cotton season, however, held limited promise. Spring planting had not been significantly reduced as the second year of the war began, and hostile military forces had not yet met on the rich Delta lands. The crops lay ripening in the summer sun, and soon the river landings would be piled with bushels of corn and bales of cotton. Certainly some of the boats could be used to move the crops to the only remaining markets at Yazoo City or Greenwood. Perhaps even Vicksburg might be reopened as a market. Even so, thirty-two captains competing to serve local shippers on a closed river system could not look forward to a prosperous season. Confederate military needs for transportation might provide economic opportunities for some of the boats. Indeed, Confederate authorities responding to military events implicitly at least and perhaps explicitly established policies that bound the steamboat captains' loyalties and self-interests to the Confederacy.[17]

Confederate navy officers came to the Yazoo River in the early spring. Robert Pinkney, commanding the *Polk* and *Livingston*, was the first to arrive, and he added the *General Earl Van Dorn* to his command in mid-May. Lieutenant Isaac N. Brown reached the Yazoo River in late May to complete the *Arkansas*, and William F. Lynch arrived several weeks later to serve as flag officer of the navy command. Brown was dismayed when he boarded the *Arkansas* at Greenwood. The hull and machinery, which had been built at Memphis, were intact, but little else had been done to complete the Confederate ram. The young lieutenant, with seemingly inexhaustible energy, retrieved a bargeload of iron rails that had been sunk in the Yazoo River, had the *Arkansas* towed to Yazoo City, built the Confederate Navy Yard with sawmills, forges, and machine shops at Yazoo City, secured a skilled and unskilled labor force from nearby plantations and from some of the steamboats, located and collected the necessary materials to put the *Arkansas* in battle-ready condition, and looked to her defense.[18] Brown selected Liverpool Landing about twenty-five miles downstream from Yazoo City as his defensive position and completed a log and chain raft across the Yazoo River by 5 June. Robert Pinkney cooperated by bringing the *Polk* and *Livingston* to the downstream side of the raft, and the *General Earl Van Dorn* soon steamed to the Liverpool raft.[19]

The Yazoo River steamers had almost unlimited access to Vicksburg via the Mississippi River until the Liverpool raft was completed in early June. After that, only the larger boats were isolated above the raft. An unknown number of steamers were moored in Lake George, a slack-water branch of the Sunflower River, and at least a dozen of the smaller boats continued steaming on the Sunflower, lower Yazoo, and Mississippi rivers. They were not blocked from Vicksburg until Ellet's ram squadron reached the mouth of the Yazoo River on 24 June. Most of the Yazoo steamers could have reached the Union flotilla at almost any time before mid-December 1862, when the Confederates completed a second raft across the Yazoo River at Snyder's Bluff, about twenty-three miles from the Mississippi River. Even after this raft isolated the Yazoo and Sunflower rivers, small steamers could have made their way through the interconnecting waterways from the Little Sunflower River to Steele's Bayou. The captains had chosen to enter the Yazoo, and they chose to remain loyal to the Confederacy. No boat left the Yazoo except on Confederate service.

From May to December 1862, the slack summer months and the weeks before the fall harvest reached its peak, some of the steamers found economic opportunities in Confederate transport service. The steamers on the Yazoo and Sunflower rivers transported supplies from the river country to Vicksburg directly by water before Union forces began patrolling the mouth of the Yazoo River. Thereafter they brought supplies to the landing at Snyder's Bluff, where the cargo was transferred to wagons, which used a road, variously know as Valley Road, Yazoo Valley Road, or Ridge Road, from Snyder's Mill on the bluff to Vicksburg. Parisot's *Dew Drop* remained active on the lower Yazoo, while the *Dixie* commanded by Milton Dent went far up the low waters of the Sunflower River in search of cargoes. The sidewheel steamer *Fair Play* was active on the Yazoo River during the summer, but she "was called out of the Yazoo" and pressed into Confederate service to transport arms and ammunition from Vicksburg to Milliken's Bend across the Mississippi River. Joshua Wiley, owner and captain of the *Argo*, actively plied the Sunflower River for Confederate authorities even though he maintained a home in Indiana.[20] The small steamers operating on the Sunflower and lower Yazoo rivers during the summer months included the *Argo*, both boats named *Cotton Plant, Dixie, Emma Bett*, and *J. M. Sharp*. Most of these boats had been on the Yazoo River during the preceding cotton season and were regarded as the regular Yazoo boats. During the summer they were not chartered by the authorities but transported small cargoes and military personnel on a voucher basis. These small boats would, in time, be pressed into Confederate service and be paid on a fee basis.

Confederate authorities impressed some of the larger boats into transport service for a charter fee. The *Mary E. Keene* earned $39,000 when chartered for fifty-two days at $750 per day in August and September. The *Magnolia* was under charter to the Quartermaster Department at Yazoo City for eight days at $650 a day in early May 1862. At the end of that month Captain Ed C. Carter of the *Thirty-Fifth Parallel* received $23,500 for a forty-seven-day charter. Carter unsuccessfully protested the $500 fee and argued that he should be paid $550 a day. The *Capitol* became the workboat for the *Arkansas*, and Brown used her machinery to hoist heavy loads and to run the steam drills. The *Fair Play* earned $1,350, the *Hartford City* received $1,000 for twenty-five days' charter "towing rafts" to Liverpool in May and June, and the *Ben McCulloch* was paid $100 a day for transporting ordnance supplies to the *Arkansas* at Yazoo City.[21] Available records suggest that most steamers remained idle but safe during their first months on the Yazoo.

Because of increasing Union activity near the mouth of the Yazoo, Brown strengthened his defenses at the Liverpool raft. Pressing an unnamed steamer into transport service, Brown sent more than eight hundred bales of cotton from Yazoo City to Liverpool. The cotton was transferred across the raft to the waiting *Polk* and *Livingston*, which with a protective sheath of four hundred bales of cotton each were moored with their bows downstream, with steam up and with orders to ram any boat that threatened the Liverpool raft. When Brown learned that the *General Earl Van Dorn* had also moored below the raft, he came to Liverpool Landing and rearranged his defenses. Removing the armaments and most of the supplies from the *Polk* and *Livingston*, he chained them together and with a liberal supply of oil and tar converted them into fireboats. When falling water levels threatened to strand the *Arkansas* at the navy yard, Brown steamed her to Liverpool Landing and rushed to prepare her for battle. Wondering whether the *Arkansas* should be held on the Yazoo to defend the "fine steamers" or be taken into battle on the Mississippi River, he sent Lieutenant Charles W. Read to confer with General Earl Van Dorn, the ranking Confederate commander at Vicksburg. Van Dorn wanted action, and soon the *Arkansas* was ordered out of the Yazoo.[22]

The Confederate naval forces at the Liverpool raft on 25 June included the armed *Arkansas* and the *Mobile*, which had been sheathed with cotton, armed with four guns, and anchored above the raft.[25] The two fireboats, *Polk* and *Livingston*, and by one account a third boat, the *General Clark*, were moored below the raft. The *General Van Dorn* lay a few yards downstream. The next morning, Alfred W. Ellet entered the Yazoo River with the Union rams *Monarch* and *Lancaster*. After proceeding upstream for about twenty miles, Ellet spotted oil floating on the river, and at one o'clock he found the carpenter of the *Van Dorn* in a skiff. On being questioned, the carpenter explained that the oil came from the fireboats, which "were all oiled and tarred." The rams continued up the Yazoo, passed the mouth of the Big Sunflower, and on rounding a bend in the river came within sight of the Confederate position. Robert F. Pinkney, commanding the fireboats, precipitously, one observer reported "cowardly," fired the *Polk* and *Livingston* and cast them adrift. The log of the *Lancaster* reported that the burning *Polk, Livingston,* and *General Clark* became entangled with the *General Van Dorn*, which exploded with a force that "shook the hills." The rams sought safety from the drifting wreckage but not before getting "a good view of the *Arkansas* lying above the raft." [24] Pinkney's sacrifice cost the Confederates three, perhaps four, boats; he was later "sent up for a Court Martial." [25]

Isaac Brown rushed to bring the *Arkansas* to battle readiness, and on 14 July he opened the Liverpool raft and took the *Arkansas* toward the Union fleet on the Mississippi River. The *Arkansas* met three Union gunboats on the Yazoo River a few miles before it emptied into the Mississippi. The ironclad *Carondolet*, the wooden gunboat *Tyler*, and the army ram *Queen of the West* were no match for the *Arkansas's* guns. Brown continued to steam the Confederate ram into the Mississippi and through the Union fleet, and after a brief but heavy battle, he moored the *Arkansas* at the Vicksburg landing. The subsequent history of the *Arkansas*, especially her effectiveness in changing the military events on the Mississippi River before her destruction near Baton Rouge on 6 August, left the Yazoo River country only lightly defended. As long as the *Arkansas* remained a threat to Union military forces on the Mississippi River, Federal commanders gave little thought to the Yazoo River. The Delta remained uncontested for several weeks. [26]

Union Lieutenant Stephen L. Phelps took a flotilla of gunboats and rams into the Yazoo River on 23 August and reached the mouth of the Big Sunflower. Because of low water conditions, Phelps sent the small *Lioness* and *Sampson* up the Sunflower, but even these relatively shallow-draft boats could not go more than twenty miles up the river. Nevertheless, Phelps reported that they came within "4 miles of the steamers in Lake George." [27] The Confederates on the Yazoo were forewarned, and they again looked to their defensive position. The Liverpool raft, which had been opened to allow the *Arkansas* to pass through, was closed when Flag Officer Lynch scuttled the old *Capitol* to close the breach.[28] Although the raft was strengthened in late August, the boom could be maneuvered to allow boats to pass.

The *Yazoo* had been the first boat to leave the river system, but she was not the last. During the late summer and early fall of 1862, four other steamers left their haven. The *Paul Jones* was a store boat on the lower Yazoo until she was ordered to Liverpool, where she transferred her stores across the raft to waiting steamers. She was subsequently ordered out of the Yazoo and, after several runs on the Mississippi River, sought refuge on the Big Black River. John C. Reives, master and owner of the *Charm*, had been on the Yazoo for several seasons, and his steamer was chartered by Confederate authorities for transport service during the fall. The *Charm*, ordered to Vicksburg on 4 November, may have steamed into the Red River for salt before joining the *Paul Jones* on the Big Black River east of Vicksburg. Retreating Confederates burned both the *Charm* and the *Paul Jones* soon after the Battle of Champions' Hill in 1863. Captain Joshua Wiley lost his *Fair Play* when she was impressed to transport arms and ammunition between Vicksburg and Milliken's Bend. Union forces captured the *Fair Play* on her second trip to Milliken's Bend. The *Dixie*, owned by Parisot and Dent, was the last steamer to leave the Yazoo. She was moored at Greenwood in mid-October, when military authorities recommended her as "proper for running after salt in the Red River and its tributaries." The *Dixie*, unmentioned again in extant records, must have steamed to the Red River with Milton Dent at the wheel before the Confederates completed the raft at Snyder's Bluff.[29]

As the summer turned into fall, Lynch reported that "twenty-three large steamers" were in the Yazoo and that an "immense amount" of corn and cotton lay on the adjacent banks. Realizing that the "barricade of sunken vessels and a raft of logs" at Liverpool, even when guarded by the cotton-clad gunboat *Mobile*, was insufficient, Lynch suggested another barricade further downstream. Three bluffs known successively as Snyder's, Drumgoulds', and Haynes' flanked the east bank of the lower Yazoo River for about two miles. Snyder's Bluff, the farthest downstream, was about twenty-three miles from the Mississippi River, and Haynes' Bluff, about twenty-five miles from the Mississippi, was the uppermost of the three. Confederate artillery emplacements, rifle pits, and an extensive log raft and boom across the Yazoo River at Snyder's Bluff effectively blocked not only the Yazoo River but also access to the Sunflower waterways. Only Steele's Bayou flowed from the Delta into the Yazoo below Snyder's Bluff. All steamboats were safe behind the Snyder's Bluff raft.30

Military commanders used several steamers to build the raft at Snyder's Bluff. The *Hartford City* earned $40 a day "towing rafts" on the Yazoo, for a total charter fee of $4,300. The larger *Hope* earned $5,911, which included the charter fee of $75 a day, wages for the officers and crew, and the cost of repairing damages sustained while working on the raft. The new terms providing for a charter fee, operating costs, and damages served as further incentive for the Yazoo captains. The *Peytona* was paid only $275 per day, but she remained moored to house those who worked on the raft, or perhaps to serve as a hospital boat, for she had drawn mattresses, sheets, and blankets from the Confederate Medical Department.31

David De Haven, captain and owner of the *Alonzo Child*, received a total of more than $100,000 for the services of his boat in 1862. The *Alonzo Child*, built in Louisville, Kentucky, in 1858, was old by steamboat standards, but her six boilers kept her active in Confederate service. De Haven chartered her for 74 of 106 days between 24 July and 7 December 1862 and accepted, with protest, the $300 a day charter fee. He received $22,200 in fee, $1,800 in salaries, and $10,050.37 to cover the damages to his boat. On or about 7 December Confederate authorities purchased the *Alonzo Child* for $35,000, and they scuttled her to reinforce the raft at Snyder's Bluff. The new owners decided to salvage the *Alonzo Child*'s engines and use them on a new boat that was being constructed at Selma, Alabama, and De Haven was paid $7,973.09 to remove and transport the engines to Selma. After delivering the machinery to naval authorities in Alabama, the captain traveled to Richmond, Virginia, where he protested the $300 a day charter fee and received an additional payment of $24,000. During the last half of 1862, the old steamer *Alonzo Child* earned her captain a total of $101,023.46, which was a substantial sum even when paid in depreciated Confederate notes.32

Steamboat captains found financial opportunities in the Confederate transport service and in charter fees for building and maintaining the rafts at Liverpool and Snyder's Bluff. The implied Confederate policy of assuming fiscal responsibility for damages and for paying a fair price for boats that were lost in Confederate service (explicit in the case of the *Alonzo Child*) augured well for establishing a commonality of interests between steamboat captains and the Confederacy. The Confederate Navy Department strengthened the policy when it asked Congress to pay $25,000 for the *Capitol*, which Flag Officer Lynch had "sunk in the Yazoo River . . . in July last" to reinforce the Liverpool raft.[33]

December was a trying month on the Yazoo River system. Thomas B. Reed, commissary for subsistence at Vicksburg, prepared storage facilities at Haynes' Bluff, but low water prevented him from reaching corn and cotton up the Sunflower River. Upriver planters took their produce to the riverbanks so that steamboats could load it when the water rose.[34] But low water was not the only problem. Union forces launched three attacks to reach the high ground east of the Yazoo.

The Union ironclad *Cairo* entered the Yazoo to test Confederate strength but struck the torpedoes that had been placed between Chickasaw Bayou and Snyder's Bluff. The *Cairo* was one of three Union boats that were sunk on the Yazoo River. A few days after the *Cairo* sank, Generals U. S. Grant and William T. Sherman launched a two-pronged attack on Confederate defenses. Grant, moving southward from Tennessee into north-central Mississippi, forced the Confederates to abandon the Tallahatchie Line and retreat to Grenada. Confederates quickly built earthwork redoubts on the ridges overlooking the south bank of the Yalobusha River near Grenada. While Union forces moved toward the Yalobusha Line, Earl Van Dorn led a cavalry raid against Grant's line of communications at Holly Springs. When Van Dorn destroyed Grant's supply base at Holly Springs, the Union general withdrew from the Yalobusha Line and returned to Tennessee. In the meantime, William T. Sherman, in coordination with Grant, tried to break the Yazoo defenses at Chickasaw Bayou. Confederate artillery and infantry fire forced Sherman to withdraw from Chickasaw Bayou.[35]

As 1862 came to a close, the Confederate Yazoo Fleet had lost one-fourth of its strength. Three military steamers were sacrificed at the Liverpool raft, and Confederate authorities scuttled the *Capitol* and *Alonzo Child* at Liverpool and Snyder's Bluff respectively. Six boats left the waterways before they were captured or destroyed. The *Yazoo* burned at Island No. 10, the ram *Arkansas* exploded on the lower Mississippi, and the *Fair Play* was captured at Milliken's Bend. The *Paul Jones* and the *Charm* went into the Big Black River, where they were later destroyed, and the little *Dixie* probably was lost on the Red River. The remaining fleet of thirty steamers continued to serve Confederate military needs with a burst of activity as 1863 began.

4/*The Yazoo Fleet at War*

The Yazoo steamboat captains had reasons to be jubilant as 1863 began. Isaac Brown's torpedoes sank the formidable Union ironclad *Cairo* in mid-December. Grant's army, responding to Van Dorn's raid, withdrew from the Yalobusha Line after Christmas and crossed the Little Tallahatchie River on the retreat to Tennessee. Sherman's invasion of the Yazoo River was stopped by the Confederate line overlooking Chickasaw Bayou, and on the second day of the new year Sherman gave up his hopeless drive against the bluffs and withdrew from the Yazoo River. The Yazoo boats were safe behind the Snyder's Bluff raft, and the captains enthusiastically looked for the winter rains, which would extend the navigable waters far up the Sunflower, Tallahatchie, and Yalobusha rivers, where quantities of cotton, corn, hay, and other produce lay on the banks waiting for the boats to come.

Throughout December Confederate authorities busily prepared to secure the upriver supplies. Thomas B. Reed, commissary for subsistence at Vicksburg, received orders to collect "rations for 10,000 men for five months." Learning that planters on the Sunflower River waterways had "an immense quantity of corn," he established a depot safely out of range of enemy gunboats at Haynes' Bluff. Reed built several "rough log houses" to supplement the leased barns, outbuildings, and pastures belonging to Benjamin Roach at the bluff. Two flatboats were built to ferry produce across the Yazoo River should farmers bring their crops overland from the Sunflower country to the west bank of the Yazoo.[1] Farther up the streams planters took advantage of the dry weeks in December and early January to carry their produce to the riverbanks along the Sunflower waterways and waited for the winter rains. They did not have long to wait. Thirty-six hours of heavy rains, with snow and sleet on Deer Creek, opened the waterways for the waiting steamers in mid-January.[2]

A dozen or more boats entered the Sunflower River system in search of cargoes. Some of the smaller boats, coming from Quiver River and Bogue Phalia, transferred their cargoes to larger boats on the Sunflower and returned to the shallow waters. Little is known about the business practices of the owners of boats on the Sunflower River system. Existing records indicate that in 1862 most steamers were paid by vouchers such as a $2.50 ticket from Vicksburg to Yazoo City, $4 per head for horses, or $1 for boxes. A few steamers were chartered for a daily fee to build rafts or perform specific services during 1862. Beginning in February 1863 on the upper Yazoo and in March on the lower Yazoo, military authorities regularly chartered steamers for transport services for a daily fee, plus expenses and damages. The absence of vouchers for small lots or, with a few exceptions, receipts for charter fees in January and February suggests that the captains made private business arrangements with the planters.[3]

Only five small boats were chartered in January and February 1863. The *Emma Bett* served for 138 days at $50 a day beginning on 1 February, and the *Ben McCulloch* earned $2,000 for a twenty-day charter that started on 18 January. Both of these boats were often reported on the Sunflower River, lower Yazoo, or in the case of the *Ben McCulloch* on Tchula Lake. The *Dew Drop* had been at Greenwood in October and was under charter at the end of January for $75 a day. The *Hope*, sometimes reported on the middle reaches of the Yazoo around Yazoo City, served under charter from 14 January to 13 February at $75 a day. Any of these boats could have been used by General William W. Loring to bring supplies and ordnance from the Yalobusha Line near Grenada, or they could have been sent into the smaller tributaries. The 180-ton *Cotton Plant* was under charter at $250 a day from 21 January to 10 February and at one time went into the Little Tallahatchie River. A few days later, 12–17 February, she ran on the Yalobusha between Grenada and Greenwood. Some of these chartered boats may have been used on the Sunflower waterways to transport the "immense quantities" of corn to Haynes' Bluff.[4]

Although there are no records detailing the private transactions between planters and steamboatmen, the steamers undoubtedly brought large quantities of produce to Haynes' Bluff, for Reed's makeshift facilities soon proved inadequate. Captain John Brooks chartered his boat the *Edward J. Gay* to authorities and with a mate, four engineers, two pilots, a steward, fireman, carpenter, watchmen, and ten slave deckhands reached Haynes' Bluff in mid-February. Brooks drew 170 pounds of nails and "one monkey wrench" from the Quartermaster Department and proceeded to install a gristmill and convert the *Edward J. Gay* into a storage boat for corn. Her cabin accommodations may have been used by military personnel because Brooks signed a receipt for blankets, comforts, sheets, towels, and pillows. The larger steamer remained moored at the landing for sixty-one days as a store boat for corn arriving from the Sunflower River. Brooks accepted, with protest, the $18,500 he received in charter fee. The *Ferd Kennett* was used for a short time as a store boat for cotton at Haynes' Bluff.[5]

While the steamers scurried about the Sunflower River system picking up cotton and corn, other boats plied the upper Yazoo, and when water permitted they steamed up the Tallahatchie and Yalobusha rivers. All seemed well until 3 February, when Union forces exploded a mine under the levee that separated the Mississippi River from Yazoo Pass. Before 1858, when the levee was built, the route from the Mississippi through Yazoo Pass to the Coldwater, Tallahatchie, and Yazoo rivers had been used by flatboats and steamers. Water from the Mississippi River pouring through the break raised the Coldwater and Tallahatchie rivers to flood stage and backed up in Steele's Bayou and Deer Creek. Within four days after the levee was broken, Union Lieutenant Commander Watson Smith steamed through the cut into Moon Lake and Yazoo Pass with a flotilla of two ironclads, two rams, six tinclads, and twenty-one transports. Confederates felled trees to obstruct Yazoo Pass, slowing the advance of Watson's flotilla, while General Loring busily prepared the major Confederate defensive position at Greenwood.[6]

Loring, who was soon to earn the sobriquet "Old Blizzards," began building a cotton bale and earthwork fortification to be named Fort Pemberton on a narrow neck of land between the Tallahatchie and Yazoo rivers west of the little town of Greenwood. Needing a large number of cotton bales for the fort, Loring took charge of several unnamed boats, issued orders that "they should not be interfered with," and sent them and the *Cotton Plant* into the swollen Tallahatchie and Yalobusha rivers.⁷ Isaac Brown, who returned to active duty following an illness, sent the *Prince of Wales* into the flooded Tallahatchie for cotton with the intention of converting her into a cotton-clad gunboat. But when the loaded boat returned, Loring commandeered her cargo for Fort Pemberton. Indeed, he retained the *Prince of Wales* and the *J. F. Pargoud* under charter to house the slaves and soldiers who were building the fort. Other defenses against the approaching Federal flotilla included a log raft across the Tallahatchie channel and a barricade of sunken boats just below the raft. The *Star of the West* and the *John Walsh* were stripped and prepared for sinking. Confederates bored and plugged 250 holes in the *Star of the West*, and when she was in position across the channel, a hundred men boarded her and, each pulling two or more plugs, sank her across the channel. The *Star of the West* so effectively blocked the river that the *John Walsh* was not sunk but was moored downstream on the Yazoo River to be used when necessary.⁸

With Fort Pemberton, the raft, and the *Star of the West* forming the first line of defense, Isaac Brown prepared secondary defenses using a squadron of cotton-clad gunboats. Deprived of both the *Prince of Wales* and her cotton, Brown pressed the *Thirty-Fifth Parallel* into service and with the government boat *St. Mary* steamed up the Tallahatchie before the raft and barricade were in place. He quickly secured enough cotton to form a protective sheath around the little *St. Mary* and proceeded upstream with both boats. After loading about three thousand bales aboard the *Thirty-Fifth Parallel*, Brown learned that a Union gunboat was approaching rapidly, and he turned his boats downstream. Ed C. Carter, captain and owner of the *Thirty-Fifth Parallel*, left the flooded Tallahatchie channel and while attempting to pass between two trees crushed both wheels of his boat. Brown ordered Carter to burn the disabled steamer and her cargo should she be in danger of capture, then transferred his command to the *St. Mary* and returned to Greenwood.⁹ Watson Smith, commanding a Union gunboat, recorded that he came upon the *Thirty-Fifth Parallel* "in flames, [and] almost consumed; [she] sank as we passed her." Smith continued in pursuit of an unnamed boat that escaped when her crew threw "large quantities of corn" overboard to increase her speed.¹⁰ Captain Carter received $500 a day charter fee, and a $70,000 appraisal reinforced the belief that the Confederate government would pay a reasonable price for a boat lost in Confederate service.[11]

The former commander of the *Arkansas* had experimented with cotton-clad boats at the Liverpool raft. The *Mobile*, at one time a cotton-clad, had been ordered from her station at the raft to the navy yard at Yazoo City, where she was being converted to an ironclad. The *St. Mary*, sheathed in cotton and armed with two guns, was the first of the cotton-clad squadron. On the day he steamed into the Tallahatchie aboard the *Thirty-Fifth Parallel*, Brown accepted the offer of Major F. G. Smith to bring up cotton from the Yazoo River. Smith went to Snyder's Bluff with orders to transfer the cotton from the *Ferd Kennett* to the *Acadia*; the latter was to bring the cotton to the waiting boats in the upper Yazoo and the former was ordered into Tchula Lake for additional bales. The demand for cotton was urgent. Smith was authorized to "give receipts for all the cotton you take, government or otherwise, and leave it to the owners to fix weights—it will be paid for." [12] Other personnel collected a thousand bales of cotton in Yazoo City and sent it upriver on the *Ferd Kennett*, while Brown secured cotton for the squadron from plantation landings along the upper Yazoo.[13]

Four steamers of the larger class, the *Magenta, Magnolia, Mary E. Keene*, and *Natchez*, lay waiting for their protective sheathing. Each boat needed approximately two thousand bales of cotton, which was about one-third the cargo capacity. The *Magnolia* had transported a record load of more than sixty-five hundred bales when running between Memphis and New Orleans. Tom Leathers's fine steamer *Natchez* was designed to carry five thousand bales of cotton, and her captain was authorized to confiscate cotton for her use along the banks of the Yazoo. Cotton from the lower Yazoo was used aboard the *Mary E. Keene* but not before her captain and part owner, William F. Corkery, removed an oil painting of the steamer from her main cabin for safekeeping. Cotton from Yazoo City, Tchula Lake, and the upper Yazoo sheathed the *Magnolia, Magenta*, and *Natchez*. The *Mary E. Keene* was the first to be completed and the last to be dismantled. The *Natchez* had the shortest career as a cotton-clad, serving only eight days. The *Magenta* and *Magnolia* were cotton-clads by mid-March and were unloaded by 16 April.[14]

The $350 a day charter fee paid to each captain while his boat was a cotton-clad was considerably below the usual fee paid for such boats. The *Natchez* and *Mary E. Keene* had received as much as $750 a day for charter service during the previous year. The *Magenta* earned between $500 and $650 a day in fees, and the cotton boat *Magnolia* customarily received $400 a day. Perhaps the fee was lower because the officers and crew were replaced by military personnel, or perhaps the boats merely remained moored on the upper Yazoo River. Because the Yazoo Pass Expedition could not breach Loring's defenses on the Tallahatchie, the cotton-clad squadron did not engage its enemy.[15]

Brown praised the cotton-clad squadron because the boats "gave confidence to other portions of the common defense." But lamenting that "the result of this experiment has not been fortunate," Brown went on to say that the squadron "promised at the outset at least peril to those engaged."[16] Did he mean peril to any enemy that should be engaged? Or did he mean peril to those engaged in preparing and manning the cotton-clads? Certainly he meant the former, but the example of the *Natchez* suggests the latter. The *Natchez*, moored at Norris Landing a few miles below the present town of Belzoni, was encircled with two thousand bales of cotton. The sheath admirably protected the boat from small arms fire but would have been effective only against the smallest artillery pieces. Fire presented the greatest danger for boats loaded with cotton in peace or in war. And a fire accidentally started aboard the *Natchez* on Friday, 13 March. Before dawn the next morning the cotton-clad burned to the waterline and sank. Leathers, with some justification, believed that the *Natchez* "was probably the finest boat then afloat, or that ever had floated on the Mississippi River." The appraisers seemed to agree for they valued the *Natchez* at $225,000.[17]

The Yazoo Pass Expedition resumed its fruitless bombardment of Fort Pemberton on the same day that the *Natchez* burned but ended the attack on Monday, 16 March. As the Yazoo Pass Expedition withdrew up the Tallahatchie, another Union flotilla entered the Yazoo River and penetrated Steele's Bayou. When the Steele's Bayou expedition began, Confederates had the three large cotton-clad gunboats, *Magenta, Magnolia,* and *Mary E. Keene,* on the upper Yazoo; the small cotton-clad *St. Mary* with her two guns was at Snyder's Bluff on 10 March.[18]

While the Confederates defended Fort Pemberton, the Commissary Department "drew large quantities" of corn from the

Yazoo and Sunflower country. Private Will H. Tunnard, who was with the Third Louisiana Infantry stationed between Snyder's Bluff and Haynes' Bluff, noted that "immense quantities of supplies of every description were transported down the Yazoo on steamers, and discharged at the landing above our camp." The bustle of activity was temporarily halted on 20 March by the sounds of "cannonading, rapid and heavy," which came from "a northwesterly direction." [19] The Steele's Bayou expedition, near Rolling Fork, was engaged by Confederate forces under General Winfield S. Featherston and Colonel Samuel W. Ferguson.

U. S. Grant had approved the combined operation of David Porter's gunboats and transports loaded with William T. Sherman's infantry. The expedition was a bold maneuver to turn the Vicksburg right flank by steaming up Steele's Bayou, through Black Bayou into Deer Creek, up that narrow stream to Rolling Fork, and from there into the Sunflower River. By turning downstream on the Sunflower, they hoped to enter the Yazoo River above Haynes' Bluff and gain the high ground in Vicksburg's rear. The Union expedition successfully navigated the tortuous channels of Steele's Bayou, Black Bayou, and Deer Creek before meeting significant Confederate resistance on 20 March. [20]

Colonel Samuel Ferguson was far up the Sunflower but rushed toward Rolling Fork aboard the *J. M. Sharp*, which he chartered at $100 a day when informed of the threat through Steele's Bayou. Ferguson sent the *Emma Bett*, chartered at $50 a day, into Bogue Phalia for his baggage, animals, and a section of artillery. [21] General Featherston had already arrived at Rolling Fork aboard the *Acadia*, which was paid $250 a day, but he was dissatisfied with the boat. Notifying John C. Pemberton that he "needed more boats," he complained that the *Acadia* "runs badly in daylight, and cannot run at all at night." The three-year-old *Acadia* was undoubtedly showing both her age and the wear and tear of service on the Yazoo River. While Porter's flotilla was stopped by rafts of willow limbs and Featherston's forces, Confederates on the Yazoo were busy. [22]

Hoping to isolate the Union gunboats on Deer Creek, Pemberton sent orders to Loring to send "two cotton clads to the mouth of Deer Creek." A second telegram, "Hurry up the boats, they must capture the enemy's boats . . . bring them down with a boarding force," reflected his ambitions and a sense of urgency. Loring replied that "Captain Brown goes down with cotton clad tonight [20 March]." In addition to asking for the cotton-clads, Pemberton ordered all boats not needed at Greenwood to steam to Snyder's Bluff, where they could be protected by Confederate artillery.[23] Before any cotton-clad reached Deer Creek, Loring received word that the Yazoo Pass Expedition was returning to Fort Pemberton. In response, General Pemberton ordered that the cotton-clads "be sent back immediately."[24] But they were not needed on the upper Yazoo. Union Brigadier General Isaac Quinby, who had obstinately ordered the return to Fort Pemberton, conducted a "boggy twelve-day reconnaissance" and agreed to a "final departure" on 5 April.[25] While Quinby caused a flurry of concern on the Tallahatchie, General Pemberton tried to trap the Union flotilla on Deer Creek.

Brigadier General Stephen D. Lee volunteered to lead a Confederate force up Deer Creek to block the stream. The expedition was organized at Haynes' Bluff and included the Third Louisiana Infantry, which marched aboard the large boat *Peytona* moored at the landing. After spending the night of 23 March aboard the fine steamer, the troops transferred to the waiting *Dew Drop*, whose name, according to Private Tunnard, "was not a misnomer by any means." The *Dew Drop*, with Parisot in command and Lee stalking the deck, was stopped temporarily by a storm but soon made her way to Wilson's Landing about twelve miles up Deer Creek.[26] Lee's efforts to blockade Deer Creek failed to entrap the Federal flotilla, which executed a laborious but successful withdrawal on 25 March. During the fifteen-day charter from 9 to 23 March, the *Dew Drop* earned $3,392, and Parisot received an additional $337.67 for transporting Lee and the Third Louisiana up Deer Creek on 24–25 March.[27] For two weeks after the Steele's Bayou expedition withdrew, the small boats scurried far up the swollen Sunflower River system. "Five or six" boats were in Bogue Phalia on 10 April before the search for supplies was again interrupted.[28]

The March rains, augmented by the waters flowing through Yazoo Pass, backed up the small streams of the Sunflower but piled driftwood against the upstream works of the Snyder's Bluff raft. The strong current threatened to break the raft, and Pemberton anticipated a renewed Federal attack on Vicksburg, perhaps through the Yazoo Delta. In fact, Union General Frederick Steele had undertaken a foray from the Mississippi River to Greenville, and some of his scouts reached Bogue Phalia. All steamers were called into action.[29]

Two small unnamed steamers busily tried to relieve the pressure against the raft, and Pemberton called for the cotton-clads. The general ordered Brown to "move downriver . . . with your cotton clad boats to operate as circumstances may require." The next day, Pemberton ordered Loring not to use the cotton-clads as transports but to hold them in service until the Synder's Bluff raft could be repaired. Stephen D. Lee, encamped near Rolling Fork and learning of Steele's presence, urged that a cotton-clad be stationed as a guard boat at the mouth of the Sunflower River.[30] The flurry of demands for the cotton-clads reached Brown a week later. On 17 April, the day after he received the orders, Brown informed Pemberton that he had already "ordered the unlading" of the cotton-clads, which action he thought had been approved by both Pemberton and Loring. The *Magnolia* had been off-loaded and had been in transport service since 9 April. The *Magenta*, according to Brown, had been damaged in "the difficult navigation of the Yazoo" while steaming from Fort Pemberton to Yazoo City. The *Mary E. Keene* was the last of the large boats in the squadron, but Brown did not believe that "anything could be accomplished by either one or two boats."[31] Two days later, the *Mary E. Keene* ended her career as a cotton-clad and returned to transport service.[32] The little forty-ton *St. Mary* remained as the last of the once impressive cotton-clad squadron.

While the cotton-clads were being dismantled, Confederate authorities pressed the small boats into government service on the Sunflower waterways. Stephen D. Lee kept the *Golden Age* at $100 a day near his camp on Rolling Fork while he sent the little *Emma Bett* with 150 troops and two howitzers up the Sunflower. The *Emma Bett* had been in government service since 1 February; before she was destroyed in July, she earned $6,900 in fees at $50 a day and $4,231.16 in salaries. The *Hope*, impressed for $75 a day, went into Bogue Phalia searching for two missing boats, the *Acadia* and *Dew Drop*.[33] She did not find them because they were far up the Sunflower. Lieutenant Colonel Edmund W. Pettus of the Twentieth Alabama left Snyder's Bluff on 5 April for the Sunflower aboard the *Acadia*, which although "tired" continued to earn her $250 charter fee. Pettus reported seeing the *Emma Bett* entering Bogue Phalia and the steamer *H. D. Mears* undergoing repairs at Garvins' Ferry above the bogue. A party from the *Acadia* went in small boats up the Quiver River in an unsuccessful search for the *Dew Drop*. While the *Acadia* waited at Quiver River, the intrepid *Dew Drop* steamed down the Sunflower to meet her. The *Dew Drop* had been twelve miles "above the mouth of Huspuckanaw Creek" to within five miles of Friars Point on the Mississippi River. She was returning with five thousand bushels of corn, eight thousand pounds of bacon, a "small lot" of cattle, and a "few hogs," all of which she transferred to the *Acadia*.[34] Presumably, the *Dew Drop* went back up the Sunflower, for as late as 11 May she was earning $75 a day transporting corn, cows, and hogs to the *Acadia* on the Sunflower.[35] None of these steamers survived to transport the crops then being planted.

The military situation changed rapidly. After failing to reach high ground east of Vicksburg, Grant decided to take his army southward and cross the Mississippi River below Vicksburg. To mask his Bruinsburg crossing, Grant sent a flotilla into the Yazoo River to demonstrate against the Confederate stronghold at Snyder's Bluff on 29 April. During the next eighteen days Grant fought his way to Vicksburg's back door. The Yazoo line was outflanked and rendered useless. Confederate defensive positions on the Yazoo were all but abandoned so that when Acting Lieutenant Commander John G. Walker, USN, entered the Yazoo on 18 May, he had no difficulty in occupying Snyder's Bluff and reported that the raft could easily be "cast adrift."[36]

As Confederate military forces evacuated the Snyder's Bluff area, Isaac Brown pressed several of the boats of the larger class into transport service to take the Haynes' Bluff supplies upriver. John W. Tobin, captain and owner of the *J. F. Pargoud*, earned more than $18,000 in the transport service from 24 April to 19 May, while the *R. J. Lackland* earned $24,250 for the ninety-seven-day charter at $250 a day. The *Magenta*, repaired and under way, joined the *Mary E. Keene*, no longer a cotton-clad, and the *Peytona*, in removing the supplies. These boats were held in the transport service at $250 a day until they were destroyed in mid-July.[37]

Brown, on learning that a Union flotilla had entered the Yazoo River, prepared to protect the fleet. Sinking the *Ivy* at Liverpool Landing, he abandoned the Confederate Navy Yard at Yazoo City, where a new ram was under construction. He burned the *Mobile*, which was being converted into an ironclad but could not be completed. The *Republic*, also moored at Yazoo City, had recently been purchased by David De Haven, former captain of the *Alonzo Child*, and his new partner John T. Shirley. Shirley and De Haven had contracted to build a Confederate gunboat at Selma, Alabama, and purchased the *Republic* for $25,000. They were removing her machinery when Isaac Brown burned the old steamer on 21 May to prevent her from falling into the enemy's hands. After burning the *Republic* and *Mobile* at Yazoo City, Brown had a fleet of eighteen boats on the upper Yazoo River and six boats on the Sunflower waterways.[38]

Brown steamed his eighteen Yazoo boats up the river and, as he went upstream on the west side of Honey Island, placed torpedoes in the channel. At Southworth's Bar, a few miles above the Head of Honey Island, the Confederate commander blockaded the Yazoo by sinking four boats abreast in the channel. In succession from east to west lay the *John Walsh, Scotland, Golden Age,* and *R. J. Lackland.* The fourteen remaining boats steamed toward Greenwood and waited there.[39]

Lieutenant Commander John G. Walker entered the Yazoo River with a flotilla consisting of the ironclad *Baron De Kalb* and the gunboats *Forest Rose, Linden, Petrel,* and *Signal.* He had no trouble passing through the raft at Snyder's Bluff and received only desultory fire at Liverpool on 23 May. Reaching Yazoo City, Walker destroyed the remains of the navy yard, including the unfinished hull of the "monster ram," and completed the destruction of the *Mobile* and *Republic.* He returned to the lower Yazoo on the same day, only to be ordered back to the upper Yazoo to seek and destroy the Confederate transport fleet. Walker returned to Yazoo City on 24 May and sent Acting Master George W. Brown with the *Forest Rose, Linden,* and *Signal* upriver in search of the Confederate transports. The gunboats did not take the Yazoo channel on the west side of Honey Island, and by steaming through Tchula Lake on the east side of the island, they missed the Confederate torpedoes. Passing beyond the head of the island, they came upon the four steamers sunk side by side at Southworth's Bar. After burning the steamers to the waterline, the gunboats returned to Yazoo City.[40]

The Union flotilla left Yazoo City and anchored on the lower

Yazoo. Walker sent the *Forest Rose* and *Linden* up the Sunflower River in search of steamboats. About seventy-five miles up the Sunflower, the *Linden* burned Joshua Wiley's *Argo* in a small bayou. The *Forest Rose* turned into the Quiver River from the Sunflower but was stopped by low water.41 The *Dew Drop* was about ten miles up the Quiver River, and her captain later reported that the gunboats, which could not come up the river, sent three armed launches into the Quiver. Parisot, loyal to the end, recorded that at about "9 O'Clock a.m." on 30 May the launches "approached" the *Dew Drop.* "When they were within sixty yards of her," he was satisfied "that she would inevitably fall into the hands of the enemy unless immediately destroyed." Captain Parisot "fired [his] boat and burned her to the water's edge." 42 The *Forest Rose* captured and burned the *Emma Bett*, and as the gunboats steamed down the Sunflower, they explored Lake George and found the small *Cotton Plant* sunk "with nothing out of the water but the top of her smokestacks." Unknown to the officers aboard the gunboats, Confederates sank the *H. D. Mears* on the Sunflower, and at the headwaters of the Quiver River the *J. M. Sharp* lay underwater. Leaving the burned and sunken wrecks, Walker steamed to the Mississippi River and filed his report.43 Forty-two days later he returned to the Yazoo country.

By Special Order 92, dated 1 June 1863, Confederate General Joseph E. Johnston placed Isaac N. Brown in command of "the boats in the Yazoo River." 44 Captain Thomas R. Smith, commanding the transports with authority to "purchase wood for [the] fleet," took the steamers to Yazoo City and the lower Yazoo in search of supplies. On the same day that Vicksburg was surrendered, Brown issued orders requiring the steamers to "assist each other in passing the wrecks now in the Yazoo." 45 While some of the transports went as far downstream as Haynes' Bluff, others scurried about to take the remaining stores to safety. The *Ben McCulloch* took twenty-four hundred bushels of corn into Tchula Lake before she was burned. The *Hope* remained at Yazoo City until the last moment. Leaving just ahead of the returning Federal squadron on 13 July, the *Hope* reached Greenwood loaded with bacon, rice, sugar, soap, candles, salt, molasses, lard, almost ten tons of corn meal, and four thousand bushels of shelled corn.46

Brown, believing that the Yazoo country was untenable, telegraphed General Joseph E. Johnston on 10 July: "In the event of having to abandon the Yazoo, what [shall we] do with the steam-boats?" Four days later he received Johnston's unequivocal reply: "You will destroy all steamboats and public property to the extent of your means."[47] Even before receiving Johnston's reply, Brown ordered Master Lewis Milliken and William F. Corkery, captain and owner of the *Mary E. Keene*, to burn the steamer and "the *Magenta* and the *Magnolia*, at the moment it becomes necessary to prevent their falling into enemy hands."[48] Others were detailed to burn the boats around Greenwood, and General James R. Chalmers, Confederate commander for the military district, named R. T. Jones and a Captain Hearvason to "burn steamboats and cotton belonging to government or private individuals."[49]

The same day that Brown gave orders to burn the large boats, John G. Walker with the *Baron De Kalb* and gunboats *New National*, *Kenwood*, and *Signal* entered the Yazoo and steamed toward Yazoo City for the third time. Just above Yazoo City, Walker found the charred remains of the *Magenta*, *Magnolia*, *J. F. Pargoud*, *Peytona*, and *Prince of Wales*. But discovering the wrecks gave him little solace. The Union ironclad *Baron De Kalb* struck Confederate torpedoes and sank as Walker attempted to beach his damaged boat a few yards below the Confederate Navy Yard.[50]

During the four days beginning 12 July 1863, Confederates burned seven steamboats of the larger class and the little *Ben McCulloch*, which was trying to hide corn on Tchula Lake plantations. When Union forces under General Francis J. Herron occupied Yazoo City by 21 July, he reported that "the cavalry captured the steamer *St. Mary*." Confederate forces abandoned the rivers, destroying the few remaining boats near Greenwood before the end of July 1863.[51]

During the following autumn farmers harvested thousands of bushels of corn, which were vital to Confederate forces operating in northern Mississippi. Andrew Jackson Dye, captain and part owner of the *J. M. Sharp*, notified Confederate authorities that his boat, which had been sunk far up the Quiver River, could be raised, repaired, and brought down the Sunflower. "She could be of great service to us," wrote a Confederate official at Grenada, for "she could be run up the Tallahatchee [sic] and Yalobusha River when it could be impossible to get the stores out with wagons." Furthermore, the boat could get "the tax in kind which could not be gathered otherwise." Captain Dye, reporting that the old *Acadia* "is now sunk in the Yalobusha River and can be raised and put in running order in two weeks," volunteered to "take the whole matter in charge."[52] The *J. M. Sharp* was raised and ran in the rivers around Greenwood until mid-February. Lieutenant Elias K. Owen, commanding the USS *Marmora*, reached Greenwood by way of the Yazoo River on 14 February 1864 and reported that "the rebel steamer *Sharp* was burned a few days ago in the Yalobusha to prevent her from falling into our hands." The *Acadia* probably had been raised, for when Confederates sank her in July, she was recorded as "sunk in the Yalloboosha [sic] River," with the notation that "she could be put in running order in two weeks." When the *Marmora* reached Greenwood, Owen found the *Acadia* sunk "about 1 mile below" the mouth of the Yalobusha.[53] The river system would claim one last boat.

Acting Master Thomas McElroy, USN, steamed up the Yazoo River in April 1864 with the gunboats *Prairie Bird* and *Petrel* supported by the transport *Freestone*. Confederate artillery and sharpshooters attacked the *Petrel* about a mile above Yazoo City. With steam escaping from damaged boilers and parted steam lines, McElroy ordered his crew to abandon the boat just before the Confederate cavalry galloped up to capture the boat, her commander, and the remaining crew. After removing eight 24-pounders, they burned the boat to the water's edge.[54]

The capture of the USS *Petrel* must have more than offset, in the Confederates' minds at least, the loss of the CSS *St. Mary* to Union cavalry the year before. But the score was far from even. The Confederates lost thirty-four steamers on the Yazoo–Sunflower River system, five on other waterways, and two by capture. Federal expeditions left the *Cairo*, *Baron De Kalb*, and *Petrel* at the bottom of the Yazoo River. The once impressive Yazoo Fleet had loyally served the Confederacy for fifteen months.

Nationalism rested on the dual bases of "common culture on the one hand" and "common interests on the other."[55] National culture and interests undoubtedly influenced the captains in bringing their steamers into the Yazoo River in April 1862. With conditions deteriorating around them, the captains remained loyal, even sacrificing their boats for the common cause. Did common culture form a strong enough bond for a captain to put a torch to his boat? Perhaps, but the question cannot be answered from available evidence. Yet, when their own interest as well as the needs of the Confederacy could be served by sacrificing their boats, the captains did not hesitate. Confederate policies of employing boats as transports and cotton-clads, of assuming fiscal responsibility for expenses and damages, and of compensating owners for their losses contributed to a commonality of interests between steamboatmen and Confederate authorities. A combination of national *and* self-interests formed the Yazoo Fleet.

Many of the steamboat captains undoubtedly found comfort in the belief that their government would pay for lost or damaged boats. The Confederate government paid for the *Fair Play, Capitol,* and *Alonzo Child,* which were lost in 1862 while in Confederate service. Authorities did not challenge Captain Ed Carter's misjudgment when they paid for the *Thirty-Fifth Parallel,* but Thomas Leathers had to go to Richmond for his payment. The problem may have had more to do with the size of the payment than with legal questions. Other captains faced delays when Richmond bureaucrats raised legal issues and temporarily suspended payment for their boats. Brown followed correct procedures after he scuttled the four boats at Southworth's Bar in May. Three steamboat captains appraised the *R. J. Lackland* at $100,000, the *Golden Age* at $75,000, and the *Scotland* at $60,000. Incomplete records preclude accounting for the *John Walsh.* These sums were approved but not paid until the end of the year.[56]

The seven boats of the larger class which were burned in mid-July were duly appraised, but payment was suspended "until certain rules for guidance of auditors office be satisfied."[57] Isaac Brown, who had been ordered to Charleston, South Carolina, supported the claims by filing affidavits that he had impressed the boats into Confederate service and that they had been burned under his orders.[58] Richard Holmes, captain and owner of the *Magenta,* went to Richmond, where on 31 December 1863 he signed a receipt for $250,000—the largest payment received for a Yazoo boat. Although Parisot received his $60,000 for the *Dew Drop* in September, other captains did not collect until December 1863 or early in 1864. Joseph Benedict and the estate of Harry Landrum, both of Louisville, Kentucky, did not receive payment for the *Peytona* until 13 April 1864.[59] Extant documents indicate that the Confederate government paid for twenty of the civilian-owned boats. Incomplete records preclude drawing conclusions regarding the remaining steamers.

Ironically, General U. S. Grant's military policies left thirty-seven wrecks in the Yazoo River, and several years after the Civil War, President Grant signed the appropriations bill providing funds to remove the wrecks.[60]

5 / A New Beginning: The P. Line

The war on the Yazoo continued for a year after the *Petrel's* capture. Confederate Scouts and Mississippi Partisans tenuously held the Delta against sporadic Union forays.[1] Steamboatmen sought only to survive; it was not yet time to begin again. As the hulls of the Yazoo Fleet and Union gunboats deteriorated into debris and the Yazoo country struggled in the backwaters of the war, only a few boats cautiously steamed around the burned-out hulls.

Records for this period are scarce, revealing only three boats on the Yazoo in the last months of the war. The *Idaho*, a "small trading steamer" of sixty-two tons, was captured by guerrillas near Greenville on the Mississippi River but managed to escape and entered the Yazoo in the spring.[2] The *Poland*, which was owned by Henry Ames & Company of St. Louis, operated on the edge of the law by dealing in Confederate cotton, which peaked at $1.90 a pound in 1865. The unnamed captain of the *Poland* offered Joseph Blackburn, a captain commanding Confederate Scouts in Washington County, "any quantity of clothing, arms and ammunitions of war" if Blackburn would let a "certain lot" of Confederate cotton reach the banks of the Mississippi in December 1864. Unsuccessful on the Mississippi River, the *Poland* steamed into the Yazoo, where she collided with the *Idaho* and sank at the mouth of the Big Sunflower. The collision cost the lives of twelve men, making it the worst steamboat disaster on the river system.[3]

The *Idaho* returned to the Yazoo periodically until she sank in December 1867. The *Freestone*, a transport on the *Petrel's* ill-fated expedition, hit a snag and sank about fifteen miles above Yazoo City in September 1865. Several months earlier, the Union gunboat *Oriole* was stationed at the mouth of the Yazoo River to "intercept a vessel said to have on board 400 bales of cotton belonging to the Confederate states."⁴ Perhaps the *Idaho*, the *Freestone*, or another unknown boat sought the rich gains of this illegal trade.

Only a few of the Yazoo Fleet steamboatmen remained on or returned to the river. Thomas P. Leathers, joining with Ed Montgomery, the former owner of the *General Earl Van Dorn*, negotiated a Confederate contract to retrieve "the engines, iron and copper work and fastenings, brasses, bells and boilers of the steamboats which [had] been sunk in the Yazoo River and its tributaries." Confederate Secretary of War James Seddon and Chief of Ordnance Josiah Gorgas approved the contract, which gave Leathers 75 percent of the value of all materials delivered to Selma. The astute Leathers wanted to be paid in Confederate cotton or tobacco, and again Seddon and Gorgas agreed. Leathers salvaged the *Natchez* and several other wrecks and stored the "machinery, riggings and outfits" in warehouses along the Yazoo. He sent some of the engines to Vaughan's Station on the Mississippi Central Railroad, but before they were transshipped to Meridian and Selma, Union forces confiscated the salvage. Leathers would spend the next thirty years unsuccessfully seeking restitution or compensation from the Federal government.⁵

Leathers began to rebuild his steamboating career at New Orleans, purchasing a one-fourth share in the *General Quitman*. John W. Cannon, who owned the remaining three-fourths, had been with the boat during the war years on the Red River. A longtime enmity developed when Leathers sued Cannon for his one-fourth of the insurance money after the boat sank in 1868. Fuming over a subsequent rate disagreement, the "feisty" Leathers met the not-so-"meek" Cannon for a "knock down" on the streets of New Orleans, but newspapers reported that "little claret was drawn." The animosity may have been present when Leathers prepared his *Natchez* for the race against Cannon's *Rob't E. Lee*. Several years before he raised the United States flag on the *Natchez*, Leathers joined Cannon, John Tobin, and Sherman H. Parisot in a business venture that ended in a fistfight on the Vicksburg streets, an economic war on the Yazoo, and a legal battle in Federal courts.⁶

John W. Tobin, former owner of the *J. F. Pargoud*, was master of the *Vicksburg* in 1865 when she steamed between her namesake city and New Orleans. Three years later, Tobin owned the beautiful *Frank Pargoud* and the "odd looking" *Economist*, which was designed "to float in 8 inches of water." In succeeding years, Tobin became part owner and captain of the "supreme triumph of cotton boat architecture," the *J. M. White*. Tobin's *Pargoud*, and later his *J. M. White*, with Leathers's *Natchez* and Cannon's *Rob't E. Lee*, became the Pool Line, which transshipped cotton on downstream runs to New Orleans from the postwar Yazoo boats owned by the survivors of the Yazoo Fleet.[7]

Several steamboatmen from the Yazoo Fleet remained on their waterways. Joshua Wiley steamed in the Sunflower trade in the *Thomas Powell*, in which he owned a half-interest. Thomas G. Ledbetter, who had been pilot aboard the Yazoo Fleet steamer *Paul Jones*, returned to his home waters and became a lifelong friend and associate of Parisot. Thomas Metzler, Yazoo Fleet engineer, probably raised the wreck of the *Hope*, for he steamed as her captain in 1866. Milton Dent, former business associate of Parisot and captain of the late *Dixie*, reappeared on the Yazoo in October 1865 as master of the sixty-four-ton *Martin Walt*. By the end of the century, six members of the Dent family had been associates of Parisot. The captain who had put the torch to his *Dew Drop* on the Quiver River made his mark on the Yazoo River after the war.[8]

Sherman H. Parisot became *the* commodore of the Yazoo and presided over, indeed symbolized, the golden age of Yazoo steamboating between 1870 and 1890. He organized the Parisot Line, affectionately known as the "P. Line" because of its logo—the letter "P"—suspended between the chimneys of his boats. Parisot prospered as a steamboatman and earned the respect and admiration of Delta citizens, who depended on his P. Line as their way to the outside world.

After burning the *Dew Drop* on the Quiver River, Parisot faced the challenge of rebuilding his career. His first task was to do something about his name, which was the same as that of the Union general, who although forced to withdraw, twice had violated the Yazoo channel. After the war, Parisot was referred to as "Shum," S. H. Parisot, Captain Parisot, or the commodore, but never again as Sherman, except by an enemy.[9] In the absence of autobiographical or biographical accounts, the captain must be known by the boats he kept. A collage of adjectives used to describe him, his boats, line, or actions reveals Parisot as seen by his contemporaries. In newspaper notices of his first boat, Parisot was referred to as *reliable, responsible,* and *reasonable.* Throughout his career he was valued for his *honesty* and was *respected* as *just, fair,* and *kind.* This *solid man of the South* exuded an *elegant* and *fine style,* characterized by an *irrepressible* and *genial urbanity.* He was *attentive, accommodating, amicable,* and *courteous* to his associates, friends, and passengers. His *grand, graceful,* and *popular* boats were *unsurpassed* for *pleasant* and *gay* times with *elegant* accommodations and *sumptuous* fare. Even the smallest of his boats was a *dandy* and showed *pride,* or *looked pretty as a daisy.* The *honored* and *staunch* P. Line was regarded in *high esteem* for its *good work in serving faithfully* and *responsibly.* Perhaps Parisot's *genial* and *urbane* personality emanated from his continental father or from the social milieu of his childhood. His *pleasant* disposition endeared him to friends, who remained steadfast even in the dark days of economic reversal.10

Shum Parisot returned to his steamboating career as master of the *Blue Wing* in October 1865. Purchasing a boat in the capital-scarce postwar South was a major feat. The day after Christmas, Parisot bought a two-thirds share in the sidewheel steamer *Calumet.* Christine Metzler, wife of the captain of the *Hope,* purchased the remaining third. Parisot refinanced the *Calumet* and owned a one-third interest in her in March 1866; G. M. Hunter and R. E. Champion, of Columbus, Ohio, each held a third interest. Carrie Hunter and Robert Bowman purchased the Ohio shares the next year. In February 1868, Thomas and Christine Metzler joined Parisot, purchasing the $3,000 interest held by Hunter and Bowman. On 24 June 1868, Parisot became full owner of the *Calumet* by buying Christine Metzler's share for $2,000. The 305-ton *Calumet* was a good-looking, three-decked, sidewheel steamer with a transom stern, and she measured 151 x 26 x 5 feet. The fine old boat served Parisot well for almost six years before he moved her machinery and abandoned the hull in 1871.11

Competition on the Yazoo River system became intense in February 1868, just at the time Parisot and the Metzlers purchased the *Calumet.* Thirteen boats, including the *Calumet,* competed for cargoes on the Yazoo River and its tributaries. The Deer Creek Slackwater Navigation Company ran the *Roma Wheeler* and *Naomi,* two small low-water boats. Four equally small boats, the *Eddie, Kate, Keoto,* and *Newsboy,* operated on the Sunflower River.

Of the two boats claiming the Tallahatchie River, the *Favorite* was a steam propeller boat and the *Myrtle* was owned by John Johnston, "a planter on the Tallahatchie River." The *Myrtle* was reported as having a "fine trip" when loaded with two hundred bales of cotton. Milton Dent owned the *Countess*, which had been rebuilt after the Confederates burned her in 1864 on the Red River, and Thomas Metzler had replaced the *Hope* with the *Plain City.* Two transient steamers from the New Orleans–Vicksburg trade, the *Big Horn* and the *Sully*, entered the Yazoo briefly during the cotton season. If the Yazoo captains had ever divided the waterways by an agreement, it was no longer observed. With thirteen steamers scurrying to pick up a cargo in unrestrained competition, any of them could have met financial disaster.[12]

Parisot, Dent, and Metzler, in an effort to establish order by dividing the trades in 1868, called the other captains to a meeting in January, but they reached no agreement. The editor of the *Vicksburg Daily Times* spoke for the steamboatmen rather than the planters when he pronounced as "most unfortunate" the practice of "every boat carrying freight and passengers at prices as each captain may determine." With the support of Dent and Metzler, Parisot called a "grand council of war" in February.[13] Following this second meeting, reports of arrivals and departures from the Vicksburg landing indicate that order had been established. Parisot's *Calumet*, Dent's *Countess*, and Metzler's *Plain City* steamed the Yazoo between Vicksburg and Greenwood. The *Favorite* and *Myrtle* ran in the Tallahatchie and Yalobusha trade and transferred their cargoes to the Yazoo boats at Greenwood, while the Sunflower boats met the Yazoo steamers at the mouth of the Sunflower River. Only one of the Deer Creek boats, the *Roma Wheeler*, occasionally moored at Vicksburg. Parisot, Dent, and Metzler coordinated their schedules up and down the Yazoo so that the two Mississippi River boats soon gave up their efforts to penetrate the Yazoo trade.

Cotton production increased from the wartime hiatus, but Delta production did not return to antebellum levels until the early 1870s. Shippers and planters estimated that fewer than one hundred thousand bales were produced annually from 1868 to 1875, and Parisot transported his share of the crop in 1868–69.[14] After securing the *Era No. 8* as a summer replacement for the *Calumet*, which was sent to New Orleans for repairs and refurbishing, the captain made an unexplained trip to Louisville, Kentucky. Milton Dent brought the "new" Calumet back from New Orleans, and, just in time for the fall cotton season, the reason for Parisot's Louisville trip became apparent. The lovely Belle Yazoo, fresh from the Louisville boatyards, steamed to the Vicksburg landing. Introducing a new boat was no trivial matter, and Parisot managed it with his customary "fine style." He planned a "flag presentation" and decorated the Belle Yazoo with bunting and flags provided by Vicksburg merchants. Parisot supplied the refreshments, and his old friend John Tobin sent the musicians from his splendid packet Frank Pargoud, which was moored nearby. At high noon, Parisot presented the flag, and after the necessary speeches, his guests toured the Belle Yazoo. Shum Parisot on his new boat, Milton Dent at the wheel of the Calumet, and John Dent aboard the Countess entered the Yazoo to do business.[15]

The next year, Parisot purchased the Lucy Keirn, a trim streamer with sidewheels twenty-five feet in diameter. She had cost $34,000 and could transport three hundred tons of cargo, but she was more than a cotton boat. She quickly earned a reputation as "the popular and the beauty and the pride of the Yazoo and Tallahatchie Rivers."[16] With four boats, Lucy Keirn, Belle Yazoo, Countess, and Calumet, Parisot organized the Yazoo River Packet Company, the Parisot Line, in 1870. When he suspended the initial "P" between the chimneys of the boats, the P. Line was born. At the close of the 1870–71 season, Dent sold the Countess for $1,000 and the Calumet "died of old age." The P. Line added the sternwheel steamer Big Sunflower, and the engines from the old Calumet were placed on the Yazoo, a new boat "built entirely" in Vicksburg. Although the Big Sunflower occasionally went into her namesake river, P. Line boats were most often reported on the Yazoo. Parisot nurtured his connections on the Sunflower River system. When Thomas Metzler's Hope, valued at $700, burned a mile from Vicksburg, Parisot helped Metzler secure a new boat, which was named in honor of Frank Beck, the P. Line clerk aboard the Belle Yazoo. The Frank Beck, Jr., was only ninety feet long, but she boasted six "pleasant staterooms."[17]

Parisot patiently forged the P. Line from its beginning in 1870 so that in 1874 the Vicksburg Daily Times editor confidently declared that the captain "has now got control of the river and intends to keep it."[18] Of the twelve to fifteen boats reported on the Yazoo system during each cotton season for the four-year period, the P. Line owned four, and Parisot was associated with several other boats, including Metzler's *Frank Beck, Jr.* George W. Bookout, who was usually known as a P. Line pilot, ran the *Nellie Thomas*, and during a difficult time with low water and probably at Parisot's request, John Tobin sent his "odd looking" *Economist* into the Yazoo. The four P. Line boats usually ran on the Yazoo and Tallahatchie rivers, while the associated small boats ran in the low-water streams of the Sunflower.

The P. Line was not significantly threatened by other small boats on the tributaries. Several competing boats in the Deer Creek trade could not have commanded much business. The little *Bluella* was only eighty-six feet long, and the *Dart* was smaller by one-half. John and Henry King organized the Yazoo Competition Line and ran the ten-year-old *Emma* and the *Vicksburg*, which was only ninety feet long. The Competition Line, started in 1874, did not return for the 1875–76 cotton season. The *Lottawanna*, a cotton boat with a cargo capacity of twenty-two hundred bales of cotton, and the six-hundred ton *Selma* offered more substantial competition, but they made only a few runs in the Yazoo trade and did not return in 1874.[19] If Parisot did not control the river, he commanded a major share of the trade, for he prospered even during the early years of the depression that began in 1873. When he built a wharfboat and elevator in Vicksburg in 1875, the local editor proclaimed that the P. Line was "the only substantial thing that Vicksburg can boast of." When he moved his headquarters to Vicksburg, Parisot changed the official name of the company to the Mississippi & Yazoo River Packet Company, but it was always known as the P. Line.[20]

Although Parisot moved to Vicksburg, changed the name of the company, and entered the New Orleans–Vicksburg trade, he did not neglect shippers along the Yazoo River. Believing that "one good line can carry the freight and passengers cheaper than two," Parisot tried to make his P. Line the best.[21] Reliability was Parisot's key to success. He maintained reliable service because he had adroit management, good boats, capable officers, and strong crews. A survey of arrival and departure notices in the sometimes incomplete newspaper collections from the three river towns of Vicksburg, Yazoo City, and Greenwood suggests that Parisot had one boat going up as another came down at almost all times during a busy season. When a P. Line boat left Vicksburg in the late afternoon, another often landed the following midday. A similar schedule was followed at Yazoo City and Greenwood. When Parisot repaired his boats in Vicksburg or New Orleans after a busy cotton season, he did not abandon the Yazoo. Instead, by staggering the downtime or chartering summer replacements, he kept three boats running in the summer. This practice attracted the attention of the *St. Louis Times*, which reported that although "the business could be handled by fewer boats it is the policy of this company to accommodate their patrons all the year round and not simply when it pays to do so."[22] The reputation of the "reliable" and "dependable" P. Line extended from St. Louis to New Orleans, and several captains of the great packets sought out the Yazoo captain.

P. Line boats occasionally ran from Vicksburg to New Orleans and back, but more often Parisot transferred his cargoes to the large packets running on the Mississippi River. The *Lucy Keirn* waited on merchandise from Cannon's *Rob't E. Lee*, and other P. Line boats transshipped their cotton aboard the *Frank Pargoud* or the *Natchez*. Thomas Leathers maintained cordial relations with Parisot. Soon after the forty-nine-year-old Parisot married Mary S. Lamkin in August 1876, Mrs. Leathers sent a gift of oysters and other "good things" to the bride and groom. A few weeks after Commodore and Mrs. Parisot returned from their wedding trip, Mrs. Leathers reached Vicksburg aboard the *Natchez*. Parisot wrote her a personal note thanking her for the delicacies, and, explaining that Tuesday was an especially busy day, he apologized for not being able to pay her a short visit.[23] Perhaps the urbane Yazoo captain more often met her husband, his old friend from the Yazoo Fleet days. Records reveal only a few meetings between Parisot and Leathers. But they were important.

Captain Parisot and his bride registered at the Lexington Hotel in Louisville, Kentucky, two days after their wedding. Perhaps they were on their way to the Chicago Centennial Exhibition, but on Thursday afternoon they were in Jeffersonville, Indiana. The Howard Ship Yards customarily launched a new steamer at 4:00 P.M., and on this Thursday Parisot's the *Yazoo Valley* slid down the ways. The new sternwheel steamer, using the machinery from the dismantled *Lucy Keirn*, was taken to Louisville for the furnishings and finishing touches. According to reports, the *Yazoo Valley* had one of the "prettiest cabins ever put on a sternwheel boat," and her bar was "a beauty." Measuring 180 x 36 x 5.5 feet, the steamer could carry three thousand bales of cotton and a "large number of passengers." Parisot and Frank Beck took her to New Orleans in October 1876 and entered her in the New Orleans–Vicksburg trade. The *Yazoo Valley* became noted for making the downstream run in thirty-six hours and the return trip in forty-five hours. She made weekly trips between New Orleans and Vicksburg until the end of the cotton season.[24]

Parisot's *Yazoo Valley* competed with the New Orleans and Vicksburg Packet Company—the Pool Line—which ran Cannon's *Rob't E. Lee*, Leathers's *Natchez*, and Tobin's *Pargoud*. These three giants certainly did not look favorably upon Parisot's intrusion into their New Orleans–Vicksburg trade. Perhaps they subtly or not so subtly implied the dangers inherent in a rate war or the needless competition if they should find it necessary to enter the Yazoo trade. Leathers seems to have done most of the bargaining with Parisot because the *Natchez* and *Yazoo Valley* often reached Vicksburg or New Orleans within the same twenty-four-hour period throughout the winter months. All four captains met in New Orleans on 21 March 1877 and signed the fateful Articles of Agreement.[25]

By this agreement Captains Cannon, Leathers, and Tobin bound themselves to transport all P. Line cargoes destined for New Orleans and to deliver to P. Line boats at Vicksburg all Yazoo-bound cargoes which they received at New Orleans. Parisot agreed to accept all cargoes arriving at Vicksburg destined for the Yazoo country and to deliver to his new colleagues all cargoes shipped from the Yazoo to New Orleans. They were agreeing to divide the trade, just as on a smaller scale Parisot, Dent, and Metzler had divided the Yazoo-Tallahatchie-Sunflower trades in 1868. But the 1877 Articles of Agreement contained other far-reaching commitments.

The Pool Line, as party of the first part, further agreed to "in no matter whatever either for pleasure, convenience or profit and for no excuse whatever interfere with or obstruct or do any act whatever to [Parisot] in his business trade or commerce of the said Yazoo River." They promised not to run any boats on the Yazoo and to refrain from "encouraging promoting or in any manner aiding or assisting other boats their agents or servants to do business" in the Yazoo. "On the contrary," they further promised to "promote and encourage" Parisot's business. Thus protected from competition, Parisot bound himself "not to interfere with, obstruct or do any act whatsoever" that would "injure or obstruct the business trade or commerce" of Cannon, Leathers, or Tobin "between the mouth of the Yazoo River [and] the city of New Orleans, Louisiana." In the final part of the document, Parisot agreed to sell one-fourth shares in the *Yazoo Valley* to Cannon, Leathers, and Tobin. Parisot would run the steamer in the Yazoo River, and the four captains would "share and share alike as to profits and losses" of the *Yazoo Valley.* Only this one of the P. Line boats was allowed to steam south of Vicksburg and then only if she had a through cargo bound for New Orleans. Finally, the four captains bound themselves, their heirs, and assigns "not only as to the steamers named herein but all other steamers and boats which any of the parties . . . may hereafter control, own, manage or direct." The Articles of Agreement signed by the four captains gave Parisot the Yazoo, but as he later found, it also confined him to his river.26

The golden age of Yazoo steamboating had arrived. Parisot had a favorable transfer agreement with the New Orleans and Vicksburg Packet Company, and he was protected against competition from that company; the U.S. Army Corps of Engineers had cleared the river channels of their worst obstructions; cotton production increased so that planters shipped 101,725 bales of cotton by water in the 1878–79 season; and the P. Line had six good boats and was adding more.27

The P. Line began the 1877–78 season with the *Big Sunflower, Carrie Hogan, Home, Sunflower Belle, Tallahatchie,* and *Yazoo.* The next year, it added the *Leflore, Hope,* and *E. C. Carroll, Jr.,* which was named for the "interesting son" of Captain Ed C. Carroll, and Parisot also temporarily chartered the *John M. Chambers.* Continuing to grow and replacing old boats with new ones, the P. Line added the *City of Yazoo, Deer Creek, Fairplay,* and *Little P.* in 1879. The hull of the *Little P.* had been built at Yazoo City, and when she burned in early 1880, Parisot replaced her with the small steamer *Alert* and made plans to refurbish the recently purchased *De Smet* for the coming season.28

The *City of Yazoo,* a sternwheel "triumph of marine architecture," was two hundred feet long with a beam of thirty-eight feet with guards eight feet wide. She was built by the Howard Ship Yards at a cost of $25,000, and Parisot added another $9,000 in machinery, outfit, and furnishings. The largest boat of the P. Line at the time, she had a cargo capacity of forty-five hundred bales of cotton, but when unloaded and "all ready for business" she drew only "seventeen inches forward and twenty-eight inches aft." Her "full length, finely furnished cabin" made her "complete . . . as a freight and passenger steamer." Indeed, "everything on her denote[d] comfort, convenience, durability, and beauty." Describing Parisot as the "little Hercules of the Yazoo," the *Louisville Courier-Journal* said that "such men as Parisot draw a full hand and play the winning cards, and the 'best' card that Capt. Parisot ever played" was the *City of Yazoo*. She was on the Yazoo in December 1879. But could such a boat be used efficiently on that river system? Where else could she run? The 1877 Articles of Agreement prevented Parisot from running her in the New Orleans trade. In mid-1880 she ran under the command of Bowling S. Leathers, son of Thomas P. Leathers, as a summer replacement for the *Natchez*.[29]

During the three cotton seasons in which Parisot enjoyed his protected position on the Yazoo (1877–80), eight or nine steamers provided the most efficient operating schedules during any given season. Parisot usually ran three of his larger boats in the Vicksburg–Yazoo City trade and kept four smaller boats running above Yazoo City. One or two small boats ran in the Sunflower River system, and the little sternwheel *Alert* was reported as the first steamer ever on Bear Creek. Parisot met variations in demand or changing water levels by moving a boat from one stream to another or adding a boat. P. Line captains and pilots knew the shippers and the rivers so well that they often anticipated and responded quickly to changing conditions.

Parisot served his patrons so that competition almost ceased to exist. The *Seminole*, a New Orleans–Shreveport packet, steamed into the Tallahatchie, where she raced the P. Liner *Home* for cargoes. The *Seminole* should have won the race for the "*Home* was always laden heavily with freight up and down, and the *Seminole* was always empty." The intruder quietly left the rivers.[30] The "produce" boat *Kate Dixon* steamed into the Yalobusha once in February 1878 and then left for her home port of Cincinnati. The *Mike Davis*, from Fish Creek, West Virginia, also tried the Yazoo waters but found no business. When the *David Stinson* had no better luck, Parisot bought her and converted her hull to a barge.[31] Charley Bocaletti of Pittsburgh, Pennsylvania, had such bad luck that he could not even leave the Yazoo. He owned the *C. P. Huntington*, which he insured against sinking, but unfortunately she burned at the foot of Honey Island in 1877, and Bocaletti had to start a "new life" with a "trade float." A few other independently owned boats steamed on the river system, but they were "specialty" boats such as "trade" or store boats, sawmill or cotton gin boats, and did not compete in the transport or passenger trade. The sometimes crusty editor of the *Yazoo Valley Flag* noted in 1878 that since Colonel Ed Richardson was regarded as the "Cotton King" of the Delta, Commodore Parisot should be recognized as the "River King." Indeed, Parisot was a mighty big frog in a not so small pond.[32]

The commodore of the P. Line built his monopoly at a time when big business enjoyed public acclaim, and even when monopolies and trusts came under attack, the P. Line retained public confidence, with one notable exception. According to local newspapers, the "regular, reliable and responsible P. Line," although recognized as a monopoly, continued to enjoy public support because the line had "never abused its powers."[33] Parisot's benevolent monopoly provided reliable transportation and stylish accommodations for passengers who looked upon his boats as their only way to the outside world. Parisot's strengths were his managerial ability and his personal relations with associates, shippers, and passengers. Although an outstanding pilot, he was at his best in the main cabin, where he presided with commendable style. Management and public relations built the P. Line on the Yazoo River system.

Commodore and Mrs. Parisot lived in a spacious home at the corner of Fayette and Locust streets in Vicksburg, a block from Christ Episcopal Church, where they were communicants. Naturally, the man who "was the ruler of all the waters of the Yazoo and its rich tributaries" conducted his business from the Vicksburg landing.[34] The P. Line wharfboat and elevator was the center of activity, with John Bell managing the store, Captain Ed C. Carroll serving as superintendent, and David B. Rundle keeping the books. Presiding over the P. Line was apparently not enough activity for the commodore. He expanded his business interests by forming a partnership with Colonel Leonidas A. Campbell, a large Yazoo County landowner. The firm of S. H. Parisot & L. A. Campbell, Cotton Factors, soon had a $5,000 merchandise inventory. Upriver, the P. Line owned a "large cotton and freight warehouse" at Yazoo City and smaller warehouses in Tchula and Greenwood. Steamboats, warehouses, and a cotton business certainly represented financial success, but could a nineteenth-century southern businessman be a complete success without land? Parisot did not neglect this aspect of economic life.35

Richard Kinkead, originally of Limerick, Ireland, became Parisot's partner and managed their extensive landholdings, which included the steamboat landings known as Avoca, Haw Bluff, Limerick, Ratcliff's, Sherrards', and Success. They rebuilt the old Galtney log home near Haw Bluff Landing and changed the name to P. Line Home. Serving as a country retreat for Parisot, P. Line Home became "the most attractive, homelike place on the Yazoo River." The business and personal relationship between the farmer and the steamboatman flourished so that in 1879 Kinkead named his sixth child Sherman in honor of the grand Yazoo captain. Farther up the Yazoo Parisot's brother, A. A. Parisot, named his first son Sherman. At the time, the brothers owned Riverside and Mound Field plantations near Silver City on the Yazoo. In 1880, Shum owned in whole or in part almost thirty-five hundred acres of good Delta cotton lands. Parisot, referred to as the commodore, or the "River King," or the "prince of navigators," seemed to be at the peak of his career as the 1879–80 season drew to a close.36

And then Captain Parisot sold the P. Line. Steamboatmen were astonished. The editor of the *Yazoo City Herald* thought that labor problems might be one reason for Parisot's action. A *New Orleans Daily Picayune* writer was so surprised that he believed the commodore "must have acted very suddenly." Extant records indicate that the *City of Yazoo* and the 1877 Articles of Agreement were at the heart of the decision.37

Although the *City of Yazoo* drew only twenty-eight inches when "all ready for business," her forty-five-hundred bale cargo capacity was too large for her to be confined to the Yazoo River. The *Louisville Courier-Journal* had reported that she had been built for the New Orleans–Yazoo City trade.38 But by the 1877 agreement, Parisot had contracted to keep his boats out of the Mississippi

River south of Vicksburg. Did the Pool Line of Leathers, Cannon, and Tobin pressure Parisot into dividing the profits of the *City of Yazoo*, share and share alike, as had been required in the case of the *Yazoo Valley*? Available records indicate only that the P. Line captain Thomas G. Ledbetter delivered the *City of Yazoo* to Leathers on 18 July as a summer replacement for the *Natchez*.39 Whatever the arrangement, Parisot was so disheartened that he told two friends that he "wanted to go out of the steamboat business entirely." Frustration and anger must have been evident in the voice of the captain who once commanded the *Dew Drop* in the Yazoo Fleet and who had built the P. Line into a near monopoly when he almost shouted to Murray F. Smith that "he wanted to have nothing more to do with steamboats."40

During the latter part of June 1880, Parisot talked with Ed Carroll, superintendent of the line, and with Colonel Leonidas Campbell, his cotton factor partner, about selling the line. Carroll and Campbell quickly formed a syndicate, which included C. C. Floweree, the Vicksburg ice merchant, Murray F. Smith, an attorney at law, and the steamboatmen George H. Smith and Frank Beck, Jr., to buy the P. Line. Murray Smith drew up a Memorandum of Agreement, which Parisot signed on 17 July 1880.41

According to the memorandum, Parisot transferred title of the *City of Yazoo, E. C. Carroll, Jr., Leflore, Carrie Hogan*, and *De Smet* to the new organization. The syndicate also secured Parisot's "undivided one-fifth" interest in the steamers *Sunflower* and *Deer Creek*, their two barges, and full ownership of five other barges, the hulls of the *Lucy Keirn, Home, Tallahatchie, David Stinson*, and "one flat barge." Carroll's company acquired title to the large freight and cotton warehouse known as the Parisot Line Warehouse in Yazoo City and the smaller warehouses at Tchula and Greenwood, "together with the good will & exclusive right to use the letter 'P' between the chimneys of any steamboat that may ply on said Yazoo River & tributaries." Parisot agreed to "complete the repairs already contracted for . . . the steamer *De Smet*," and he bound himself not to "hereafter either directly or indirectly, for & on his account or the account of any other person, persons or corporation engage in the business of running boats or other water craft" on the Yazoo River system "unless it be the associate or in the interest of" the new P. Line. The syndicate agreed to pay $110,000 for the P. Line.42

Three days after the Memorandum of Agreement was signed, more than seventy-five "handsome young fellows" from the "far-famed and invincible P. Line" gathered in the late afternoon at the corner of Fayette and Locust streets and were invited into the "spacious parlors" of the Parisot home. The commodore of the "immortal P. Line," was known for his "popularity, stainless integrity, generous liberality, his steadfastness to friends and his matchless steamboat experience," faced his men. Murray F. Smith stepped forward and, speaking for the P. Liners, offered a "beautiful double neck chain of etruscan gold" to the commodore's wife. Then, turning to the captain, Smith presented on behalf of all who steamed under the letter "P" a "handsome gold watch and chain of the Louis Napoleon style," which was inscribed "In Token of Esteem to Commodore S. H. Parisot, from officers and members of the P. Line, July, 1880." Smith's obligatory speech soared with the eloquence and hyperbole demanded by such an occasion, but even so, he clearly reflected the P. Line mystique. He praised the special relationship that existed between the commodore and the P. Liners as "ties which are unparalleled in the history of any business." Because of Parisot's "courtesy, kindness and liberality," no P. Liner "in times of trouble or adversity ever hesitated as to whom they should apply for assistance and advice, and no one of them ever applied to [Parisot] in vain." Smith described the commodore's business as one that "towers aloft" in "majestic proportions" for the "wonder and admiration of all." High above all that Parisot built "glitter[ed] the mystic letter 'P'." It had become the symbol of "honesty, courtesy, liberality and fair dealing." The "elegant entertainment" came to an end. The P. Line did not.[43]

6/ Parisot Fights Another War

C aptain Carroll, steamboatman, and Colonel Campbell, merchant-planter, quickly put together a syndicate to purchase the P. Line. In addition to the two principals, the group included C. C. Floweree, Murray Smith, George H. Smith, and Frank Beck, Jr.[1] As the summer months wore on, the syndicate expanded to include Charles C. Carroll, Jr., and John A. Scudder, both of St. Louis, and A. Nye Spencer of Delta, Louisiana.[2] Murray Smith advised his fellow investors to form a corporation, and, believing that Mississippi had no general corporation law, he "examined the corporation laws of several states" and recommended that the investors "take out a charter according to the laws of Louisiana." [3] On 30 August 1880, the investors crossed the Mississippi River to Delta, a small town in Madison Parish, Louisiana, and there formed a "body corporate" bearing the name and title of the Mississippi and Yazoo River Packet Company. This company, the new P. Line, was capitalized at $100,000, which was divided into one thousand shares at $100 each. E. C. Carroll, former superintendent of the P. Line, was elected president, and David B. Rundle, P. Line bookkeeper, was named secretary.[4] Three weeks later, Parisot transferred his entire interest in the P. Line to the new corporation.[5] Carroll began the active management of the P. Line. Parisot was reported as devoting "most of his time to looking after his planting interests." [6]

Ed C. Carroll was born on the Eastern Shore of Maryland, but his family moved to St. Louis when he was an infant. He began working at the age of fourteen and soon became second clerk on a steamboat. After serving on a number of boats, Carroll moved to Vicksburg in 1867 and in time became a cashier in Duff Green's

Vicksburg wharfboat, which served the Parisot Line. In 1873 he became superintendent of the P. Line, a position he held until he was named president in 1880. He was an astute businessman, serving as an officer or director for a hotel, a timber company, a cottonseed oilmill, the cotton compress, an insurance company, an ice company, the Vicksburg Gaslight Company, two banks, and the P. Line. He was "an all around solid and substantial citizen." Carroll was clearly a managerial and financial success. His experience with the P. Line, however, suggests that he lacked the finesse of Shum Parisot in public relations.[7]

Carroll's P. Line ran seven boats in 1880, and the *De Smet* was the grandest of them all. She was built in 1872, and after one or two trips in the Red River trade she ran in the Missouri River. In 1873, she traveled up the Missouri to Fort Benton, Montana, and then returned to the Missouri and Ohio river trades. Parisot bought the old boat in 1880 before he sold the P. Line, and she was rebuilt and refurbished to his specifications. This sidewheel steamer measured 188 x 34 x 5 feet and could carry twenty-six hundred bales of cotton. "Almost everything aboard the *De Smet* [was] brand spanking new," and her large and comfortable rooms could "accommodate about fifty persons handsomely." She had "two bureaus, one under decks and one in texas," for "colored passengers." The *De Smet*, consistent with Parisot's attention to detail, "did not suffer by the comparison" when she moored next to the *J. M. White, Natchez,* and *Ed Richardson* at Vicksburg on her maiden voyage to the Yazoo. Indeed, she outshined the large Mississippi River packets. She had electric lights—four Brush electric arc lights, two in reflectors on the boiler deck and two on the roof, "lighted up the river for miles" the night she "came into port." Captain Parisot, although no longer associated with the company but with flags flying and the "magic P." between the chimneys, proudly introduced the "new candidate to the public." With Captain Thomas G. Ledbetter in command, the *De Smet* entered the Yazoo River, and the marvelous electric lights reached Greenwood on 2 December 1880. The bright example of the *De Smet* was slightly dimmed by events on the Yazoo.[8]

Captain Charley Bocaletti, who had lost his steamer the *C. P. Huntington,* rebuilt his career until he became known, albeit derisively, as the "Commodore of the Yazoo coal-oil barrel and soda bottle fleet" when the Greenwood boatyard built him three boats "in three days." But peddling notions, penny candy, fruits, vegetables, and a small assortment of housewares at steamboat landings paid off, for Bocaletti purchased the steamer *Josephine Spengler.* Taking her to Greenwood, he sold shares in her to local investors.9 Other investors at Yazoo City organized the Yazoo River Merchants and Planters Transportation Company in August 1880 and purchased the *Charles H. Tompkins* to run with Bocaletti's *Josephine Spengler* against the P. Line.10 Carroll countered by slashing freight rates to one dollar a bale and by sending the little *Timmie Baker* into the Yalobusha. The *E. C. Carroll, Jr.*, with new electric lights, went eighty miles above the "head of usual navigation" in the Tallahatchie to bring out 181 bales of cotton. The Vicksburg newspapers, always friendly to the P. Line, reported that the new competitors "intended to crush the P. Line, but it didn't P-an out very well." At the end of the 1880–81 cotton season, Murray Smith successfully brought suit against the *Charles H. Tompkins*, and a few months later the *Josephine Spengler* was condemned by admiralty court.11 The old P. Line had never treated its opposition so badly. Parisot beat his competitors, but he allowed them to leave the rivers quietly or absorbed them through purchase or charter. Public opinion on the upper Yazoo, the Tallahatchie, and the Yalobusha rivers increasingly tended to accuse Carroll's P. Line of monopolistic practices.

The cotton season beginning in the autumn of 1882 was an exceptionally bad one for Carroll's line. A short crop, low water followed by floods, a freight rate controversy, and growing antimonopoly sentiments combined to cause shippers in the upper river lands to yearn for Parisot's return. The strongest attack on the P. Line came from J. M. Liddell, Jr., the editor of the Greenwood *Yazoo Valley Flag*, who also supported the Farmers' Union in the Tallahatchie and Yalobusha river counties.12 Yazoo City shippers remained relatively quiet, though the Vicksburg newspapers continued to praise Carroll's line.

Three exceptionally dry months in the fall left the upper Yazoo and Tallahatchie navigable only to very small boats, and the Yalobusha was essentially closed to steamers. Liddell, complaining that Carroll did not furnish "boats sufficient to move the cotton lying on the river banks," charged that the P. Line wanted to "carry out the entire crop" with only "one or two little crafts [sic] which pay for themselves every two trips." Continuing his attack, Liddell noted that "weeks and weeks have passed and gone," and hundreds of bales of cotton "are still awaiting shipment." Local shippers, said the editor, "are afraid to try to get another line to come in" because they know that anyone supporting another line will find that P. Line boats will drive out the competition and leave his cotton to "waste upon the land." People are afraid to "speak out against the P. Line except in a whisper to a confidential friend."[13]

Carroll tried patiently to explain that during low water he made every effort to get boats into the upper Yazoo and Tallahatchie. He ran the only two boats that had a chance of navigating the treacherous channels, and when the *Leflore* ran on a snag, the line was "one boat short." During the worst of the low water, Carroll said that he secured an independent boat for the Yazoo, and even though he gave her "the entire receipts of the trip" and furnished her a barge "free of charge" the captain refused to return to such dangerous waters. But low water was not the only problem facing Carroll.[14]

In New Orleans representatives from the Cotton Exchange, the Produce Exchange, and the Chamber of Commerce attempted to establish uniform freight rates for the lower Mississippi River and its tributaries. They recommended that the maximum rate for public landings on the Yazoo River be the same as the rate from New Orleans to Vicksburg and that way landings should be no more than an additional 20 percent of the Vicksburg–Greenwood rate. When Carroll did not adopt the recommended rates, the *Yazoo Valley Flag* attacked.[15]

Liddell charged that Yazoo shippers would not benefit from the recommended rates because the P. Line "will charge whatever it pleases." He recalled that "these rivers have long been owned and controlled by the P. Line," which had "succeeded heretofore in freezing out any competition." Regretting that the line has "become careless of the interest of the patrons," the editor complained that shippers were "at the mercy of the whims of the P. Line." Using stronger language, Liddell observed that "the monopoly in this river has resulted in untold damage" and the people of Leflore County "have suffered more from this monopoly . . . than any people ever did." Waxing eloquent, the fearless editor seemed to shout that the "planters and merchants have been at the mercy of a soulless corporation that has grown fat and powerful from exorbitant rates."[16]

Carroll's reply to these charges did nothing to change public opinion. He said only that since the rate schedule was made by New Orleans merchants without consultation with the rivermen, he "very properly refused to recognize it." Attempting to contradict the charges that the company was growing "fat and powerful," he offered to "give the receipts of the Line for the past 90 days if [he] could have the disbursements refunded," or he would "cheerfully sell" the P. Line and "all its property, at cost," with "only a fair rate of interest." [17] The winter rains did more to end the attack than any resolution of freight rates. But the rains brought new problems.

Rapidly rising water quickly sloshed around the bales of cotton that had been left on the riverbanks during the drought. Water backing up over the lower Delta floodplain remained so shallow that boats could not reach farmers' cotton, which had been moved to higher ground. During the flood Carroll sent the *De Smet*, *Headlight*, and *Sunflower*, each "manned with a full complement of men, skiffs, axes, and other necessary utensils," into the Yazoo. Going as far as they could into the high waters, the boats anchored and sent skiffs with "medicine, stimulants, etc." in "each direction to look for the sufferers." After a hard day, the boats rescued 350 people, and when the *Sunflower* returned to Vicksburg her "deck was crowded with cattle they had picked up." The *St. Louis Post-Dispatch* praised the "good work" done by the P. Line in relieving the "sufferers in the over flowed lands" and lauded Carroll as "one of nature's noblemen." In Yazoo City, "A Friend" praised the P. Line as the "best monopoly ever known." Such service and publicity helped restore public confidence in the P. Line. It also reminded Delta shippers and planters of the good old days when Parisot was in command.[18]

Parisot's activities after he sold the P. Line are a matter of conjecture. A Vicksburg newspaper suggested that Parisot sold his steamboat interests because he wanted to devote his energies to his Yazoo River cotton plantations. Undoubtedly, he worked closely with Kinkead, his farming associate, at P. Line Home because they won the third prize for long-staple cotton at the 1883 Cotton Exposition. He was not associated with the P. Line except for a brief period in the 1880–81 season when he allowed Carroll to name him as director during the short struggle against the Merchants and Planters Transportation Company. Murray Smith affirmed that Parisot was a director without authority and that it was even suggested that he be given one share of stock and named president, but no stock changed hands. When the old commodore died in 1917, the *Vicksburg Daily Herald* printed a ten-paragraph obituary summarizing Parisot's business career. This summary, although containing several errors, suggests the most probable set of circumstances. After leaving the P. Line, Parisot, in addition to his planting interests, continued in the firm of Parisot & Campbell, and "discovering that he had lost a large amount of money, he decided to enter the river trade again." For whatever reason, Parisot did return to steamboating, but not on the Yazoo.[19]

Parisot made his decision during the 1881–82 cotton season. Perhaps as early as January 1882, he contacted the Howard Ship Yards of Jeffersonville, which had built the *Yazoo City* and the *City of Yazoo*, about another steamer. John Howard wrote that he would build the boat Parisot described for $25,100 excluding machinery, and Parisot approved the price by endorsing the letter, which became the contract for his new boat. The boatyard began building the hull, and in May Parisot sent a "rough sketch of [the] cabin & Texas," which did not have "quite so many rooms as fore." He wanted the rooms to be three inches larger because "6 ft. is rather too short for some of our long and hungry fellows." Frank Beck, Jr., a former P. liner, made the first payment for the boat, giving Howard a draft for $2,000 drawn on the New Orleans steamboat captain A. McVay and dated 10 May 1882. Subsequent drafts by Parisot, McVay, or Beck made between May and 18 October completed payment for the boat. The new steamer was named *S. H. Parisot*, and when she was enrolled according to law, her owner was S. H. Parisot, president of the New Orleans and Bend Packet Company of Louisville, Kentucky. The certificate was dated 18 October 1882.[20]

Before the steamer was enrolled and while Carroll tried to cope with the low water in the Yazoo, Parisot, McVay, and Frank Beck, Jr., met in Louisville, where on 23 September 1882 they incorporated the New Orleans and Bend Packet Company. Parisot held 298 shares of stock, Beck 161 shares, and McVay 141, for a total of 600 shares at $100 each. The three riverboatmen, as the board of directors, elected Parisot president, Beck vice-president, and Richard H. Woolfolk, who owned no stock, secretary of the Louisville-based corporation. The *S. H. Parisot*, on her maiden voyage, reached New Orleans on 30 October 1882.[21]

The Washington Artillery Band struck up a lively welcoming tune as the graceful *S. H. Parisot*, with her two Brush electric arc lights blazing, reached the New Orleans landing at 7:30 in the evening. As she touched the wharf, the Washington Artillery honored her with a twenty-gun salute. This sternwheel boat was the largest Parisot had ever owned. She measured 225 x 40.5 x 7.5 feet for a total tonnage of 563.57 tons; she could carry fifty-five hundred bales of cotton. Her four 24-foot-long boilers produced the steam to turn her giant sternwheel, and she gleamed as only a Parisot boat could. Her main cabin, 200 feet long, must have been a brilliant spectacle with new furniture, stylish decorations, and spotless white linens. Each of her skylight glasses sparkled as they caught the sun, for each was decorated with a cotton plant in bloom. Naturally, she was described as the "finest sternwheel ever built."[22]

The *Daily Picayune* reported that the *S. H. Parisot* was "owned by two of the most popular and thorough steamboat men in the country." The reference was not to Parisot but to Captains McVay and Beck, who entered the boat in the New Orleans and Bends trade. Apparently, neither Parisot, Beck, nor McVay made any effort to correct the announcement. The *S. H. Parisot* continued to be advertised as a weekly packet in the New Orleans and Bends trade under the command of McVay and Beck.[23] But the steamboat fraternity could not keep secrets long, and before the year was out knowledgeable persons, including Leathers and Tobin, knew that Parisot was an owner of the boat.

The *Vicksburg Herald* tried to untangle a series of events that took place in January and February 1883 but came to the conclusion that the "bottom facts are hard to find." Earlier, the *Picayune* reported that the "long threatened war . . . has at last assumed shape," and the paper erroneously reported that Beck, of the *S. H. Parisot*, was planning to enter the Yazoo in competition with the P. Line. The *Picayune* was correct only in forecasting that it "will be a bitter war."[24] The war raged from December 1882 until 5 April 1884. The combatants were Parisot and the P. Line on one hand and the Pool Line of Leathers, Tobin, and the heirs of the late John Cannon on the other. The battleground stretched from the streets of Vicksburg up the Yazoo, down the Mississippi, and finally into the United States Fifth Circuit Court.

Even before Parisot, Beck, and McVay made their last payment for the steamer *S. H. Parisot*, the old commodore reluctantly came back to the P. Line. When L. A. Campbell, the cotton factor, died in 1881, Parisot scrutinized the firm's books and discovered that Campbell was in debt to the business and therefore to the surviving partner. Parisot was prevailed upon to accept Campbell's 225 shares of P. Line stock rather than a Yazoo River plantation. According to Murray Smith, Parisot "was at first unwilling" to take the stock but accepted it as the "readiest means to realize his money."[25] The stock transfer was completed in early January 1883, and when Parisot returned to the P. Line, the newspaper reported that he was president. At the time, Parisot and Carroll were the only P. Liners who knew of the 1877 Articles of Agreement, and apparently they continued to transship Yazoo River cargoes on boats of Leathers's New Orleans and Vicksburg Packet Company. The *S. H. Parisot*, making its weekly trips up and down the Mississippi River and taking in receipts estimated at $4,000 per trip, was not yet part of the P. Line.[26]

Captains Tobin and Leathers of the New Orleans–based Pool Line could not stand idly by while Parisot invaded their territory. They contacted their attorneys, and the New Orleans firm of Bayne and Denegre entered a suit on behalf of John Tobin, his wife, Mary F. Tobin, Thomas P. Leathers, Louisa H. Stout, and William Campbell (the latter two representing the estate of the late John W. Cannon) against S. H. Parisot on 31 January 1883 in the Civil District Court of Orleans Parish. The plaintiffs asked for $75,000 in actual damages and $20,000 in exemplary damages on the grounds that Parisot had violated the 1877 Articles of Agreement by running his steamer, the *S. H. Parisot*, south of Vicksburg. Parisot's New Orleans attorney, W. S. Benedict, filed exceptions, and when they were overruled by the court, he entered a petition to remove the case from the state court to the Circuit Court of the United States for the Fifth Judicial Circuit because of diversity of citizenship. The case was duly removed on 17 February 1883, and the wheels of justice slowly began to grind.[27]

Parisot had been in New Orleans at the end of January when the suit was filed, but he returned to Vicksburg two days later and immediately resigned as president of the P. Line. Within a day or two after filing his resignation, Parisot met Thomas Leathers on a Vicksburg street. The wartime comrades and former business associates, now adversaries, exchanged a few words, which became increasingly unpleasant. Their meeting came to an end when Leathers called Parisot a "d——d liar" and Parisot responded by giving Leathers a "bl——k eye." The combatants separated or were separated, and the battle shifted to the Mississippi and Yazoo rivers.28

Friends and shippers in the Yazoo country did not know what was happening. Indeed, neither did the New Orleans newspaper, for the editor sent the "pressboat" the *Susie B.* into the Yazoo. Frank Beck went "up the Yazoo in the interest of his popular boat the *S.H. Parisot*" in January, which was about the same time that the steamer *Headlight* entered the Yazoo and advertised as connecting with the *S. H. Parisot*. Liddell, the antimonopoly editor of the *Yazoo Valley Flag*, exuberantly reported that the *Headlight* and *S. H. Parisot* were running in "opposition to the P. Line." Believing that Captain Parisot was connected with both boats, Liddell anticipated better times on the Yazoo because Parisot was "the man to correct the abuses that had crept into the management of the P. Line."29 The editor was only partly right. Conditions did improve, not because Parisot was in opposition to the P. Line but because he was connected with his old line.

River business in March, the last month of the cotton season, was deceptive. The *S. H. Parisot* was withdrawn from the New Orleans–Bends trade and was "laid up" at Gretna, Louisiana. John Tobin's boat, the *J. M. White*, tied up at Vicksburg to wait for the P. Line steamer *De Smet*, which was coming down the Yazoo with a cargo destined for New Orleans. Shum Parisot was reported as returning to the "active management" of the P. Line. And Thomas Ledbetter noted that since the winter floodwaters were falling, planters were beginning to clear their fields for the next crop.30 Spring was at hand, summer not far away, and all seemed back to normal. But behind the scenes, Parisot busily prepared the P. Line for the coming battle against the Pool Line.

"Sometime in the late spring, or the early summer of 1883," the P. Line made an agreement with the New Orleans and Bend Packet Company to purchase the *S. H. Parisot* for 600 shares of P. Line stock. E. C. Carroll called the stockholders of the P. Line to order at 2:00 on 30 May 1883, in Delta, Louisiana, to amend the company's charter according to law. The eight stockholders voted their 1,250 shares, without a dissenting vote, to increase the stock of the company by 600 shares valued at $100 each. Sometime later, when the *S. H. Parisot* was inspected and new enrollment papers completed, she was owned by "D. B. Rundle, Secretary" of the P. Line.[31]

Parisot, with the support of Carroll, who remained as president of the corporation, was determined to break the Pool Line's stranglehold on the lower Mississippi River trade. Arguing that the 1877 agreement was an unenforceable contract because it was "illegal, immoral, and in restraint of trade," he prepared to fight the larger monopoly. The P. Line repaired and refurbished its largest boats, *S. H. Parisot, City of Yazoo*, and *De Smet*, for the coming battle and began advertising in mid-September that the *City of Yazoo* and the *S. H. Parisot* would be run as "through packets" from the Yazoo River to New Orleans.[32]

Soon after the advertisements appeared in the *Daily Picayune*, Captain Leathers of the Pool Line met Murray Smith at the Vicksburg lawyer's office. Leathers was more than willing to fight, and he threatened that if the P. Line carried through its plans to invade the Mississippi River south of Vicksburg, his Pool Line would enter the Yazoo. A few weeks later, editor Liddell of Greenwood visited Leathers in New Orleans and reported their conversation to readers of the *Yazoo Valley Flag*. Leathers, Liddell said, vowed that "there [was] and can be no compromise between him and the P. Line." The editor was confident that if Leathers leaves "'that man Parisot' master of this [Yazoo] River it will be because he (Leathers) is a pauper."[33]

The battle lines were drawn. When by late September the Yazoo River system became fully navigable and enough cotton was waiting for shipment, Parisot began scheduled runs from Vicksburg to New Orleans. Learning of developments in the litigations with the Pool Line, Parisot went by train to New Orleans on the last day of September. He launched the *S. H. Parisot* on her first regular weekly run of the season to Vicksburg. The war had started. The Vicksburg editor thought the "whole teaparty [was] no good any more." In Greenwood, Liddell issued a clarion call to his readers that it was "now high time that the patrons of this soulless monopoly rise in their might and thunder" to support the Pool Line "against the rapacity and ingratitude of this satrap [Parisot] of the Yazoo and Tallahatchie Rivers." River commentators for the *Picayune* admiringly reported that "the little commodore is beginning to make the fur fly in the Vicksburg trade."[34]

Parisot's battle fleet was composed of twelve tried and trusted P. Line steamboats. The *S. H. Parisot* (fifty-five hundred bales capacity), the *City of Yazoo* (forty-five hundred bales capacity), and the *De Smet* (twenty-six hundred bales capacity) formed the main battle line to steam between Vicksburg and New Orleans, the enemy's territory. And they would occasionally run as through boats from Yazoo City to the Crescent City. The nine boats of the P. Line's support fleet were scheduled and assigned trades as only Parisot could do. The *Silverthorn, E. C. Carroll, Jr.,* and *Leflore* usually ran in the Vicksburg–Greenwood trade, but the *Carroll* and *Leflore* were sometimes reported on the Tallahatchie. The *Sallie Carney* operated out of Greenwood for the Tallahatchie and Yalobusha trades, but when she had a full cargo, she ran straight through to Vicksburg. The *Golden Era* and the *Charles Rebstock* ran daylight round trips between Yazoo City and Belzoni on the upper Yazoo, and when the water was high, the *Rebstock* went into the Yalobusha. The small *Alert, Alice,* and *Deer Creek* ran with their barges in the Sunflower River trade, and the *Alert,* when the need arose, steamed into Lake Dick or the Yalobusha. Delta planters, shippers, and passengers had never experienced such service.[35]

The Pool Line's major battle fleet, managed by Tobin and Leathers, far outweighed that of the P. Line. The *Natchez* (No. 7) was 303.5 x 46.5 x 10 feet with a cargo capacity of almost six thousand bales of cotton. The *Ed Richardson* was 309 x 49 x 12 feet, and her guards made her main deck 95 feet wide. She was named for Colonel Ed Richardson, the Delta Cotton King and cotton factor par excellence in the firm of Richardson & May of New Orleans and Vicksburg. Everything about the Pool Line's third boat, the *J. M. White,* was monumental. Including guards, she measured 321 feet long and 91 feet wide; her bow and stern were 17.5 feet deep. She had two bridal chambers, hot and cold running water in all her bathrooms, and her main cabin, built with 170,000 feet of lumber, was 8 feet longer than the total length of the 225-foot *S. H. Parisot.* The bell of the *J. M. White* weighed 2,880 pounds; her chimneys were 6 feet, 3 inches, in diameter and towered 80 feet above the roof. Her cargo capacity was computed at ten thousand bales of cotton.[36]

The main battle fleets were obviously unevenly matched. The three P. Line boats had a combined capacity of 12,600 bales, whereas the Pool Line could carry more than 25,000 bales, or twice as many. Delta planters did not market enough cotton to fill the boats in any given week. To win the war, the Pool Line had to take enough cotton from the Yazoo country to make the P. Line run from Vicksburg to New Orleans unprofitable. And Parisot, conversely, had to retain control of the Yazoo shipping lanes to compete successfully on the Mississippi River run. On the Yazoo, Parisot's secondary fleet was far superior.

When it became obvious that Parisot had entered the New Orleans–Vicksburg trade, Leathers charted the small, one-boiler *Hope* to enter the Yazoo and connect with the *Natchez*. By mid-October, Leathers organized the Choctaw Line and purchased two boats, *Era No. 10* and *Hard Cash*. Leathers sent the Choctaw Line boats with their logo, a replica of a cotton bale painted red suspended between their chimneys, into battle on the Yazoo. Within two weeks, John Tobin added the *Clara S.* to the Choctaw Line fleet. But the four invading boats could do little damage to the P. Line on its home waters. Indeed, when the *Clara S.* sank at Christmas time, she was not replaced.[37]

The P. Line was remarkably successful during the first seven weeks of the fall cotton season. The *S. H. Parisot* rarely left Vicksburg with less than 3,000 bales and a substantial load of cotton seed. The *City of Yazoo* loaded 1,300 bales on 10 October and 2,800 on her next reported trip, while the *De Smet* reached New Orleans with a "full load" on her first trip in November. In Yazoo City, the Parisot Line warehouse alone shipped 10,631 bales by Christmas. Parisot was so successful in commanding the shipping of the Yazoo that he scheduled the *S. H. Parisot* as a regular steamer from Yazoo City to New Orleans. When the P. Line flagship neared the Yazoo City landing on her maiden voyage up the river, the Yazoo City Silver Cornet Band greeted her with a resounding serenade.[38]

Leathers's Pool Line was busy transporting "fine loads" of merchandise from New Orleans to Vicksburg, but when the *Hard Cash* left Vicksburg for the Yazoo as a connecting boat for the *Natchez*, she carried no upriver freight. Shippers and consignees stipulated that freight from New Orleans be transferred to P. Line boats for the Yazoo River run. Leathers went along on the *Hard Cash* for a Yazoo River run hoping "to renew his old acquaintances," but he returned with a very small cargo.[39]

Whatever the Pool Line did to make freight or passenger rates attractive, Parisot did it one better. Yazoo freight rates fell to one dollar a bale as clerks began bidding for shipments. By November, the P. Line steamer *Silverthorn* was taking cotton at seventy-five cents. Passengers enjoyed the competition as never before. Parisot offered half-fare rates to Yazoo country passengers going to the Cotton Planters Convention in Vicksburg, and Leathers responded with the announcement that he "would not be outdone in liberality toward any good enterprise."[40] As fall turned to winter, Parisot was in full command of the Yazoo, but then his luck changed.

Parisot was wracked by three stunning blows in November and December 1883. Richard Kinkead, his old friend and farming partner, was severely ill during November and did not live to see Christmas.[41] The captain presumably took on the added burden of completing the harvest, marketing the crop, and preparing for the planting season. Perhaps Shum Parisot stopped at Limerick to visit his dying friend as the *S. H. Parisot* made her maiden run to Yazoo City in mid-November.

The Yazoo City Silver Cornet Band, greeting the P. Line flagship with a serenade, was unknowingly playing her requiem. Leaving Yazoo City, the *S. H. Parisot* safely navigated the Yazoo channel and completed her load in Vicksburg. With a "good load" of 3,564 bales of cotton, 1,296 sacks of cottonseed oil cake, 500 barrels of cottonseed oil, and fifty-one passengers, the fine steamer began her run down the Mississippi River. Six miles above Natchez, an accidental fire reached her highly flammable cargo, and the grand steamer burned to the waterline. She was a total loss, and damages were estimated at $225,000. She was insured but not for the full amount.[42] As quickly as possible, Parisot secured the *Cherokee* as a replacement and continued the fight against the Pool Line.[43] But Tobin and Leathers, unable to secure Yazoo River cargoes, outflanked the P. Line. The third blow came from the courts.

On 29 September 1883, the day before Parisot inaugurated the regular weekly schedule of the *S. H. Parisot*, John Tobin, Thomas Leathers, and others signed a bill of complaint to the United States Fifth Circuit Court praying that the court grant them "the most gracious writ of injunction" against Parisot and his boats. After reviewing the complaint, accompanying documents, and depositions, Morrison R. Waite, chief justice of the United States Supreme Court, signed the writ of injunction on 15 December 1883. Six weeks later, U.S. Marshal W. Pitkin served a "true copy of the Injunction" on Parisot by "handing it to him in person" in an office "under the St. Charles Hotel" in New Orleans. The chief justice of the highest court in the land, sitting on the U.S. Circuit Court for the Fifth Circuit, "commanded and strictly enjoined [Parisot] under penalty of the law" from managing, assisting, or running "any steamboat in the route or trade described in the agreement of March 21st, 1877." The New Orleans Pool Line had won, but the battle still raged on the Yazoo.44

When asked about the injunction, E. C. Carroll replied that because he "was president and superintendent of the Parisot Line," and because Captain Parisot "has nothing to do with the management of the P. Line," the injunction would have little effect. And he continued the fight.45 During the peak of the cotton trade in mid-January, the *Hard Cash* left Vicksburg for the Yazoo without any upriver freight, and at the same time Captain Leathers's *Natchez* received only 156 bales of cotton while Parisot's *City of Yazoo* loaded 1,260 bales of cotton and 2,500 sacks of seed. A few days earlier, Parisot's *Cherokee* had steamed to New Orleans with 2,192 bales, 3,552 sacks of seed, 1,201 sacks of oil cake, 800 sacks of cottonseed meal, and 277 barrels of oil. The P. Line steamer *De Smet* managed to work in a three-day excursion from Greenwood into the Tallahatchie as five inches of snow lay on the ground at Sharkey's Landing, the head of navigation.46 While the battle raged, and with Carroll's bluster about the injunction, negotiations must have started between the two lines. The *Cherokee* was "temporarily withdrawn" in March.47

The desk clerk of the St. Charles Hotel registered three guests who had just arrived from Vicksburg by train on Saturday, 5 April 1884. Commodore S. H. Parisot, Captain E. C. Carroll, and C. C. Floweree had come to New Orleans on business. The next morning, the *Picayune* printed a short announcement under the heading "A DISASTROUS FIGHT ENDED." The story noted that "a compromise was effected . . . between the New Orleans and Vicksburg Packet Line and the Parisot Line." The terms were simple: the P. Line withdrew from the trade south of Vicksburg, and the Pool Line removed its boats from the Yazoo. In addition, Parisot turned the *City of Yazoo* over to Leathers, "for a certain sum of money," and the Pool Line withdrew its $95,000 suit against Parisot. The Pool and P. Lines agreed to connect at Vicksburg as before.[48] The war was over. The Pool Line had the Mississippi and Parisot retained the Yazoo.

The Vicksburg editor used clichés to report that "the war is over" and "the lion and the fox will lie down together." Leathers and Parisot, the editor noted, "have buried the hatchet and smoked the pipe of peace." In Greenwood, Liddell printed a verse commemorating the battle between the Choctaw Line with its red emblem and the black letter "P" of the Parisot Line in which he gave "only a sigh for the worsted red / A cheer for the valiant black." When the fall cotton season began, the once anti–P. Line editor acknowledged the success of the "irrepressible and popular autocrat of our river—Commodore S. H. Parisot."[49]

Although denied the Mississippi River trade, Parisot retained his standing on the Yazoo, where small boys and young men continued to regard "Commodore Parisot and the officers of his steamers . . . with awe and envy."[50] The P. Line fraternity of captains, pilots, and clerks remained as Parisot's "family," even when the commodore reached unquestioned planter status by more than doubling his landholdings. Commodore, planter, merchant, and cotton factor Parisot was at the peak of his many-faceted career as 1884 began.

7 / P. Line Family and Fortunes

The fraternal nature of steamboatmen is legendary. Mark Twain convincingly portrayed rivermen as members of an informal brotherhood and described the pilots' association as the "compactest" organization in the world. Recent writers, including Frederick Way, Jr., and the editors of *Waterways Journal*, present rivermen as a select group. Another writer noted that crews of modern towboats often regard " 'their' boat as if it were a second home," and many rivermen consider the crew a "surrogate family."[1] The P. Line as a microcosm of the larger Mississippi River fraternity had its own mystique and the characteristics of a brotherhood.

The P. Line captains, pilots, mates, and clerks had their specific duties aboard a steamer, but they were bound together by common cause and daily routine. Sharing meals, quarters, and duties aboard a Yazoo steamer for days or weeks during the harsh winter months of the cotton season fostered comradeship that must have given the "boys of the P. Line" a sense of family. The boat's officers were separated from the main deck crew by class and race. Twelve or more white officers aboard the *De Smet* or as few as five on the *Yazonia* had cause to be on the main deck only to supervise loading and unloading cargoes or to greet distinguished passengers. The brotherhood of the P. Line officers who worked together in the boat's office, main cabin, and lofty pilothouse was strengthened by physical proximity, class, race, and common interest.[2] Commodore Parisot presided at the apex of the fraternity.

Shum Parisot, without children of his own, found his family in the P. Line, and the officers returned his confidence and affection. A Vicksburg newspaper recognized this relationship by heading its article on Parisot's 1880 retirement with the title "THE BOYS OF THE P. LINE." The seventy-five young men marched to Parisot's home to demonstrate their "high esteem" and "affection" for "their best friend." These rivermen, who were generally "friendly in their disposition, generous in their impulses, and never forget a kind act or let one pass unrewarded," gathered on Locust Street to express their appreciation for Parisot's "generous liberality" and for a "thousand pleasant associations."3

Given the commodore's urbane personality, his penchant for elegance in the main cabin, and his congenial nature, one may assume that Shum Parisot rewarded his boys from time to time. Perhaps the reward or one of the "pleasant associations" was a dinner in the main cabin of a P. Line steamer, or a summer fish fry or fall hunting party at his country retreat at P. Line Home, or certainly a friendly conversation over drinks at the P. Line head-quarters in Vicksburg after a successful run into the Yazoo and back. When Murray Smith spoke of the "mystic letter 'P'" during the presentation ceremony at Parisot's home, he reflected not only the insiders' recognition of a fraternal mystique but also that of the larger community of river watchers, planters, and merchants, who, viewing from the outside, saw the P. Line as more than a business organization. Indeed, the relationship between Parisot and his officers extended beyond the narrow confines of the pilot house, main cabin, or P. Line wharfboat on the Vicksburg water-front.4

Vicksburg was not a large city in the late nineteenth century. Mark Twain referred to it as a "country town" after a change in the Mississippi River channel almost isolated Vicksburg on Lake Centennial.5 Vicksburg's 1880 population of 11,814 lived in four wards, and when the census takers recorded names and occupa-tions, there were steamboatmen in all four wards, though they appear to have been concentrated in three neighborhoods. Levee Street along the waterfront was the home, perhaps temporary, for a large number of black men who gave their occupation as deckhand or raftsman with an occasional female steamboat cook or steam-boat chambermaid. A smaller number of white men along Levee Street listed their occupation as steamboatman. Pearl and Klein streets in the southwest quarter contained another concentration of steamboatmen, including pilots and captains. Although only a few of these names were found in association with P. Line boats, the majority in this quarter of town were apparently connected with Mississippi River steamboating. The second ward in the northeast quarter of Vicksburg was bounded by Jefferson Street, North Third on the east, Clay Street to the south, and Cherry Street to the west. Locust Street ran north to south about the center of the second ward.[6]

Fifteen P. Liners lived in the northeast quarter, and an additional dozen or so men associated with the P. Line lived within a couple of blocks of the second ward. Locust Street had the largest number of steamboatmen. George Smith, John Wilson, John L. Dent, Thomas Murray, Charles Pare, Charles Dent, and Joseph Dent lived a few blocks from the commodore. P. Liners Thomas Young, John Young, C. C. Floweree, Murray Smith, and Frank Dent lived just south of Clay Street. Captain Carroll lived closer to the P. Line wharfboat in the southwest quarter, as did the young steamboatman James Dent. Opportunities in the neighborhood for casual conversations, chance gatherings during the less active summer seasons, and myriad possibilities for the social amenities of a small town contributed to a sense of family. Not surprisingly, a number of steamboat families were associated not only by social and business ties but also through marriage.[7]

The young Parisot, steaming as pilot aboard the *Lewis Whitman*, which was the largest steamer on the Yazoo in the 1850s found a lifelong friend in David Lamkin, the first clerk aboard the *Whitman*. David's sister Mary married Parisot in 1876, and the newlyweds made their home on Locust Street. In the meantime, David had established himself as a cotton factor with his offices at 196 Mulberry Street in Vicksburg. When David died in the yellow fever epidemic of 1878, his widow, Martha, and four children moved into Parisot's home. Months later, the Vicksburg newspaper carried an advertisement for "Parisot & Campbell, Cotton Factors," with offices at 196 Mulberry Street. In 1880, Martha's oldest boys listed their occupations as store clerks, presumably for Parisot & Campbell.[8] Parisot's nieces, Lizzie and Emily, the daughters of Josephine Parisot and Fountain Barksdale of Yazoo City, married the cousins Thomas and Robert Craig. When Shum Parisot dismantled his real estate holdings, the P. Line sold the Yazoo City warehouse to Thomas and Robert Craig.[9] Family connections seemed to have permeated the P. Line.

The Wilson and Dent families offer good examples of marriage connections within the P. Line. Mary A. Dent, a widow with seven children, lived in Vicksburg in 1840. Her son Milton P. Dent was Parisot's friend and business associate with the antebellum steamers *Ranger, Roebuck, Dixie,* and *Dew Drop,* and a second son, John L. Dent, was a P. Line clerk for many years after the Civil War. Milton and his wife, Sarah, had three sons, Joseph, John, and Charles, all of whom became P. Line officers. After Milton's death in the 1870s, Sarah married another P. Line captain, Charles Pare, and they lived a short distance south of the commodore. Milton's sister Margaret married Charles G. Wilson in 1847, and their eldest son, John W., became a P. Line pilot as did his son, John W. Wilson, Jr. Margaret's son John and his wife maintained a household in 1880 on Locust Street that included four generations: the matriarch Mary Dent, her daughter Margaret, John and his wife, and their two children.[10] Victor Wilson, probably related to Charles G. Wilson through a collateral line, was an antebellum Vicksburg ice merchant, and his daughter Ellen became the bride of Captain Carroll in 1875. P. Line stockholder and business confidant of the commodore C. C. Floweree married Jennie Wilson in 1867. She may have been related to Victor because Floweree became the city's ice merchant and they named their son Victor. Records regarding James Dent are elusive. He first appears in the 1880 census as a thirty-year-old unmarried steamboat pilot who boarded near the P. Line wharfboat.[11] He may have been a nephew of Milton P. Dent, but the records are not clear. He was a well-known P. Line officer and married Annie Kinkead, the daughter of Richard Kinkead of P. Line Home. The bonds established through career associations, neighborhood friendships, and family relationships were obviously part of the P. Line mystique as the company and its founder reached a turning point.

Captain Parisot was reported as saying that when the Civil War ended he owned only "a piano and a pony." The captain, who began the P. Line with the sidewheeler *Calumet,* reached the peak of his business career in the 1883–84 cotton season. When the P. Line owned twelve steamers in 1883, Parisot expanded his landholdings. Previously the *Yazoo Sentinel* editor commented that he "would not be surprised" if Parisot "goes on until he owns as many plantations as he [owns] steamboats."[12] The editor turned out to be right. In 1884, Parisot owned in whole or in part twelve plantations, and Mary owned two sections of land near Fish Lake in Yazoo County. Parisot's holdings amounted to more than twelve thousand acres of rich Mississippi–Yazoo River Delta land and more than a dozen city lots in Yazoo City and Vicksburg.[13]

Parisot purchased from his brother, A. A. Parisot, two pieces of land known as Riverside and Mound Field plantations (879 acres) on the Yazoo River about thirty-one miles above Yazoo City, but four other plantations formed the core of Parisot's Yazoo River holdings. Richard Kinkead and Shum Parisot began their business association with each owning an "undivided one-half interest" in the lands known as P. K. Plantation (460 acres), P. Line Home, and Avoca Plantation (1,050 acres), and Parisot purchased Limerick Plantation of 300 acres from Richard and Mary Ann Kinkead. These four contiguous holdings were on the east bank of the Yazoo River about ten miles below Yazoo City. Parisot also owned an "undivided one-half interest" in Belle Yazoo Plantation (779 acres) on the west bank of the river about twenty-five miles below P. Line Home.[14] He owned other plantations located on Silver Creek near its confluence with the Big Sunflower River.

The Silver Creek plantations were part of Colonel Campbell's estate. When Campbell, Parisot's cotton factor partner, died in 1881, his debt to Parisot was only partially paid by transferring Campbell's stock in the P. Line. Other portions of the debt were secured by Campbell's lien to Parisot on certain lands along Silver Creek. Parisot was not the only lienholder, and all creditors waited until Campbell's heirs defaulted on their indebtedness. When six plantations along Silver Creek were sold in March 1884, Parisot submitted the high bid for the plantations known as Grand Oak, Valley Home, Grosvenor, Cottonwood, Wildwood, and Alluvia containing 7,281 acres "more or less."[15] In March 1884, Parisot owned in "whole or in part" 12,019 acres and the P. Line still ran on the Mississippi River. But Parisot's economic situation changed rapidly.

The loss of the *S. H. Parisot* a few months earlier and the cost of replacing her with the *Cherokee* undoubtedly damaged the financial standing of the P. Line, but such corporate indebtedness did not necessarily extend to the stockholders. When he made peace with Leathers in April 1884, Parisot may have been hoping to rebuild his financial standing through farming. But that was not to be.

Parisot's farming ventures, organized under the name of S. H.

Parisot & Co., carried a heavy debt burden. Parisot owed almost a quarter of a million dollars in 1884. Most of his debt was caused by bad weather conditions, especially floods that resulted in very small crops for the three years beginning in 1882. Cotton factor Parisot was a creditor at the local level, but planter Parisot was a debtor to larger firms. His principal creditors were the First National Bank of Lexington, Kentucky, represented by Samuel L. Wooldridge, and the cotton factors Richardson and May of New Orleans. The Kentucky bank, which financed Parisot's purchase from the Campbell estate, held a lien of $36,000 on the Silver Creek plantations.[16] Parisot borrowed $64,750 from the Kentucky bankers in 1883 and gave them promissory notes alternating in amounts of $5,000 and $2,500 payable periodically between 7 August 1883 and 5 January 1884 for a total of $75,000, including interest. Existing records do not indicate how Parisot spent this money. He may have used part of it in the fight against Leathers, or in his cotton factor offices, or for his farming operations. When Parisot was unable to meet the notes, Samuel L. Wooldridge extended the original debt and loaned him another $75,000 on 4 January 1884, which made "a total indebtedness now existing . . . amounting to the sum of One Hundred & Fifty Thousand Dollars." This considerable debt was secured by a mortgage, rather than a lien, on Parisot's interests in the Yazoo River plantations. The mortgage included not only the land but also the livestock, machinery, implements, and any crops to be harvested on the Yazoo River lands as well as the crops from the Silver Creek plantations.[17]

In addition to the $186,000 owed to the First National Bank of Lexington, Parisot owed Richardson and May of New Orleans $56,400. In late 1884, the New Orleans factors claimed the right "to sell [Parisot's] crop to reimburse themselves."[18] Richardson and May's claim against the cotton held on the Yazoo River plantations created a cash-flow problem for Parisot and started a chain reaction. Wooldridge, acting for the Kentucky bank, instituted legal proceedings against Parisot for $56,400, the value of the cotton in dispute, and the suit was transferred from Warren County to the Federal Court for the Southern District of Mississippi on 6 December 1884. Richardson and May also entered a suit in equity against Parisot for the cotton.[19]

Newspapers from New Orleans to Greenwood learned of Parisot's financial difficulties in early December, and they expressed sympathy for his "embarrassment." Federal District Judge Robert Hill appointed George S. Irving, a Vicksburg commission merchant, as receiver to "take charge of the property until the matter of the crops [could] be adjudicated." Irving gave a partial listing of Parisot's assets, stating that the debt was about a third and certainly no more than half the value of the assets. According to the newspaper reports, the "sympathy of the whole community" was with the captain, and the editor was sure that "every creditor [would] be paid every cent." Receiver Irving was so confident that he named Parisot "as the best possible agent he could select." Liddell, the formerly antagonistic editor of the *Yazoo Valley Flag*, agreed that Parisot's "honor as a businessman was untarnished." [20] As the extent of Parisot's indebtedness unfolded, however, Richardson and May as "cross complainants" joined Wooldridge of the Kentucky bank to protect their interests.

Parisot, unable to satisfy his creditors, lost the Silver Creek plantations in January 1886, and a year later, the court ordered the sale of his Yazoo River lands. The claims did not end until six claimants joining with the Kentucky bank won a favorable judgment. When the court orders to seize any property were returned, the clerk noted that "all lie *Nulla Bona* Nov. 7th 1892." [21] All that was left was his Locust Street house, which he had deeded to his wife. Although Parisot retained no property, his once extensive landholdings, even though in other hands, continued to be important in steamboat activities. George S. Irving, whose offices were a block away from Parisot's Mulberry Street business, managed the breakup of the captain's holdings as ordered by the court. The available court documents and the deeds for the land suggest that Irving, Wooldridge, and others, all acting under court orders, tried to help Parisot retain his holdings, but failing, sought the best possible solution for all concerned. Plantations continuing to be associated with the P. Line included the Yazoo River plantations contiguous to P. Line Home and the Silver Creek plantations.

Mary Ann Kinkead emerged as the heroine of P. Line Home. Through a series of complex title exchanges, each secured by a deed of trust to the previous title holder when necessary, the "undivided one-half interest" to the Yazoo River plantations passed from Parisot to Irving the receiver, then to Wooldridge of the Kentucky bank, then back to Irving, who sold the lands to

Mary Ann Kinkead. By May 1888, she held title secured by deeds of trust to Limerick, PK, P. Line Home, and Avoca plantations.[22]

An economic depression beginning in 1893 and a suit involving the remaining debt on the Kinkead original one-half interest created unimaginable problems for Mary Ann, a widow with six children. Wooldridge and Irving helped by temporarily postponing payment on the principal, but not the interest, owed to them. Ten years after she borrowed money to buy the lands, the clerk of the Chancery Court entered the marginal notation that the lands "were released" from the deeds of trust, and deeds of release were duly recorded in the county records in March and April 1898.[23] During the ten hard years that the "accomplished and pleasant lady" of P. Line Home fought to maintain her lands, she earned the enviable reputation as "one of the best planters on the river."[24]

Although Mary Ann's financial distress was caused by the failure of the S. H. Parisot & Co., the "gracious hostess" of P. Line Home continued to regard the P. Line with affection. Even the meanest of Parisot's steamers, the *New Evergreen*, was greeted at the landing with refreshments, and James Dent blowing "five blasts from the whistle" from his station in the pilothouse of the *F. Barksdale* was especially welcomed. Perhaps Annie Kinkead, watching from one of the three dormer windows on the second floor of P. Line Home, saw the approaching steamer before Dent announced his arrival. Several years after marrying James Dent in 1892, Annie purchased a portion of the lands from her mother. When the matriarch died in 1930, she bequeathed one-sixth of the land to Annie and the remaining five-sixths to her second daughter, Mary, better known as Mrs. Molly Turnage. Molly returned to P. Line Home, and like her mother before her, she kept the lands intact through the Great Depression of the 1930s.[25]

George S. Irving acquired title to the Silver Creek lands. Parisot seemed to have had little attachment to these lands, and perhaps he had purchased them reluctantly from Colonel Campbell's estate. He held a deed of trust to Grand Oak and Valley Home, and W. B. Pittman and Irene C. Whitehead held liens on other plantations.[26] Parisot, the high bidder for six plantations when the Campbell estate was sold at public outcry on the courthouse steps in Vicksburg on 17 March 1884, borrowed $36,000 from Samuel Wooldridge of the Kentucky bank to pay for the lands.[27] Irving, acting as receiver for Parisot's property, sold eight hundred acres to W. A. Campbell for $8,000 in December 1885, but this relatively small sum did little to stem the mounting claims against Parisot.[28] In a court action transferred from Warren County to the Federal District Court for the Southern District of Mississippi, the First National Bank of Lexington, Kentucky, forced the sale of Parisot's Silver Creek lands. Edmund H. Wooldridge of Vicksburg was the high bidder at $27,000, and he transferred title to Samuel Wooldridge of the Kentucky bank.[29] At ten-thirty in the morning of 8 December 1886, the Yazoo County chancery clerk filed two instruments. One was a deed from Samuel Wooldridge to George Irving for the plantations known as Grand Oak, Valley Home, Grosvenor, Cottonwood, Wildwood, and Alluvia; the second was a deed of trust executed by Irving to Samuel Wooldridge creating a lien on the six plantations for $55,970.15, which included the purchase price of $36,680, interest on the six promissory notes covering the amount for the next six years, and a $10,000 advance for the forthcoming planting season. Within three years the clerk noted that the "lien created by this Deed of Trust [was] released and discharged and the indebtedness paid—September 27th, 1889."[30]

George Irving, onetime receiver for Parisot's holdings, expanded his Vicksburg grocery until it became known as the G. S. Irving Grocery and Provision Company. A large portion of his plantation supply business undoubtedly was conducted along the Sunflower River and Silver Creek. Indeed, his six plantations would have consumed a significant portion of the plantation supplies sold by the firm. The southernmost boundary of Irving's Silver Creek holdings included Campbellsville Landing on the Big Sunflower River. Extant records regarding subsequent relations between Parisot and Irving are tantalizingly suggestive. The Sunflower River Packet Company, with Parisot on the Board of Directors, was organized soon after Irving purchased the Silver Creek lands in 1886, and during the following three cotton seasons, P. Line steamers did not enter the Sunflower River system. No documents exist to explain the business agreement, if any, between Parisot, the Sunflower packets, and Irving the merchant-planter, but the Sunflower trade appeared to have been profitable until a steamboat accident in 1889 caused the demise of the Sunflower Packet Company. Nevertheless, Campbellsville remained as the transfer point even after the Yazoo River steamers were divided into three companies, each operating in separate trades, in 1897.[31]

Parisot was observed as "getting along very well in years" after passing his sixtieth year in 1886. His physical appearance must have shown the effects of forty cold, damp winters in the Yazoo River cotton trade. Certainly, the fight with Leathers, the long-drawn-out legal battles, and the financial collapse of his farming ventures left their mark on him. Perhaps the burden which the failure of S. H. Parisot & Co. unintentionally placed on the Kin-keads, other business associates, and his friends weighed heavily on the captain. Even though he was regarded by some as an old man in the last half of the 1880s, Parisot was "still vigorous and full of business, enterprise, and energy." [32] Concentrating on the mainstay of his economic life, the commodore rebuilt the P. Line with style even when facing greater competition than ever.

Although too late to be of significant help to planter Parisot, the two cotton seasons beginning in the fall of 1885 and ending in summer 1887 reflect exceptionally good crops and consequently a heavy freight business for steamboats. The P. Line transported almost 225,000 bales of cotton (55,362 tons) and an equal tonnage of cottonseed during the two shipping seasons. Commercial statistics as reported by the Corps of Engineers did not list grain or provisions as separate categories but estimated that the upriver freight had a value of more than $5 million. [33] In addition to a good freight business, the P. Line retained mail contracts acquired in the early 1880s.

In 1882, Parisot had successfully bid for the mail contract for both the Sunflower and the Yazoo river routes. The Sunflower contract, requiring one weekly round trip between Vicksburg and Faisonia, paid $3,000 annually. The contract from Vicksburg to Greenwood earned the P. Line $4,800 annually for biweekly trips on the Yazoo. The postal service renewed the contracts in 1884 but reduced the number of stops, the number of round trips, and the fee. P. Line steamers took the mail up the Sunflower once a week until the Sunflower Packet Company was organized. Presumably, Parisot, holding the contract and serving on the Board of Directors, made a satisfactory agreement with the new company. Beginning in 1884, the Yazoo contract stipulated seventeen stops during one round trip each week between Vicksburg and Greenwood, and the reduced service was reflected in the $3,000 contract fee. Parisot used the shallow-draft *Golden Era* and the *Tributary* as mailboats in 1886. [34]

During that year other P. Line boats reflected the style associated with Parisot steamers. The "reliable" *Katie Robbins* and the "splendid" *F. Barksdale*, named for Parisot's brother-in-law Fountain Barksdale, provided "regular and reliable" freight service, as well as the elegant passenger accommodations that had become synonymous with the P. Line. At the same time that Parisot ran the two mailboats and two packets, he used four smaller steamers for the cotton trade. The "popular" *Ike Bonham* and the "slow" *New Evergreen* ran with the *Headlight* and the *Birdie Bailey* before being sold to a new Yazoo steamboat interest. No wonder that the P. Line, running eight steamers in 1886, continued to earn praise for "serving its patrons promptly and faithfully."[35]

During the mid-1880s, Parisot experienced not only increasing pressure from his creditors but also a threat from the railroads that were beginning to penetrate the Delta cotton lands. In addition, the indomitable commodore confronted increased competition on the rivers that had been his exclusive province for several decades. George Quakemeyer ran both the *Alice*, the last side-wheeler on the river, and the *Alert* in association with his Yazoo City mercantile business. At the same time, the Yazoo City Oil Company ran the *Beta* under the command of Captain White, but these three boats did not seriously threaten the commodore.[36]

When F. M. Andrews, G. W. Faison, John Auter, and others organized the Sunflower River Packet Company in 1886, P. Liners Parisot, Marcy Johnson, and George W. Bookout joined the new company as director, stockholder, and manager, respectively. Parisot sold the old steamer *Headlight* to the company, which after rebuilding her at Marietta, Ohio, renamed her the *Addie E. Faison*. The new packet company, relieved of competition from the P. Line on the Sunflower River, ran the *Addie E. Faison*, *Crown Point*, and *Josie D. Harkins*. Three years after receiving its corporate charter, the Sunflower Packet Company ceased to exist, and Parisot not only became owner of the *Addie E. Faison* but reestablished control over the Sunflower trade. Competition from the three Yazoo City boats and the three Sunflower boats did not materially affect the P. Line, but a more formidable competitor, the Pugh Line, emerged during the last half of the decade.[37]

William D. Pugh was a twenty-three-year-old businessman with a young wife and a three-month-old son when Parisot first organized the P. Line in 1870. Fifteen years later, Pugh bought his first steamboat, the *Lake City*, which for two years had steamed under the P. Line logo.[38] When Parisot's boat *Ike Bonham* burst her boiler below Vicksburg, Captain Pugh purchased the wreck and towed her to Paducah, Kentucky, where she was rebuilt and fitted with new boilers. With five newly furnished staterooms, the *Ike Bonham* returned to the Yazoo trade as a Pugh Line boat in time for the record-setting 1886–87 cotton season. Before the season was half finished, Pugh purchased his third boat, the *New Evergreen*, from Parisot.[39] Steaming from the Yazoo City landing, Captain Pugh organized his operations in response to the realities of railroad competition and Parisot's declining activities on the upper river.

During the 1880s, railroads on the east bank of the Yazoo River and a line touching the Tallahatchie on the west forced steamboatmen to reconsider their opportunities. While Parisot reduced his activities on the rivers above Yazoo City, Pugh correctly assessed the possibilities of short hauls on the upper Yazoo and Tallahatchie. Small, low-water boats could transport cotton, cottonseed, staves, lumber, and passengers profitably in short runs to and from Yazoo City, Belzoni, and Greenwood. Pugh Line steamers brought farm produce to markets, warehouses, and railroads in Yazoo City and Greenwood, where they were transshipped to more distant markets.[40] Four years after beginning his line, Pugh took an estimated ten thousand bales of cotton to Yazoo City and Greenwood, while Parisot took more than thirty thousand bales and twenty-five thousand tons of cottonseed to Vicksburg. P. Line boats made only sixty trips into the Tallahatchie during the season, but the Pugh Line made three round trips weekly and brought out more cotton than did the P. Line. Pugh often unloaded the Tallahatchie cotton at Greenwood, while Parisot's boats steamed through to Vicksburg.[41]

Short hauls on the meandering upper Yazoo and especially on the Tallahatchie were hard on small boats. Realizing that his steamers would need frequent service, Pugh built a boatyard at Yazoo City. The *New Evergreen* towed two barges to Yazoo City in 1887, where Pugh converted them into a dry dock for his small boats. Two ship carpenters, James and W. A. Craig, rebuilt the *New Evergreen*, and when she came out of dry dock, she was "bright as a pin, and as tight as a champagne bottle." But she belied her name for now her hull was bright red. Captain Pugh, repairing and refurbishing the *Lake City* and the *Ike Bonham* at his boatyard, earned the title "commodore."[42]

Commodores Parisot and Pugh did well during the record 1886–87 season when planters shipped more than 133,000 bales of cotton by steamers. But their prosperity was short-lived. The next two seasons were noted as "short-crop" years, and riverboats transported about 70,000 bales each season. Even so, Parisot believed that he did not have enough boats to maintain his position on the rivers. When the shipping season began in 1887, he formed a temporary pool with Charles D. Mulholland of Vicksburg. The P. Line contributed the *F. Barksdale* and the *Katie Robbins,* and Mulholland added the *Lake Washington* and the towboat *Helen Meade.* The four steamers had access to eight barges when needed.[43] The pool may not have lasted the season for Parisot added a new boat to the P. Line in October. The first enrollment certificate for the *R. L. Cobb* named M. S. Parisot as "sole owner," but the next year the steamer was owned by the P. Line. Although "many friends [were] delighted" when Parisot piloted the *R. L. Cobb* on her maiden voyage to Yazoo City, newspaper announcements lacked the enthusiasm customarily expressed for P. Line boats. Perhaps indicative of Parisot's declining fortunes or the lessening importance of steamboats, the *R. L. Cobb,* which was the longest of the P. Line boats then in service, was described only as having "ample accommodations," which were "convenient and roomy."[44]

Financial exigencies and the decreasing river trade may have been the reasons for a reorganization of the P. Line. The Mississippi and Yazoo Packet Company, chartered at Delta, Louisiana, in 1880, was superseded by the Yazoo and Tallahatchie Transportation Company, incorporated under Mississippi law in 1888. Even though the corporate title changed, the logo and the affectionate P. Line sobriquet remained, as did President Parisot, Secretary Rundle, and Superintendent Carroll. The new corporation, chartered for $50,000, which was less than half the capitalization of the old company, had thirty-five stockholders including Parisot, M. S. Parisot, and several P. Line captains and pilots.[45] In 1888 the new corporation owned the *Birdie Bailey, Blanks Cornwell, F. Barksdale, Golden Era, Katie Robbins, R. L. Cobb,* and at least four barges. Six P. Line steamers, three Pugh Line boats, three Sunflower packets, at least three independently owned steamers, and several sawmill boats could handle the needs of the river system. When the *D. O. Fogel*, a Mississippi River "tramp steamer," reached Yazoo City, the protective editor bluntly announced that "outsiders are not welcome."[46]

Captain Pugh, however, increased his line by adding two boats at the beginning of the 1889 season. The *Mountain Girl* with sixteen staterooms and accommodations for sixty-six passengers made daily runs between Yazoo City and Belzoni, and the *John F. Allen*, described as a "splendid packet for the local trade, having good accommodations for passengers and plenty of freight room," steamed south of Yazoo City to Irving's Campbellsville Landing seventeen miles up the Sunflower. Commodore Pugh rapidly built the line to accommodate short-haul needs, and Parisot continued to dominate the Yazoo trade to and from Vicksburg. But each line experienced costly accidents.[47]

Two of Parisot's fine steamers were destroyed within days of each other. The *F. Barksdale* burned on 4 January, and within the week, the reliable *Katie Robbins* sank on Tchula Lake. The *Barksdale* was a total loss, and the *Robbins* remained in the mud for sixteen months before she was raised. Pugh's steamer *Lake City* hit a snag at Holt's Landing, "careened over," and sank for a $3,600 loss in February. During the summer, the *Ike Bonham* was at Pecan Point when she hit a snag and sank causing a $4,000 loss for Captain Pugh. Pugh raised both the *Ike Bonham* and the *Lake City*, rebuilt them at his dry dock, and had them back in service for 1890. Parisot raised the *Katie Robbins* in 1889, but she sank again as a total loss in 1890.[48] Costly accidents in addition to a bleak shipping season, when all steamers transported only 72,054 bales of cotton, forced a realignment of steamboat interests.

Parisot, for the last time, used his "enterprise and energy" to organize the Yazoo steamboating business. Newspapers reported that the P. Line purchased the Pugh Line in August 1889. Such business transactions were usually recorded in the files of the Vicksburg Customs Office, but these records have not been preserved. Given Parisot's financial condition in 1889, the reorganization might more properly be described as a merger rather than an outright purchase. When the negotiations were completed, Parisot retained the presidency of the line, but Pugh replaced Carroll as superintendent. The company continued officially as the P.

Line, but it was often referred to along the rivers, especially in Yazoo City, as the "P. & P. Line." With the two Pugh boats back in service and the *Katie Robbins* steaming again, albeit for a short time, Parisot ran nine boats. Soon after the Sunflower River Packet Company's boat *Josie D. Harkins* rammed the *Katie Robbins*, Parisot acquired ownership of the Sunflower packet *Addie E. Faison*, and the tributary line went out of business.49 Commodore Parisot was again in command of shipping on the entire river system, but after having once more demonstrated his organizational expertise, Parisot made a decision.

The stockholders of the Yazoo and Tallahatchie Transportation Company met in Yazoo City in October 1890 to elect officers for the coming year. The old P. Liner Rundle remained as secretary, Captains Carroll and Pugh were named to the Board of Directors, and F. M. Andrews, former president of the late Sunflower Packet Company, was elected president of the P. Line. Captain Sherman H. Parisot, nearing age sixty-five, was not present at the stockholders meeting.50 After a career spanning more than forty-five years on the Yazoo River, the founder of the P. Line left steamboating. Unlike his retirement a decade before, no known ceremony marked the commodore's passing from the P. Line. A brief return to the Yazoo in the twentieth century would be recognized by old friends and simple ceremonies.

8 / *Yazoo Boats*

P. Line boats continued to steam the Yazoo channels into the twentieth century. For a half-century before Parisot's death on the eve of World War I, commodores, companies, and combinations formed a large segment of Yazoo steamboating history. Even though captains, clerks, and crews provided the human dimension, the boats exhibited uniquely identifying qualities. Passengers and river watchers praised their favorite boats, ridiculed the ungainly steamers, expressed dismay at accidents, or exhibited sadness when a boat was lost or abandoned. Many river watchers saw the boats not just as wooden hulls, iron boilers, and brass fittings but as personalities full of sound and color and action. Personified as they were, the boats were a living part of the Yazoo Delta.

Almost three hundred known boats plied the Yazoo River system from the Civil War to World War I. Of these, 90 percent (272) were powered by steam, and when the remaining twenty-six entered the Yazoo powered by gasoline or oil, the internal combustion engine forever altered the romance of river transportation. The change in form of power was a twentieth-century innovation. In the nineteenth century, the major changes were relocating the paddle wheel from the side to the stern and redesigning the bow to tow barges. These changes, although slowly adopted after the Civil War, made late nineteenth-century steamboats significantly different from the antebellum sidewheel steamers.

The steam power plant changed little during the late nineteenth century, except that coal, rather than wood, was used for fuel. Steamboatmen along the Ohio and Mississippi rivers developed new valves, better reversing gears, and steam-powered capstans

Left: *Natchez* (ca. 1860). Thomas P. Leathers' *Natchez* served in the Cotton Clad Yazoo Fleet until she burned, March 1863. (Photo courtesy of the Area Research Center, University of Wisconsin–La Crosse) Below: *Peytona* (ca. 1860). Confederates used the *Peytona* to build the Liverpool and Snyder's Bluff defenses. (Photo courtesy of the Area Research Center, University of Wisconsin–La Crosse)

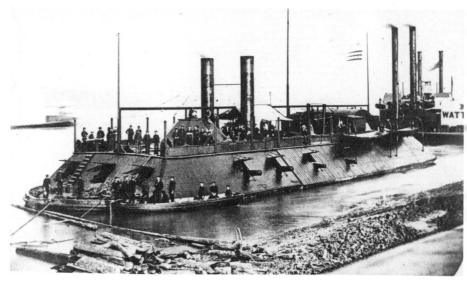

Top: *Cairo,* US Ironclad. The first of three Union boats sunk on the Yazoo during the Civil War. (Photo courtesy of the Area Research Center, University of Wisconsin–La Crosse) Directly above: *Forest Rose,* US Gunboat. Active on the Sunflower River; when her armed launch went up the quiver River, Parisot burned the *Dew Drop.* (Photo courtesy of the Area Research Center, University of Wisconsin–La Crosse, and Missouri Historical Society, by Geo. E. Perrine, River 207)

Above: Business at the New Orleans landing in 1859. The steamer *Col. T. H. Judson* (far right) is shown accepting freight for her return trip to the Yazoo River Delta. (Photograph courtesy of the Murphy Library, University of Wisconsin, La Crosse, Wisconsin, and Tulane University)

Left: Letterhead of P. Line stationery, 1876. Below: The Vicksburg landing in 1883 showing the P. Line offices. *Leflore* and *Sallie Carney* in the foreground; *Will S. Hays* with billowing smoke; *Ed Richardson* with tall chimneys; from left to right in the background: *Clara S., Deer Creek, Aglia* (ferry), *Helen Meade*.

(Photos courtesy of Gordon Cotton, Old Court House Museum, Vicksburg)

Above: The Yazoo City landing (ca. 1895). Looking downstream; from left to right: *Yazonia, Hibernia, Des Arc, Maggie,* and *Fifteen.* Below: The Yazoo City landing. Same as above, except looking upstream. From left to right: *Hibernia, Des Arc, Maggie, Fifteen* with the ill fated "river queen" *Blanks Cornwell* in the background. (Photos courtesy of the Memphis Room, Memphis/Shelby County Public Library and Information Center)

Top: *Frank Pargoud.* In 1869 Captain John Tobin sent her band to the ceremony Parisot presented the *Belle Yazoo* to the public at Vicksburg. Directly above: *Natchez* (1870). The sixth boat to bear the name as she looked without her landing stages while preparing for the race against John Cannon's *Rob't E. Lee.* Left: *J. M. White* (ca. 1878). This, the largest steamer in the New Orleans Steamboat Pool Line, replaced the *Frank Pargoud.* (Photos courtesy of the University of Wisconsin–La Crosse, Murphy Library)

Right: *Yazoo* (ca. 1877). One of the first stern-wheelers in the P. Line. (Photo courtesy of the Area Research Center, University of Wisconson–La Crosse) Below: *De Smet* (before 1883). "Commodore Parisot's pet" as she looked before she was rebuilt and electric lights added. (Photo courtesy of the University of Wisconsin–La Crosse, Murphy Library, and Missouri Historical Society, by Robert Goebel, River 235)

Opposite page, top: *F. Barksdale* (ca. 1886). Annie Kinkead's "favorite" P. Line steamer. Opposite page, bottom: *Katie Robbins* (ca 1885-6). With banners flying and the mystic P. between her chimneys, the *Katie Robbins* rushed to Vicksburg. (Photo courtesy of Gordon Cotton, Old Court House Museum, Vicksburg)

Hallette (ca. 1902). Captain Pugh's steamer proudly wearing the P. Line emblem long after Parisot's line came to an end. (Photo courtesy of Gordon Cotton, Old Court House Museum, Vicksburg)

and hoists, but the basic steam plant remained relatively unchanged. The boilers continued to be located in the forward third
of the boat and the cylinders in the after third. If the steam plant
appeared unchanged, the boat itself underwent several seemingly
radical changes. Hog chains, often metal rods with turnbuckles to
allow adjustments, were developed in the 1850s and made it possible to move the wheels from the side to the aft end of the hull. The
hog chains, which ran longitudinally from bow to stern above the
boiler deck, strengthened the hull and supported the heavy sternwheel. Sidewheels were supported in part by an extension of the
main deck known as guards, but with sternwheel boats, the guards
were structurally superfluous and were narrower than on sidewheelers. Sternwheelers with less breadth of main deck than
sidewheel boats of the same tonnage became the dominant design
after the Civil War.[1]

Steamboat builders made additional changes that were incorporated on the Yazoo boats. The balanced rudder, extending fore and
aft of the rudder post, became standard on sternwheel boats.
Indeed, most steamers had two balanced rudders, and some of the
larger ones had as many as five. Another change in design occurred
in the 1870s on the Ohio River and quickly spread to the Mississippi and its tributaries. The fore main deck was redesigned so that
steamers could push barges ahead of them. The modeled hull remained intact, but builders strengthened the bow section with
additional braces and "squared" (or rounded) the fore main deck.
Steam-powered propellers were tried on small boats during and after the Civil War, but they did not become the major propulsion
system for low-water boats until the internal combustion engine
of the twentieth century. Steamers with hog chains, narrow
guards, sternwheels, balanced rudders, and squared fore decks
served as the workhorses and thoroughbreds during the late nineteenth century.[2]

Yazoo steamboats may be divided into several categories based
on design, size, and function, of which the three main ones included 18 sidewheel steamers, 20 steam propeller boats, and 194
sternwheel boats. The sternwheelers may be further divided into
categories based on size. The large boats are defined as those
having hulls of 150 feet or longer; small boats are those less than
75 feet long. Length of hull was used for comparative measurements because the regulations for measuring tonnage were

changed four times after the Civil War. The mythical "average" Yazoo boat may be described as a sternwheel steamer, about 120 feet long, with room for cargo and deck passengers on her large main deck and with a main cabin for meals, an office, perhaps a bar and staterooms for passengers on her second deck; at the top were a small texas and pilothouse, or perhaps just a pilothouse on the roof. Such a steamer may have towed barges, but she should not be regarded as simply a towboat. A towboat was a sternwheeler designed to handle a tow but having little cargo and no passenger space; it was a specialty boat. Function defines a last category. Either large or small, sidewheel or sternwheel, a number of service boats plied the Yazoo waterways after the Civil War. The ubiquitous trade boat, the sawmill and cotton gin boats, and certainly the circus and showboats performed special functions on the Delta waterways. Although these service boats contributed to, they did not interfere with the fundamental job of moving freight and passengers safely, reliably, and sometimes with style.

Sidewheel steamers had long been noted for their ability, speed, and style, but the efficient sternwheel quickly replaced them after the Civil War. Only eighteen sidewheelers have been reliably documented on the postwar Yazoo, and thirteen of these were reported on the river during the first five years after the war ended.[3] Parisot seems to have preferred sidewheel steamers. Both the *Blue Wing* and *Calumet*, his earliest postwar boats, were sidewheel steamers. Milton Dent's *Countess* and Thomas Metzler's *Hope* and *Plain City* were sidewheelers. Indeed, the first P. Line fleet, consisting of the *Calumet, Countess, Belle Yazoo, Lucy Keirn*, and the summer replacement *Era No. 8* were all sidewheel boats. The sidewheel *Lucy Keirn*, known as "the popular and the beauty and the pride of the Yazoo and Tallahatchie Rivers," served until 1876. When she was taken to Louisville and dismantled, her machinery was used on the *Yazoo Valley* and her hull returned to the Yazoo as a barge.[4]

The *De Smet*, the grandest of the sidewheel packets, won the praise of many steamboat enthusiasts. William Stokes reflected the admiration of all who boarded the *De Smet* when he wrote:

We sing the steamer *De Smet*
Commodore Parisot's Pet;
Finest boat on the Yazoo yet.[5]

The graceful steamer was part of Parisot's main battle fleet during the fight against Leathers and Tobin. Characteristic of Parisot's insistence on reliable service, she delivered the mail during high water in 1884, but because she could make few landings most people came out to the steamer in skiffs to receive their mail. Nevertheless, Parisot decided to deliver the mail directly to Captain D. G. Pepper's home at Lousy Level Landing. He lowered the stage plank into Pepper's "front hall," but when withdrawing from the front yard, the steamer knocked down a section of the fence. No serious damage was done, and the *De Smet* continued on her appointed rounds.6 After serving the P. Line for almost five years, the *De Smet*, according to the enrollment certificate was sold to Milt R. Harry, identified only as "the husband of Josephine Harry," of Memphis.7

Two other sidewheelers in addition to the *De Smet* were active on the Yazoo at the same time. The *Home* was a P. Line boat with James Dent as her pilot, but she was later sold to Captain Ben W. Sturdivent, who ran her from his Tallahatchie River plantation, Twilight, to Greenwood and back. When she occasionally ran to Vicksburg, Parisot's line served as her agent.8 The *Alice* had the distinction of being the smallest and the last of the sidewheel steamers on the Yazoo. After steaming for the P. Line, the *Alice* was purchased by George Quakemeyer, a Yazoo City merchant. She was reported as the "only sidewheeler in the river" in 1886, and she was steaming for the merchant as late as 1889.9

If sidewheel steamers reflected the past, steam propeller boats suggested the future. Six known propeller-driven steamboats plied the Yazoo during the ten years after the Civil War. Two of these, the *Dart* and the *Fairfield*, were documented as "canal style" boats; two others, the *Carrie Williams* and the *Dime*, were probably of the same style. The little *Favorite*, size unknown, was described only as a "small sized propeller." The *Dart* was often reported in the Deer Creek and Sunflower trades, and the *Favorite* also went into Tchula Lake and the Tallahatchie River.10 The *Trade Palace* was a major exception to these early small-propeller boats. She measured 154 x 29.5 x 5 feet and steamed on the Yazoo as a trade boat in the fall of 1868.11 Shum Parisot purchased the *Tributary*, a propeller boat, which he used as the "tri-weekly" mailboat between Vicksburg and Greenwood after the Parisot–

Pool Line war.[12] The eleven propeller-driven steamboats reported on the river system after 1890 tended to be towboats without passenger service and were often found steaming from the Mississippi into the Yazoo River. For example, the *J. B. O'Brian* made ten trips into the Yazoo over the five-year period 1893–97, most of them to and from Natchez, and the *Josephine Lovinza* made seven trips into the Yazoo from Vicksburg in 1897–98.[13] Propeller-driven boats, powered by steam or the internal combustion engine, replaced the sternwheel by the third decade of the twentieth century.

Sternwheel steamers dominated the Yazoo waterways from the Civil War to the early twentieth century. The largest and the smallest, the most elegant and the most ordinary boats were sternwheelers. Because tonnage measurements are misleading for the late nineteenth century, length of hull is better for determining the relative size of the sternwheel boats. An 1895 photograph of the Yazoo City landing offers a good illustration of misleading impressions based on tonnage measurements. The photograph shows the *Des Arc, Maggie,* and *Fifteen.* The *Des Arc* was 95 x 18 x 3 feet and measured 40.88 tons. The *Maggie* was 85 x 19 x 3.5 feet and measured 50 tons; the largest of the three, the *Fifteen*, computed at 75 tons, was 103 x 18 x 3.5 feet. Also shown are the ill-fated *Blanks Cornwell*, 140 feet long and measured at 232.4 tons, and the *Hibernia*, 135 feet long and computed at 157.06 tons.[14]

Of the postwar boats, 194 have been identified as sternwheel steamers, and of these, 160 have been further defined by linear measurements. More than three-fourths of these sternwheel boats measured between 75 and 150 feet, and approximately one-half ranged between 90 and 130 feet. A typical Yazoo River sternwheel steamer, excluding the service boats, would have been about 120 feet long, with two decks topped by a pilothouse.[15]

The small sternwheelers measuring 90 feet or less were usually, but not always, found on the smaller tributaries. The *Roma Wheeler, Naomi, Eddie, Kate,* and *Keoto* were small sternwheel steamers in the Sunflower and Deer Creek trade when Parisot, Dent, and Metzler first organized the river in 1868. Two years later, when the P. Line was born, the 86-foot-long *Bluella* ran in competition against Parisot for a short time. As the P. Line grew, Parisot used small sternwheel boats such as the *Deer Creek* and the *Alert* for the tributary trade and even on the Yazoo during low-water seasons. When the P. Line boat *Golden Era* was first reported on the Yazoo in 1883, the newspaper noted that she had a new hull that would "make it twenty feet longer." Two years later, inspectors measured her at 69.1 x 13.2 x 3.3 feet. The *Golden Era* could "trim in 10 inches," and she ran as a regularly scheduled mailboat alternating with the propeller boat *Tributary*. The little sternwheeler earned a reputation for reliability and was praised as "a fine little boat" steaming under the "letter P." [16]

The 75-foot-long *Lake City*, built at Yazoo City in 1885, was described as a "little breech loading steamer." Local river watchers praised the "fine appointments" of her main cabin and her four staterooms, which were arranged in "the Mann Boudoir style." [17] The *Maggie* was 85 feet long but was not representative of the small steamers because her pilothouse was located on the fore boiler deck rather than on the roof. During her eight years of the Yazoo she made 664 round trips from Yazoo City, most of them weekly round trips to the mouth of the Big Sunflower River. She was busiest in 1902, when she made 125 biweekly round trips between Yazoo City and the Sunflower with more than five hundred passengers. [18] The smallest recorded sternwheel steamer was the *L.L.B.*, which measured 36.6 x 16.7 x 2.3 feet and was computed as 6.5 tons. She was not a regular Yazoo boat, for she made only two trips into the river system, and on each trip she towed a barge from her home port of Brashear, Louisiana, to the Tallahatchie River. [19] There may have been many other sternwheel boats that never entered recorded history. The largest sternwheel steamers, because of their size, were noted when they reached the Yazoo City or Greenwood landings.

Twenty-three sternwheel steamers measured 150 feet or more in length. Eleven of these steamed under the "mystic P."; [20] six, including Leathers's *Hard Cash*, unsucessfully attempted to break Parisot's hegemony on the Yazoo. [21] The remaining six large boats ran on the rivers at the turn of the century. [22] The four largest sternwheelers were the *Yazoo Valley*, the *City of Yazoo*, the *S. H. Parisot*, and her replacement, the *Cherokee*. If the sidewheel *De Smet* was Parisot's pet in the 1880s, the *Yazoo Valley* must have been her sternwheel counterpart nine years earlier. The *Yazoo Valley* was built by the Howard Ship Yards in 1876 with "one of the prettiest cabins ever put on a sternwheel boat." Henry Whemhoff did "a most excellent job" on her carpets and upholstery, and other

Louisville merchants did similar high-quality work on all other appointments, including the bar, "which was a beauty."[23] Having to sell equal shares in the *Yazoo Valley* to Leathers, Cannon, and Tobin must have disheartened the gallant Yazoo captain, but he rebounded to build the *City of Yazoo* and the *S. H. Parisot*. The *City of Yazoo*, an "A 1" boat with a "full length, finely furnished cabin," was powered by three steel boilers producing steam for a "driving wheel 22' in diameter and 26' length of bucket." In addition, the steamer had a "donkey boiler" 10 feet long, which supplied steam for the "freight hoisting, stage lifting and capstan engines." The *S. H. Parisot*, said to be "the finest sternwheel ever built," made only one trip up the Yazoo before she burned a few miles above Natchez. Her replacement, the *Cherokee*, did not capture the imagination of Yazoo patrons as had the other three large boats.[24]

The *F. Barksdale*, somewhat shorter than the 200-foot length of the largest boats but still ranking among the boats of the larger class at 155 feet, generated excitement during the five seasons she steamed the Yazoo. She was photographed at the Vicksburg landing with her guards nearly touching the water when she was loaded with thirty-five hundred bales of cotton stacked to her hurricane deck.[25] Her texas, topped by the pilothouse, suggests that the *F. Barksdale* was more than a workboat; she was a Yazoo River "favorite." Annie Kinkead of P. Line Home and the daughter of Parisot's old friend Richard Kinkead had a fondness for more than the steamer, for she became the bride of James K. Dent, pilot of the *F. Barksdale*. When she wrote a poem entitled "My Favorite," was she thinking of the boat or of Dent?

Last night I heard the mighty puffing,
  Oh, could it be a dream?
No. Twas the noble P. Line Packet
  Sailing down the stream.

It was the steamer *Barksdale*
  Coming down to land,
Was she ever known to fail
  With Capt. Marcy in command?

And when she came around the bend,
  We knew it was the guiding hand
Of Jim Dent—the expert of the line—
  That brought her so gracefully to land.[26]

The sternwheel steamer *Hallette,* measuring 161 x 30.5 x 4.5 feet, but without a texas, steamed the Yazoo from 1902 through 1905. When photographed at an unidentified Yazoo River landing, the *Hallette* proudly wore the"mystic P" between her chimneys. The presence of the P. Line logo on the *Hallette* is both astonishing and revealing. Commodore Parisot left steamboating, and the P. Line as a corporate entity went out of existence before the *Hallette* reached the Yazoo River. The *Hallette* made fifty-eight round trips with 550 passengers between Vicksburg and Greenwood in 1904, but she was seldom mentioned in river town newspapers, which may indicate declining public interest in steamboats.[27]

The large Yazoo sternwheelers measuring more than 150 feet and the small ones of less than 90 feet, though often popular, were not typical Yazoo steamers. At least half of the known sternwheel boats measured between 90 and 130 feet; boats in this size range would be better described as representative of those on the river system during the late nineeenth century.

Two small but typical boats of approximately the same size also reflect different eras in Yazoo steamboating. The *Sallie Carney* was built in Nashville, Tennessee, in 1876, and three years later she was given a new bow. When she steamed to Vicksburg in 1883 she measured 96 x 24 x 3 feet. She was described as a "beautiful little boat," perhaps because of her proportions, the railing around the fore hurricane deck, her handsome pilothouse, and windows in the roof above her main cabin. The *Sallie Carney* served the P. Line for several years before she burned just before Christmas 1885, and after her hull was rebuilt and lengthened to 120 feet, she returned to service.[28]

The *Yazonia,* built at Yazoo City by Captain William D. Pugh in 1894, reflected changed conditions on the rivers. The *Yazonia* measured 95 x 19.8 x 3.5 feet. A photograph of her when loaded with cotton in a bleak winter scene does little to promote a romantic view of river life. The *Yazonia* made 103 round trips between Yazoo City and the Big Sunflower River with 977 passengers and untold bales of cotton in the 1894–95 season but remained unsung in verse and unpraised in prose. Records of her trips appear as numbers in the prosaic reports of the chief of engineers and an occasional announcement in a river town newspaper. Publicly unmourned when she sank at Glendora on the

Tallahatchie River, she was only one more wreck lining the river's banks.[29]

The *Birdie Bailey*, measuring 111 x 22 x 3.5 feet, was slightly larger than either the *Sallie Carney* or the *Yazonia*, and she reflected Shum Parisot's touch. He purchased her from J. H. Sannoner of Little Rock, Arkansas, where she had been built in 1885. The *Birdie Bailey* reached the Yazoo waterways in November 1886 and served her patrons well for eleven years. As they did many other P. Line boats, river watchers admired the appointments of her "full cabin, office and bar." A Yazoo City writer, "impressed by her ability," regarded her as a "little Dandy" and "quite proud." During a yellow fever epidemic in 1888, many boats were quarantined, and although P. Line boats were ordered to stop running, Parisot announced that his boats, including the *Birdie Bailey*, would stop, "except whenever the people are in need of their services." The *Birdie Bailey* was most often reported as running in the middle reaches of the Yazoo between the mouth of the Sunflower River and Belzoni. The *Birdie Bailey* set an astonishing record in the Corps of Engineers District Office in Vicksburg reports of annual round trips and numbers of passengers. Steaming from Yazoo City to the Sunflower or Belzoni, the *Birdie Bailey* made 784 round trips and safely transported 8,292 passengers during a four-year period from early 1893 until she sank in January 1897.[30]

The *Leflore* and the *Carrie Hogan* are typical of the early years of the P. Line. The *Leflore*, built in the Jeffersonville boatyard in 1878, entered Yazoo service in November. Like other P. Line boats, she had ample room for passengers. She was fully loaded with six hundred bales of cotton "piled to her pilot house." Captain Carroll used the *Leflore* during the low-water months during the fall of 1882, until she hit a snag and was withdrawn from service. The *Carrie Hogan* at 136 feet was about seven feet longer than the *Leflore*, but she boasted a carrying capacity of a thousand bales of cotton and forty passengers. Parisot purchased the *Carrie Hogan* for $11,000 in 1878, and she built her reputation for being "staunch and strong."[31]

Two still larger boats may also be considered as representative of Yazoo steamers. The *Katie Robbins*, built in 1884 at Jeffersonville, measured 141 x 28 x 4.9 feet with a computed tonnage of 162.54 tons. During her regular service in the P. Line she earned the nickname of "Old Reliable." She unloaded a record load of "3,671 packages" at the Yazoo City landing. When coming to a landing with a "big load," the *Katie Robbins's* crew strained from 8:00 P.M. until 3:00 A.M. to unload. No wonder the crew was known as the "strongest on the river." With her guards touching the water, the *Katie Robbins* made a majestic sight as she steamed to Vicksburg with billowing smoke, banners flying in the wind, and the "mystic P." between her chimneys. While praising her "Favorite," Annie Kinkead noted that the "*Katie Robbins* of the Line / Is a noble steamer too." [32]

The *Blanks Cornwell*, built by the Howard Ship Yards at a cost of $48,650 in 1886, soon carried the letter "P" between her chimneys. She had so many accidents on the river during her nine years in service that her engineer's son reported he could "not remember how many times she was on the bottom." When she sank for the last time at Dew Drop Landing in 1896, Annie Kinkead Dent published "The Ill Fated *Blanks Cornwell*," as a farewell salute to "the River Queen." [33] Many other boats may have been favorites and might be classified as representative boats during the late nineteenth century, but their records have failed to survive.

Large and small, sternwheel or sidewheel, the steamers offered the Yazoo country farmers and townspeople some relief from isolation and monotony. During the long, hot summer weeks, after one cotton season had ended and before another began, steamers added a holiday spirit by offering excursions. Some were short day trips, upstream or down from Yazoo City or Greenwood, others were longer trips to Vicksburg or New Orleans.

Occasionally a steamboat captain advertised an excursion in a local newspaper. The *Sallie Carney*, for example, was advertised as offering an excursion "if enough people showed interest." A similar advertisement by Parisot for an excursion on the *Calumet* resulted in so few people showing interest that the newspaper reported that the *Calumet* "did not leave." More often, local organizations and social groups made special arrangements for excursions. The *Beta*, owned by the Yazoo Oil Works and under the command of Captain D. C. White, was often used by Sunday school classes or social clubs. When a black fraternal organization chartered the *Beta* for an excursion, 273 members enjoyed the round trip to Vicksburg. The *Beta* conducted the "first excursion of the season" in 1887 when she towed a barge equipped with a refreshment stand and a "good floor for dancing" from the Yazoo City landing. The barge may or may not have had sufficient facilities in case of inclement weather for one excursionist wryly commented that they "enjoyed good ventilation."[34]

Most of the excursions reported in local newspapers were daytime trips from the point of origin and return. The little *Alert* hosted an excursion and fish fry at Fish Lake, ten miles below Yazoo City, and a few weeks later black citizens in Yazoo City chartered the *Sallie Carney* for a one-day excursion to Belzoni and return. Sixty-eight people chartered the *Charles Rebstock* to take them and the Yazoo City Orchestra upstream to Lodi Plantation for dancing and a fish fry. The *Rebstock* left Yazoo City at 7:00 in the morning as scheduled, but just as the steamer passed under the new railroad bridge, she began to leak. While the captain and officers reassured the passengers, the crew quickly repaired the damage, and the excursion continued as planned. The potential danger was quickly forgotten, and the party arrived at Lodi Plantation in the early afternoon. After feasting and dancing, the group boarded the *Rebstock* at 4:30 and arrived in Yazoo City at 8:30 in the evening.[35]

Some steamers provided longer excursions. The *Blanks Cornwell* carried a party to Vicksburg for $2.50 round trip fare, which probably did not include meals. Sometime later, the *Ashland City* offered an excursion to Vicksburg for $3.50 for the round trip and $6.00 with meals. The *Katie Robbins* towed a barge equipped with tents and tables "for eating," for a militia encampment at Vicksburg in 1886, with the steamer serving as a cook boat. The grand steamer *Yazoo Valley* ventured farther, conducting a Mardi Gras excursion to New Orleans for $25 in 1878. The returning travelers rated the excursion "a great success." The large sidewheel steamer *Issaquena* went in the opposite direction, leaving Vicksburg with 225 excursionists to view the Yazoo River and Yazoo City.[36]

Shum Parisot, never one to miss an opportunity to cultivate the goodwill of Yazoo patrons, especially during his war with Leathers's Pool Line, offered a midwinter excursion to Sharkey's Landing when five inches of snow were reported on the upper Tallahatchie River. The *De Smet*, with her four arc lights blazing, successfully navigated the tortuous upper river channels and so pleasantly entertained her guests that William Stokes rhapsodized on the trip in verse. He offered a "cheer" for the captain, the officers, and "all the jolly crew" of the "finest boat" on the river. He praised the "pleasure and diversion" provided by the "sumptious fare," the "mellow wine," the "entrancing" music, and "joyous" dancing. Stokes even managed a "huzza" for the "noise and racket" and for the "electric lights that illumined the winding way." Strangely, Stokes did not mention the snow.37

Sometimes a regular trip took on a holiday or excursion atmosphere. Thirty "cabin passengers" aboard the *Myrtle* in 1868 celebrated their trip to Vicksburg by cheering the captain and his boat. Thirty years later, fifty-one passengers aboard the *Rees Pritchard* turned their trip to Satartia into a holiday. The exuberance of an excursion even erupted aboard the tired old *New Evergreen*. When she stopped at Mary Ann Kinkead's P. Line Home, the gracious hostess served "ice cream, cake and wine" to the officers, crew, and passengers. The *New Evergreen*, however, soon became the butt of a joke. The *Yazoo City Herald* reported that an alligator that made its home near Lake Dick heard the *New Evergreen* steaming upriver one summer day and came out to challenge the steamer to a race. The editor took pleasure in reporting that the alligator won. George Bookout, master of the *New Evergreen*, and his entire crew sought revenge. They steamed after the 'gator on their next trip upriver and met it with "loaded Winchesters, shotguns, and pistols." The alligator lost this race "at his old place below Lake Dick," and Captain Bookout was known as the "best shot" on the rivers with either "rifle or pistol." Excursions continued to be popular into the twentieth century.38

The bars aboard many of the steamers may have contributed to the holiday mood. Parisot and Carroll often sold or leased the bars on P. Line boats. Richard Smith "purchased" the bars on the *Yazoo* and the *Big Sunflower*, but as the P. Line grew, Parisot leased the bars on all his boats on a seasonal basis. In 1882, J. J. Tanner of New Orleans "purchased" the bars on all of Carroll's P. Line boats, and at the beginning of the next season, when Parisot once more was active in the P. Line, the franchise was sold to W. H. Andrews & Bro. of Vicksburg. At one time the bar on the *Yazoo Valley*, described as "a Beauty," was owned by a I. R. Levie. Perhaps some of the smaller boats, such as the *Yazonia*, did not have bars. One Tallahatchie River watcher erroneously recalled, when reminiscing many years later, that the Yazoo boats "seldom had bars, as did the palace steamers of the Mississippi River." Nevertheless, he reported, "there was no scarcity of alcoholic drinks." The captain or clerks always kept a "plentiful supply of whiskey aboard for both passengers and those of the crew who were permitted to imbibe."[39]

Although the packets took passengers on holiday excursions, and even the meanest boats provided some diversion, showboats brought entertainment to the landings along the river system. "Hardly a year ever passed without a showboat" on the rivers. Newspapers, surprisingly, rarely mentioned showboats, and when the circus boat *Belle* visited the Yazoo River in 1868, the Vicksburg newspaper mentioned only her return to Vicksburg. The existing announcements indicate that the showboats entered the rivers in the fall, "when money was plentiful." Few names of showboats survive in the existing records; perhaps small sternwheel steamers were converted to "handle a show" on a temporary basis. The *New Idea* was especially "built to handle a show," and the *Electric*, owned by Ruth Rice of New Orleans, was mentioned as a showboat in the *Annual Report of the Chief of Engineers* several times at the turn of the century. She made one trip to Greenwood from New Orleans in late 1897, and in January 1898 she left Greenwood for the Tallahatchie and then went downstream to Yazoo City before returning to New Orleans. In 1899 she was reported as a "show boat" making "local trips" from Greenwood.[40]

Captain W. M. Howell recalled that "some of the more pleasant memories of the past" included "Show Boat Nights" at Belzoni. Every year a showboat, announced by the music of a calliope, would stop at Belzoni and give "weekly performances" to which "everybody went." These shows had a "group of impressive entertainers," which included "singers, comedians, dramatic characters and musicians." The players "never failed to bring out a crowd," and the young men found "the dancers with their low cut bodice, short skirts and blondined [sic] hair" to be "especially alluring."[41]

An observer on the Tallahatchie River agreed with Captain Howell only in that the "piercing wails from the calliope" announced the arrival of a showboat. Showboats on the Tallahatchie, according to this report, were "common and tawdry." Regardless of what show was "put on," the audience responded with loud applause for "no reason than the monotony of existence was invaded." People cared "little for the talent," and most in the audiences found that the "tough jokes, music and dancing were sufficient entertainment." Steamboats occasionally brought a circus to the Tallahatchie River, but one river watcher recalled that "the only animal show on the smaller rivers was an occasional flea-ridden monkey or a jaded parrot."[42]

Yazoo steamboating involved more than the graceful steamers *Calumet, De Smet,* or *Katie Robbins* revealing a world of excitement, fine accommodations, large cargoes, and happy summer excursions. It also included the more mundane world of the little *Deer Creek,* the monotonous regularity of the mailboat *Golden Era* or the slow *New Evergreen* and bleak *Yazonia.* Yazoo boating, in addition to the "alluring" or "tawdry" showboats, included the everyday world of indigenous service boats such as trade, sawmill, and cotton gin boats.

The trade boat was both reminiscent of the peddler's wagon and a presage of the later "rolling store." Keelboats and flatboats, more often than steamers, were "in trade" before the Civil War. A one-masted keelboat with a cabin equipped with shelves and counters was advertised in 1842 as "suitable for trading up any bayou with either dry goods or produce." Several years later, the "trading flatboat" *Rover* sold "corn, bulk pork, flour, apples, vinegar, potatoes, castings, stoneware, brooms, cheese, bear meat, &c &c" to customers at the water's edge.[43] "Trading floats" appeared on the waterways after the Civil War. After losing his steamer to fire, Captain Charley Booker started his "river life" with a "trade float." Captain Charley Bocaletti, who lost his steamer *C. P. Huntington* by fire, began to rebuild his career with a trade float and became so successful that he was known as the "commodore" of his small trading fleet. As late as 1890 the Yazoo City newspaper reported "two sails," which were trade floats "loaded with tropical fruit" for customers along the Yazoo. Evidence is too scarce to suggest the extent of trade floats after the Civil War.[44]

Steamers appeared "in trade" on the Yazoo soon after the Civil War. The *Trade Palace,* a propeller-driven steamer built by the Howard Ship Yards, entered the Yazoo for several weeks in 1868. By Yazoo standards she was a large boat, but she was described only as "a box." She was probably not very successful for she was soon sold to buyers in Mobile, Alabama.[45] Several other steamers appeared on the Yazoo as packets but were also reported occasionally as trading boats. The *Trader,* as her name suggested, was listed as a trading boat on the Sunflower River. The *B. H. Hurt,* "a small trading boat," returned from the Sunflower River with 1 barrel of flour, 3 beer kegs, 1,334 staves, and 69 bales of cotton. Apparently, boats such as the *B. H. Hurt* not only sold merchandise but also purchased local agricultural produce. Bocaletti's *C. P. Huntington* and the *Ed Foster* were other steamers engaged in trade. Ira Hale of Pope Station and A. T. Wimberly of Coffeeville in Yalobusha County jointly owned the steam trader *George Baker,* but they soon sold her to G. F. and J. D. Powell at Graball Landing on the Tallahatchie. The Powell brothers also owned the *Arkansas City,* a small propeller-driven steam trader. Captain Pugh, the last commodore on the Yazoo, used his little *Lake City* as an iceboat during the summer, and his advertisements promised to "deliver ice to your door." [46]

Charles Mann of Shell Mound on the Tallahatchie River provided a different service with his sternwheel steamer *Alpha.* With two decks and measuring 110 x 20 feet, the *Alpha* was a "steam gin and trade boat." The main cabin on the upper deck was divided into two rooms. The forward room, equipped with counters and shelves, was the trade room, while the aft part of the cabin served as the "lint" room. The *Alpha* went up and down the waterways ginning cotton for small farmers who did not have a gin and buying less than bale lots of unginned cotton. The trade room merchandise was readily available for farmers who sold cotton to the captain. The *Alpha* was apparently successful, for in 1876 Mann replaced her with the *Beta,* a newly built gin boat measuring 116 x 22 x 3.5 feet. The *Beta* had a cotton gin and a press so that rather than handling loose lint as did the *Alpha,* Mann was able to compress the ginned cotton into compact bales. The *Beta* served as a gin boat until 1885, when she was overhauled to become a transport boat for the Yazoo Cotton Oil Company. The *Beta,* steaming under the command of Captain D. C. White, then served the oil company and local patrons, including excursions, for three years before an accident destroyed the old hull. The machinery was placed on a new hull 85 feet long. When the *Beta* was no longer serviceable, she was replaced by the *Gamma,* a sternwheel steamer running for the oil company. The two-decked *Gamma* had six rooms for passengers, and Captain White's room was "as long as a small bedroom, adjoining was a bathroom." [47]

Sawmill boats were one of the more remarkable of the service boat genre. They were indigenous but not unique to the Yazoo. Henry Hall, when writing his "Report on the Ship-Building Industry of the United States," for the 1880 census, visited Evansville, Indiana, where he saw a sawmill boat under construction. He noted that in 1881 "there were eight or nine of this class of boats in the South." Four of these sawmill steamers were on the Yazoo waterways between 1879 and 1882. Sawmill boats were usually built on a flatboat hull with square fore deck and sternwheel. The main deck, sometimes with guards four feet wide, was "entirely open," and the upper deck contained cabins for the crew and a pilothouse. The sawmill machinery was on the main deck between the boilers and the engines. Logs were hauled over the bow, "run aft, sawed and discharged over the side amidships." The *Orange, Thomas B. Florence, Granger*, and *Lumberman* were actively sawing lumber on the upper Yazoo and Tallahatchie rivers during the winter of 1878–79. The *Thomas B. Florence* had one boiler with the stack behind the pilothouse. Operating out of Greenwood as a sawmill boat, she was chartered by the Corps of Engineers to cut overhanging trees in 1880, and she was later purchased by the Corps of Engineers, converted into a snag boat, and operated in the Vicksburg District until 1918. The *Granger* was advertised to "cut timber to any dimensions" and sawed half a million feet of lumber on the Tallahatchie in 1879 before she was replaced by the *Lumberman*, which offered expanded services. The *Lumberman* had "an 'edger' to facilitate squaring up lumber, and still more important had a planer to dress, tongue and groove lumber to any desired breadth and thickness." Impressively, especially to an energy- and environment-conscious twentieth century, the *Lumberman* burned sawdust for fuel.[48]

Although towboats such at the *Eva Alma* and the *Shawnee* were towing logs directly to riverside sawmills in the late 1890s, three sawmill steamers operated on the Yazoo until the end of the century. The sawmill steamer *Bill Nigh* burned near Belle Prairie in 1890, and a few years later the *Rover* entered the sawmill business, but she served for less than a year before she sank in 1897. The *C. H. Woods*, replacing the *Rover*, was a sternwheel "combination sawmill and low water packet" with a "scow bow" and tin roof. She was last reported on the rivers in 1899.[49]

Steamboats meant more to the Yazoo River country than taking cotton to market, merchandise to upriver towns, and cabin passage for planters finding a way to the outside world. The boats were woven into the fabric of everyday life in the Delta. Plantation hands used deck passage to go to town or to visit friends and families, and construction workers on the railroads often traveled by boat when going to or from work. Trade boats making periodic stops at river landings served the isolated farmer's house and the field hand's cabin, while the gin, sawmill and showboats provided patrons with their special services. Who cannot imagine that the coming of the mailboat or Captain Pugh's iceboat *Lake City* was a welcome event? But all the boats, whether fine packet, workhorse, or specialty boat, steamed on the rivers at their own risk. And the dangers were real, for more than a hundred steamers found watery graves in the Yazoo River system.

9 / Of Wrecks and Rivers

R eminiscing about steamboat days, one river watcher sadly
commented that "there remains little evidence . . . except
for the hulls of the wreck[s]." [1] More than a hundred steamers and
an uncountable number of flatboats, barges, and fishermen's
houseboats littered the riverbanks. Indeed, twenty-eight antebellum wreck heaps and the thirty-seven hulls left from the Civil
War clogged the rivers with so many obstructions that pilots had a
difficult time navigating the waterways. These pre-1865 wrecks
brought the U.S. Army Corps of Engineers to the Yazoo River in
1873, and after clearing the worst obstructions, the engineers
helped remove parts of more than sixty hulls that sank between
the Civil War and World War I. Although *Yazoo* has been translated
as *river of death*, Major Joseph L. Willard of the Corps of Engineers
boasted that the Yazoo was an "ideal stream" because its relatively gentle flow "can never attain destructive speeds." [2] If the
river belied its name in some ways, its meandering course contained many dangers.

The twisting channels slowed transportation, and floods and
low water relocated or made previously innocuous debris into new
hazards. Sandbars, snag beds, sunken logs, and wreck heaps could
spring hull timbers, damage planking, or rip out bottoms. Of all
the chances for accidents aboard steamers, fires and boiler explosions presented the greatest threat. The wrecks lining the riverbanks at the end of the steamboat era reminded observers not only
of the golden age but also of the dangers inherent in steamboating.

Although the mainstem Yazoo and Tallahatchie rivers may have
looked stable to an engineer's eye, local rivermen had problems
with their meandering course. One pilot reported that the "upper

[Yazoo] River is more tortuous than the lower [and] its writhings, like those of a wounded snake, are difficult to follow." He pointed out that at Cape Horn, sometimes known as Rick's Bend, the "river winds for four miles and returns to within 20 paces of its starting point."[3] The series of bends known as Oxbows on the Tallahatchie were even more convoluted. Careful pilots navigated the twistings and turnings with little more than loss of time or an occasional minor collision.

Floods were both a boon and a curse for pilots. High water caused tree-bearing banks to cave in, creating new obstrutions. Local newspapers reported "serious slides" above Yazoo City and at the Head of Honey Island after heavy summer rains in 1886. Usually flood stage meant broad and safe channels, but when the streams overflowed and covered the floodplain with shallow water, steamers could not make a landing. The *De Smet* ran into such a problem as she tried to deliver the mail, and when the *Timmie Baker* went into the Yalobusha for two weeks in 1882, farmers were unable to move their cotton across the floodplain to meet the steamer. Floods were destructive for planters and an inconvenience for boatmen, but low water severely handicapped shipping, narrowed the channels, and brought boat bottoms into range of unsuspected dangers.[4]

A few sandbars slowed steamers at almost all times except during high-water stages, and smaller bars became major obstacles during low water. Shum Parisot liked to tell the story, perhaps with embellishments, of Captain Joshua Wiley and his boat the *Tallahatchie*, which was stuck on a bar in the Tallahatchie River for several weeks.[5] Several shoals proved troublesome during low water. The four steamers scuttled during the Civil War compounded problems at Southworth's Bar, and White's Bar near Yazoo City and a long bar with a snag bed near Satartia sometimes impeded traffic. The *Lottawanna* was grounded twice in one week at Brown's Bar, and the *Beta* was stuck for thirty hours at McCormick's Bar. The P. Line steamer *Belle Yazoo* was reported in "the bar scraping trade" during one dry season. A shifting bar at the mouth of the Yazoo River created recurring problems, and the *R. L. Cobb* and the *Birdie Bailey*, finding only eighteen inches at the bar, scraped bottom. Three bars on the Sunflower River, sometimes carrying less than twelve inches, made navigation next to impossible, even for the small boats that usually used the Sunflower.

During one low-water season the *Delia No. 2* took four days to pass Rolling Fork.[6]

Snags and sunken logs were responsible for sinking more boats than any other source of danger. Most boats that sank after hitting an underwater obstruction were raised, or the machinery was transferred to a new hull, and the steamer was back in service for the next cotton season. The sidewheeler *Myrtle* hit a snag and sank about three miles above the mouth of Tchula Lake, but she was raised and repaired. When she returned to the trade on New Year's Day 1868, she was reported as the only steamer with insurance. The *Lizzie* had several mishaps, beginning with a fire that was controlled by scuttling the steamer on White's Bar near Yazoo City. Soon after returning to service, the *Lizzie* hit a snag but suffered only minor damages. A few years later, with George Bookout serving as her pilot, the *Lizzie* "tried to climb up a snag." She "was persuaded not to do so," according to her first mate, because "it was not appropriate for a female to be seen climbing a tree." After the *Lizzie* was repaired, her owners sold her to steamboatmen in Galveston, Texas.[7]

During Captain E. C. Carroll's stint as president of the P. Line, the *Leflore*, one of two low-water boats able to reach the upper Yazoo, struck a snag and barely made it back to Vicksburg with all her pumps going. Later, the P. Line mailboat *Golden Era* was interrupted in her rounds when she hit a snag and had to be towed back to port. After the *Beta*, commanded by Captain D. C. White, hit a sunken log, he "backed her against a bar," built a bulkhead, pumped her out, and continued as if nothing had happened. Before the next season began, the *Beta* had a new hull. Captain William D. Pugh built a new hull for the *Lake City* after she hit a snag, careened over, and sank. With a sound, new hull, the *Lake City* boasted four staterooms, new furniture, and "fine appointments." When the P. Line favorite *Katie Robbins* hit a snag and sank on Tchula Lake, she was lamented as the "late steamer." But Parisot refused to let her die, and sixteen months after she sank, the *Yazoo City Herald* proudly announced in bold-faced type: "*Katie Robbins* Floats." She was soon back in service, but the fine old steamer sank as a total loss seven months later.[8]

The *Blanks Cornwell*, another P. Line favorite, was under "full headway" on the Yazoo when a snag ripped out her bottom at 6:30 in the morning at Dew Drop Landing. Captain James Dent's wife, the former Annie Kinkead, commemorated the accident in a verse titled "The Ill Fated *Blanks Cornwell.*" The passengers and crew were wakened by the warning bell and shouts of danger. Captain and officers "stood firm," and while the clerks saved the "books and funds" the mate "skillful and true" secured the boat to the river bank. When her "blue top kissed the wave" the steamer lay on her starboard side, "shifted once" and all was quiet.9 The River Queen *Blanks Cornwell* was gone, and a sand bar quickly formed round her hull.10

Although many other steamers hit snags or sunken logs, officers, crew members, or passengers rarely suffered more than minor injuries. The *Maggie* was an exception. Harper Thompson, who had been an officer aboard the *De Smet* with James Dent, and who had married Maggie Kinkead, a sister of Annie K. Dent, was clerk aboard the *Maggie.* The small boat was steaming on Wolf Lake loaded with lumber and plantation supplies when she hit a snag and careened over. Thompson jumped overboard but drowned before he could reach shallow water. Collisions, fires, and boiler explosions were more destructive of both life and property than underwater obstructions.11

One steamboat authority reported that collisions "did not rank as a major class of steamboat accidents" and that most glancing blows or "sideswiping kind of collision" were "lightly" regarded by steamboatmen.12 Such may have been the case on the Yazoo River system, for a relatively small number of collisions were reported in the local newspapers, and most of these reports indicated no more than minor damage. The *Myrtle*, a "Tallahatchie River boat," and Thomas Metzler's *Plain City*, competing for cargoes and the "right of way" before Parisot organized the Yazoo River trades in 1868, collided at Oxbows on the Tallahatchie River, but both boats sustained only light damage. The P. Line steamer *E. C. Carroll, Jr.* and her competitor the *Josephine Spengler* of the Merchants and Planters Transportation Company had a minor collision in 1880 with no damage as they raced for cotton on the upper river. James Dent and W. D. Pugh, colleagues in the P. Line and its successors but at the time piloting competing boats, collided in the Yazoo River near Freedman's Bureau Landing in 1890. The stage of the *Addie E. Faison*, piloted by Dent, struck Pugh's *Birdie Bailey.* Tearing through the *Bailey*'s ladies' cabin, the stage scattered "furniture, lamps, dishes, passengers and stoves" before it broke and fell to injure slightly a "lady passenger" aboard the *Bailey.* The *Birdie Bailey* sustained $250 in damages, but the damage to the *Faison* was estimated at $25. In another instance, the *R. L. Cobb* owned by Mrs. Sherman H. Parisot collided with the *Helen Meade* of a Memphis line. Neither boat sank, and the damages were soon repaired. But the first mate of the *Cobb* was accused of drunkenness and lost his license, and the pilot of the *Meade* was suspended for thirty days.[13]

Although most collisions were minor events, two steamboat disasters occurred because of collisions. The collision between the *Idaho* and the *Poland* took twelve lives in early 1865. Both boats had been in the Yazoo and Sunflower river systems in search of cotton, and they collided on 2 January 1865. Little is known of the accident, but perhaps the smaller *Idaho* (62 tons), loaded and going downstream, rammed the 161-ton *Poland*, broke through the hull, and caused the larger boat to career over and sink quickly. The loss of twelve lives from the *Poland* made this accident the worst disaster on the Yazoo River system. The *Idaho* continued on the Yazoo, but she sank near the mouth of the river when loaded with "old iron" two years later.[14]

In January 1890 the editor of the *Yazoo City Herald* reported "with great regret" that the P. Line steamer *Katie Robbins* sank at "fifteen minutes after twelve o'clock on Sunday morning." The *Katie Robbins*, which had been raised from the bottom of Tchula Lake only a few months earlier, was steaming up the Yazoo and was just above the mouth of Little Deer Creek when a competitor, the *Josie D. Harkins*, towing a barge, changed course. The barge rammed the *Katie Robbins*, breaking through her hull and causing the boat to fill and sink in three minutes. Captain Mose Smith commanded the *Robbins*, although Shum Parisot was aboard, and when the barge tore into the hull, Smith roused the sleeping passengers and crew and led them to safety by having them cross the barge to reach the *Harkins*. Ed McElroy, pilot of the *Robbins*, remained at the wheel until his boat touched bottom and then "stepped off the hurricane" onto the barge. After serving as a gangway, the barge filled with water, and as she sank the *Katie Robbins* slipped from the bank into the channel until only the top of her derrick showed above the water. She was abandoned as a total loss. Three of the seven men thrown into the water by the collision were pulled to safety, but four deckhands were swept away and drowned.¹⁵ The accidents involving the *Birdie Bailey* and the *Katie Robbins* both occurred at night, and the ascending boat sustained the greatest damage. Significantly, none of the collisions that were reported in local newspapers involved two boats steaming under the "mystic P." at the time of the accident. Such a record affirms Commodore Parisot's reputation for safety and efficient management.

Fires usually caused the most extensive property damage of all the accidents. Fire was reported as destroying twelve steamers from the Civil War to the end of the century. The highly flammable cargo of cotton, cottonseed, and cottonseed oil enhanced the likelihood of fires on boats burning wood or coal to produce steam power. Steamers destroyed by fire ranged in size and value from the *Novelty*, 107.5 feet long to the grandest of all P. Line steamers, the *S. H. Parisot*. After making four trips from the Sunflower to Vicksburg in 1899, the *Novelty* accidentally caught fire and burned about one mile above Vicksburg. The *S. H. Parisot* was 225 feet long and was valued at $225,000. Fire on the famous P. Line steamer started when a "jug" of spirits was accidentally knocked over, caught fire, and spread to the cotton and cottonseed oil. The *S. H. Parisot* burned to the waterline about six miles above Natchez on the Mississippi River. When Joshua Wiley's steamer, *Thomas Powell* burned in 1871, he sold the wreck for $700. Charley Bocaletti's trade boat *C. P. Huntington* was a total loss.

The *Hibernia* made more than two hundred trips from Vicksburg and safely transported more than two thousand passengers during her five seasons on the Yazoo before she burned at Vicksburg in 1899. The *Silverthorn* also burned at Vicksburg. The little *Ella Belle* burned on Black Creek above Steele's Bayou. The sawmill steamer *Bill Nigh* was tied up for the night near Belle Prairie landing when she burned as a total loss, and when the workhorse *Yazonia* burned at Glendora on the Tallahatchie, her loss was recorded only in the official reports of the Corps of Engineers. The beautiful little *Sallie Carney*, loaded with 480 bales of coton, burned as a total loss a few miles from Greenwood just before Christmas 1885.¹⁶

Annie Kinkead described the action when her favorite, the *F. Barksdale*, came to a landing:

Five blasts the whistle blew,
    And in a moment more was landed,
Then the rousters set about to do
    What the mate commanded.

The freight all off, the cotton on,
    Then the silvery bell was rung,
And away from the port she steamed.
    That's how business on the P. Line's done.[17]

Perhaps such a scene was taking place when the *F. Barksdale* burst into flames at Hendrick's Landing below the mouth of Tchula Lake on a cold January day in 1888. While the boat hugged the left bank of the Yazoo and flames raced through her cabin, Pilot George Stevens "stood nobly by the wheel" until the captain ordered him "from his post." [18] No lives were lost in any of these cases when fire destroyed the boats. The *Carrie Hogan* was an exception. This P. Line steamer was described as "staunch and strong" with a cargo capacity of a thousand bales of cotton and accommodations for forty passengers. Parisot paid $11,000 for the steamer when he purchased her in 1877, and she was insured for $6,000 when she burned with a "fine" load of eight hundred bales of cotton in 1881. The *Carrie Hogan*'s cabin boy, whose name was unrecorded, lost his life in the fire.[19]

Boiler explosions usually took more lives than fire, but of three instances aboard Yazoo boats, only one resulted in the loss of life. The large P. Line steamer *Yazoo Valley* burst a boiler when she was above Greenwood in 1878, but no one was injured and the boiler was soon replaced. When a boiler burst aboard the *Frank Beck, Jr.*, while she was steaming on Deer Creek, no one was injured and the boat was towed to Vicksburg for repairs. But when the boiler on the small *Ike Bonham* burst while she was a few miles below Vicksburg on the Mississippi River, the explosion killed six deckhands, and the boat settled in shallow water. She was later repaired and returned to the Yazoo trade, only to sink as a total loss at Pecan Point on the upper Tallahatchie River in 1888.[20] Between the Civil War and World War I, steamboat accidents left sixty-three known hulls to litter the rivers. Some of these wreck heaps compounded the navigational hazards created by the hulls from the Civil War.

The wreck heaps of sixty-five steamers that were left on the river bottoms before 1865 severely handicapped navigation after the Civil War. Local salvage efforts had removed some of the metal from the Civil War boats, but salvaging the boilers, engines, and fittings of most of them required professional wreckers. The Salvor Wrecking Company of St. Louis, using James B. Eads's *Submarine No. 11* and *No. 12*, salvaged materials from some of the wrecks in 1866 and 1867.[21] When Captain Buchanan of *Submarine No. 12* salvaged the *Natchez*, Thomas P. Leathers instituted a suit to recover $20,000 in damages. Failing to collect, Leathers continued to press the United States for payment. As late as 1894, the indomitable Leathers was still trying to get Congress to provide funds for what he considered the illegal salvage of the *Natchez* as well as for the material confiscated by Federal forces even before the Civil War ended. Shum Parisot did not fight the salvage operations but joined in the work and steamed the *Calumet* into Vicksburg harbor with one hundred tons of old iron from the wrecks. When the *Idaho* sank in 1867 while loaded with scrap iron, she became another impediment to shipping.[22] But these were salvage operations rather than an effort to improve the river channels, and many of the wreck heaps remained, creating serious obstacles to navigation.

In 1872, after the Mississippi congressional delegation returned to Congress, Representative George C. McKee of Vicksburg sought Federal aid to clear the Yazoo River of wartime obstructions. The initial report from the House Committee on Commerce did not include funds for the Yazoo River system. McKee must have worked behind the scenes beause the chairman of the committee, Philetus Sawyer, amended the bill during debate to include the Yazoo River. Funds were provided for an initial survey, recommendations, and cost estimates for clearing the river of "wrecks, gunboats, steamers, and other obstructions placed in the Yazoo River during the war." The United States Army ordered Lieutenant Colonel William F. Raynolds to conduct the survey. He and Assistant Civil Engineer J. D. McKown reached the Yazoo by October 1872. Five months later, McKown presented his final report, which noted that nineteen wrecks formed obstructions on the Yazoo, and he estimated that the eight most "serious obstructions" could be removed for $40,000.[23]

Perhaps because of Reconstruction era politics, the Committee on Commerce preparing the 1873 Rivers and Harbors Bill did not include an appropriation for the Yazoo River. Congressman

McKee introduced an amendment during the House debate, but he made a tactical error by proposing $50,000 rather than the $40,000 recommended by the Corps of Enginers. McKee's resolution also approved removal of forty-one wrecks, which included those on the Yazoo and all of its tributaries. McKee's impolitic amendment was defeated, and he responded by facetiously moving that the Yazoo be considered as lying within the boundaries of Michigan and Wisconsin, for then, he said, "my amendment would get through."[24]

After two days of private negotiations, McKee reintroduced an amendment asking for the recommended $40,000 and passionately pleaded that it was "due to the great cotton growing region of the South." His amendment was adopted and sent to the Senate, where James Lusk Alcorn quietly urged that a "great deal of charity ought to be extended to the rivers of the South." The Rivers and Harbors Bill was approved and sent to President U. S. Grant, who signed it on 3 March 1873. Ironically, his military decisions had caused the obstructions which he now agreed to remove.[25]

Captain William Henry Harrison Benyaurd of the U.S. Army Corps of Engineers arrived in Vicksburg to assume command of clearing the Yazoo River of the eight most dangerous obstructions. The Underwriters Wrecking Company of Cincinnati and the New Orleans Wrecking and Salvage Company submitted bids. The Cincinnati company's bid of $40,200 was rejected as too high, and Benyaurd awarded the contract to the New Orleans company, which offered to remove the obstructions for $35,450 provided the company kept the salvage. The company removed parts of nine wrecks which formed dangerous obstructions by the early spring in 1873.[26]

Joseph Burney, assistant civil engineer, examined the Yazoo River and made a comprehensive report before the end of the fiscal year. He noted that sandbars, snags, and overhanging trees presented problems to navigation on the Yazoo. Seven wrecks offered no serious problem, but eleven others formed obstructions. In addition, beds of snags caused serious difficulties at eighteen places, and there were innumerable single snags that should be removed. Burney estimated that a snagboat purchased at a cost of $52,030 with a $12,100 operating budget for six months could clear the Yazoo of its major obstructions. He further estimated that $120,000 expended over a four-year period was necessary to make the Yazoo River a fully improved waterway.[27]

Congress, exercising spending restraints in a depressed economy, provided no funds for improving the Yazoo River for the fiscal year ending 30 June 1875. Benyaurd remained in Vicksburg and resumed clearing the rivers when Congress appropriated $12,000 in 1875, $15,000 two years later, and $25,000 in 1878. The Corps of Engineers purchased the snagboat *O. G. Wagoner* and used her on the Yazoo in 1875 and in 1877. On her first trip into the Yazoo, the *O. G. Wagoner* pulled 512 snags, cut 903 overhanging trees, destroyed four wreck heaps, and removed parts of the *Star of the West* and the *Capitol*. Justin Straszer, returning with the boat in 1877, cleared snag beds that made approaches to twenty-three landings dangerous, removed 612 "single obstructions," cut 576 overhanging trees, and removed parts of four wrecks. During four working seasons, the Corps of Engineers made significant strides in improving navigation for the mainstem Yazoo River, which by 1877 had become Commodore Parisot's highway.[28]

The P. Line was noted as Vicksburg's "most substantial" business in 1874, and three years later Parisot signed the agreement with Thomas Leathers which gave the P. Line control of the Yazoo. The Corps of Engineers certainly recognized the growing importance of river transportation on the Yazoo system, and Parisot encouraged the efforts to improve navigation of the river. When Benyaurd received no appropriations for 1874–75, he reported that "no work has been carried on except in the office where a map of the river was prepared." This Yazoo River map, completed in early 1875, reflected the cooperation between the P. Line and the Corps of Engineers.[29]

The 1875 Yazoo River map contained range, township, and section lines for the river area, and a comparison of this map with modern quadrangle sheets shows it to be remarkably accurate. Furthermore, the 1875 map located more than three hundred steamboat landings. The place names and locations suggest a close working relationship between the Corps of Engineers and the P. Line. Abel C. Tuttle, in his *Complete Directory of the City of Vicksburg*, published in 1877, included a list of steamboat landings on the Yazoo and Tallahatchie rivers. Although several P. Line pilots, including George and Benjamin Bookout, provided information, the publisher made a few errors and omitted many landings, and he published a revised edition two years later. P. Line pilot Thomas F. Young met with Tuttle on 24 June 1879 and "revised and corrected" the list of landings on the Yazoo and Tallahatchie rivers. Almost all of the place names on the 1875 Yazoo River map are in script and appear to have been written by two people at different times. The largest number of names seem to be in the same hand and correspond to the list of landings in Tuttle's 1877 *Directory.* Corrections and a few additions appear to have been written in a different hand and are remarkably consistent with the new landings noted in the revised *Directory* of 1879. Because the 1875 map, unlike earlier ones, precisely located landings in relation to section lines, geographical features, and on the left or right bank of the river, P. Line pilots, especially Thomas Young, must have assisted Benyaurd's mapmakers.30

The 1875 Yazoo River map also locates wrecks, snag beds, and sandbars. The notations showing the wrecks were probably added to the map in 1887, when the Corps of Engineers asked Parisot and Thomas G. Ledbetter to assist in locating obstructions to navigation. This list of obstructions, compiled by two outstanding Yazoo River pilots, was published in a local newspaper and added to the Yazoo River map.31 Benyaurd and others, recognizing the growing importance of river transportation as the P. Line reached the zenith of Yazoo steamboating, recommended that the Corps of Engineers extend its work into the Yazoo tributary streams.

The chief of engineers included in his 1879 report recommendations for improving the Big Sunflower, Tallahatchie, and Coldwater rivers. The Sunflower River was navigable for 250 miles to Clarksdale during high water, but during normal water, Garvins Ferry, 135 miles from the mouth of the Big Sunflower, was the head of navigation. In low water, boats had considerable difficulty in this low-water stream. The Sunflower River system was becoming increasingly important because steamers brought out about two-thirds of the crops in the Sunflower country. The remaining third was shipped by Mississippi River steamers. Benyaurd estimated that $66,000 would be needed to clear the Sunflower of snags, logs, leaning trees, and two sandbars. Snags, logs, and overhanging trees formed the major obstructions on both the Coldwater and Tallahatchie rivers. He estimated that $25,000 spent for the Coldwater and $40,000 for the Tallahatchie would greatly improve those streams and the entire Yazoo River system.32

Congress responded by making annual appropriations for the

Big Sunflower, Tallahatchie, and Coldwater rivers in 1879. Just as the Parisot-Leathers war began in 1881, Congress funded improvements on Tchula Lake and the Yalobusha River; Steele's Bayou was added to the Corps of Engineers' responsibility in 1884. Congressional appropriations only occasionally included funds for a major project, notably on the Sunflower. Most of the funds were expended in maintenance projects of pulling snags and cutting overhanging trees. Major flood control projects became a responsibility of the Vicksburg District offices after the great flood in 1927. Between the initial $40,000 appropriations in 1873 through the fiscal year ending in 1926, a period of fifty-three years, Congress provided almost $2 million for improving the Yazoo River system. Funding for work in Tchula Lake, Steele's Bayou, and the Yalobusha River ended about the same time that railroads replaced steamboats as the major means of transportation.33

Funding for the Big Sunflower was greater than that for the Yazoo because several large projects for the Sunflower system were included in annual appropriations. Wing dams were authorized in a successful effort to scour the channel and improve navigation. In addition, the Corps of Engineers built a single lock and dam at Little Callao Landing about sixty-three miles from the mouth of the Big Sunflower just before World War I. Another major construction project, funded separately, relocated the mouth of the Yazoo River.34

When the Mississippi River changed channels opposite Vicksburg in 1876, the old river bend, known appropriately as Lake Centennial, fronted the city. Though seemingly isolated from the Mississippi River, Vicksburg continued as a port city because the Corps of Engineers conducted several projects to maintain an appropriate channel and to keep Lake Centennial from silting up. Because the shifting bar across the mouth of the Yazoo River continued to plague steamboatmen, Major Joseph L. Willard, Vicksburg District engineer, proposed to change the course of the Yazoo River so that it would flow through the Old River and through a diversion channel to Lake Centennial. The relocation of the Yazoo helped solve both the problems of a bar at its mouth and the city's threatened isolation. Congress began funding the project in 1892, and the canal was completed in 1905 at a cost of more than $1 million.35

Once given the responsibility of improving the Yazoo River, the

Vicksburg District of the Corps of Engineers maintained the river system as an improved waterway throughout the remainder of the steamboat era. Each season, the engineers removed parts of wrecks, pulled snags, cut trees, and dredged dangerous shoals. Although railroads reduced the need for boats on the Yalobusha River and Tchula Lake and these streams no longer received maintenance appropriations, the mainstem Yazoo-Tallahatchie rivers and the Sunflower River with its small tributaries continued as major concerns for the Vicksburg District. The cost of maintaining these waterways paid off handsomely for steamboatmen and Delta farmers. The District Office, in its annual reports and requests for renewed funding, compiled economic data to show the importance of river commerce for the Yazoo basin. The commercial statistics published in the *Annual Report of the Chief of Engineers* from 1879 through 1929 provide an illuminating history of waterborne commerce on the river system.

The reports beginning in 1879 refer to cotton and cottonseed shipped on steamers. In the mid-1880s, the District Office prepared a blank form that steamboatmen could use to provide shipping information. Not all steamboat captains responded, and during these early years the reports were occasionally noted as being incomplete. The Corps of Engineers refined their data-collecting system so that records beginning in 1890 and continuing through 1920 reported commercial statistics in a uniform format with only slight variations. For thirty years these relatively consistent reports listed the major commodities by number and/or tons for each river and estimated the value of riverborne commerce. These annual reports also listed boats by name and dimensions and recorded the number of round trips between specified points as well as the number of passengers each year. The engineers devised a more sophisticated reporting form in 1921, which included ton/mile rates and new commodities, indicating changes in river commerce. The *Annual Report of the Chief of Engineers* reflects only part of the golden age of Yazoo steamboats, but perhaps more important, the reports from 1890 through 1926 chronicle the decline of a major transportation system as railroads pushed steamboats into obsolescence.

A superficial look at compiled commercial statistics leads to the same conclusion as a more detailed study: river commerce almost ceased to exist by 1930. Although conclusions are sometimes so obvious that they have become part of the general wisdom, further analysis of existing data suggests subtle and not so subtle changes. The changes during the decades encompassing the long decline of river transportation illustrate the complexity, the variations, and the resiliency of steamboating on the Yazoo.

10/ The Long Decline

Capable captains steaming good boats on improved waterways could not retain forever their supremacy in transporting passengers and freight. Railroads penetrated the Yazoo–
Mississippi River Delta in the 1880s, offering a second way to
the outside world. The futility of naming any one year as the high
point of Yazoo steamboating demands the expansive phrase *gold-
en age.* Over the more than a century after steamboats entered the
Yazoo River system in the 1820s until the last reported steamer
plied the river in 1934, two decades stand out. The twenty years
beginning in 1870, when Parisot launched the P. Line, and ending
with his retirement in 1890 were the golden age of Yazoo steamboating. A cursory glance at commercial statistics suggests a
different high point, for figures representing total annual tonnage
indicate a peak of activity during the first decade of the twentieth
century. The three years before the 1927 flood formed another
impressive period. These twentieth-century high points, characterized by towboats with vast log rafts, lack the ingredients
needed to define a golden age. Considering not only commercial
statistics but also the number and size of boats, the subjective
element of beautifully designed packets, the quality of their accommodations, and the élan with which steamboat service was
conducted, the years from 1870 to 1890 leap out as preeminent in
Yazoo steamboat history. That this period ended with the fall of
Commodore Parisot's P. Line does not imply a precipitous end to
steamboating. Nor did railroad expansion in the 1890s automat-
ically signal the demise of steamboats as a transportation system.
Steamboats continued to serve the Yazoo River basin for four more
decades.

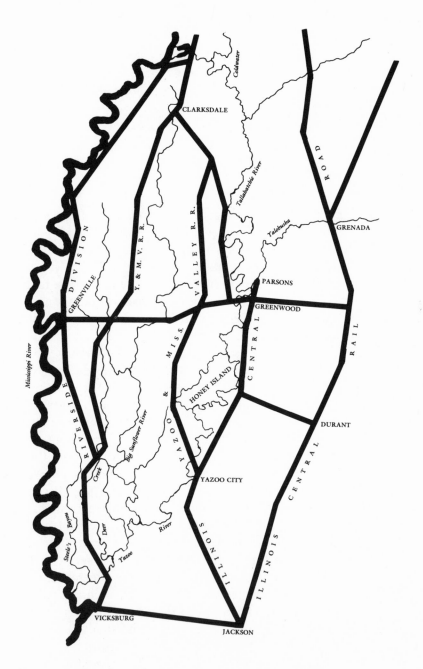

Map 2. *Railroads in the Yazoo River System, Ca. 1905*

Conventional wisdom has maintained that steamboating in the United States ended with the nineteenth century. A study of the Yazoo Delta specified that by the end of the century, the Yazoo River was used only by the lumber industry and that "any other kind of river traffic has *long since* dried up."[1] The obituary of Yazoo steamboating, like another premature notice, was greatly exaggerated. Steamboat traffic and services changed in response to the railroads, and steamboating went through a long decline before the steamboat whistle was no longer heard. Before gasoline-powered boats completely replaced steam power, railroads competed with and then superseded steamboats in providing the way to the outside world.

Several factors contributed to railroad development in the Yazoo Delta during the late nineteenth century. Antebellum plantations prospered on the rich sedimentation of the natural levees along the Delta waterways. But a rudimentary levee system seldom made it possible to develop the back swamp (or natural depressions) between the streams. These primeval forest basins remained relatively untouched until after the Civil War. Beginning in the 1870s, Federal levee construction along the Mississippi River began to protect vast areas of the Delta swamplands, and land speculation ran rampant. When lumber companies harvested the rich forest resources, the former swamplands of the Yazoo basin quickly became productive farmlands. A protective levee system, land speculation bringing in more and more farmers, and lumber companies clearing the back swamps of the great forests generated an agricultural bonanza in the Delta. This agricultural expansion not only benefited steamboat traffic but also offered economic opportunities for railroads. In time, the Illinois Central Railroad provided an acceptable "marriage of interests" to Delta planters.[2]

The Mississippi Central Railroad from Jackson to Grenada crossed the Yalobusha River before the Civil War. The railroad's western branch continued to Memphis, Tennessee, while the main line ran northward through Oxford and Holly Springs into Tennessee. In its effort to rebuild from wartime destruction, the Mississippi Central incurred a heavy debt load and was purchased by the Illinois Central system in 1877. Although railroads reduced the need for steamboats on the Yalobusha, they had little effect on the Yazoo River system until the Illinois Central laid a line of track roughly parallel to the eastern bank of the Yazoo. The branch line from Yazoo City northward to Parsons on the Yalobusha touched at Yazoo City, Tchula, Sidon, Greenwood, and Parsons. It was connected to the Illinois Central line by a spur from a switching yard near Tchula to Durant on the main line. By the time the Illinois Central completed the line from Yazoo City to Jackson, Mississippi, the railroad had begun to siphon freight from river traffic. Indeed, even the P. Line warehouse shipped most of its cotton by railroad in low-water periods. During the 1887–88 season steamboats took 13,652 bales of cotton from Yazoo City and the railroad handled 29,484 bales. The Illinois Central improved this ratio until at the end of the century it transported 52,211 bales and steamboats loaded only 2,054 bales at Yazoo City.[3] A 25-to-1 ratio would seem to prove that railroads had ended the usefulness of steamboats. Such a conclusion ignores the three salient points that steamboats developed a lucrative short-haul business, that riverboat service was based on more than bales of cotton, and that the railroads did not yet dominate the west bank of the Yazoo. But railroads were moving into the Yazoo Delta west of the Yazoo at the turn of the century.

Railroads had been planned through the Delta from Memphis to Vicksburg before 1880. Two lines, the Mississippi Valley and Ship Island Railroad, and the Memphis and Vicksburg Line, secured rights-of-way through the Yazoo basin but had only a few miles of track, which were south of Vicksburg. Investors headed by Collis P. Huntington purchased these lines in 1882, renamed them the Louisville, New Orleans and Texas Railroad (LNO&T), and began constructing a line from Memphis through the Delta. The main line from Memphis went through Clarksdale, then southward between Bogue Phalia and the Sunflower River to Rolling Fork, and then to the Redwood bridge and Vicksburg. A branch known as the Riverside Division, opened in 1903, connected with the main line above Clarksdale and paralleled the Mississippi River through Greenville and the areas west of the Big Sunflower before returning to the main line at Rolling Fork. Another branch of the LNO&T penetrated the Tallahatchie River lands east of Clarksdale and touched on that river at least five times. The major area untouched by railroads lay between the Sunflower and Yazoo rivers, and many farmers in this area depended on river transportation. But the LNO&T had plans for this region.

The Illinois Central purchased the LNO&T line before the branch from Clarksdale to Belzoni on the Yazoo was completed. In a vain effort to promote the fiction that it was not a monopoly in the Delta, the Illinois Central renamed the LNO&T the Yazoo and Mississippi Valley Railroad (Y&MV). The Y&MV laid track to Belzoni and extended it to Yazoo City. By the time the bridge at Yazoo City was completed in 1905, railroads offered their services to all the areas that once relied on steamboats. One final line, the Georgia Pacific, was the only east-west line. It passed through Greenwood and, although completed soon after the Civil War, did not threaten river traffic. As the railroads expanded their service area, steamboats responded to the increased competition.[4]

The romantic vision evoked by the words *steamboat* and *cotton* usually includes gleaming packets, elegantly dressed passengers enjoying the luxury of the cabin, and the main deck piled high with bales of cotton. The few early references to passengers and cargoes preclude a complete analysis of the antebellum steamboat business. Statistics compiled by the Corps of Engineers after 1878 help to define Yazoo steamboating. Passenger and freight statistics place Delta river transportation in perspective.[5] For decades after the first steamboat entered the Yazoo River in the 1820s, uncounted passengers found the steamers to be the way to the outside world.

The number of passengers carried on steamboats was as elusive as antebellum freight statistics until the Corps of Engineers reported them from 1890 to 1917. Slightly more than 125,000 people found passage aboard steamers in the Yazoo basin during these twenty-seven years. Although some passengers boarding the *Yazoo Valley*, the *De Smet*, or any other of the P. Line's larger boats enjoyed an experience that was not inconsistent with the romance of steamboating, the records suggest another perspective. For example, during the four seasons beginning in the fall of 1890 and ending in the summer of 1894, steamboats made 3,124 round trips between points on the Yazoo River system with 24,486 passengers, or a rough average of only 8 people per trip. During one season, the "river queen" *Blanks Cornwell* made 67 round trips between Yazoo City and Vicksburg with a total of 855 passengers, who were not necessarily destined for either of the terminal ports. At the same time, the *Birdie Bailey* made 158 round trips with 3,100 passengers between Yazoo City and Belzoni. A few years later, the *Maggie* made 114 trips with 500 passengers between Yazoo City and Campbellsville on the Sunflower, while the *City of Greenwood* took 1,500 people during 139 round trips between Yazoo City and Belzoni. The *Annual Reports* indicate that a large majority of the passengers reported during any given year boarded a steamboat for a trip of less than seventy-five miles. Steamers provided the way out for some travelers, but they served as a short-distance commuting, or ferry, service for most passengers, who probably traveled on deck rather than in the main cabin. Just as a revised perspective on passenger service emphasizes the typical passenger as traveling on deck between nearby landings and towns, an analysis of freight services provides a broader perspective than steamboats loaded to the hurricane deck with bales of cotton.[6]

The Yazoo River system carried more than 10 million tons of reported freight from 1878–79, when the Corps of Engineers started publishing annual data, until 1928, when traffic in the major commodities ceased to be statistically significant (Figure 1). During the years covered in the *Annual Reports of the Chief of Engineers*, the Yazoo River, including Tchula Lake, accounted for about 59 percent of the total commerce, with the Tallahatchie-Coldwater rivers adding 14 percent and the Sunflower River with its tributaries amounting to 27 percent of the total tonnage. Figures representing total tonnage, although impressive, may be misleading. A superficial glance at annual tonnage statistics indicates that 1925 was the record year when the Corps of Engineers reported more than half a million tons of river commerce. In fact, three-fourths of that commerce was in logs, which were rafted rather than transported on deck or on barges.

A small amount of sawlog tonnage was barged, especially on Tchula Lake, Deer Creek, and Steele's Bayou. Logs rafted and towed by steamers to sawmills at Greenwood, Yazoo City, Vicksburg, and several other points along the rivers did not provide a source of income for many of the steamers serving the river system. A few of the towboats consistently towing logs out of the Tallahatchie or along the Yazoo were described as sawmill boats, which probably referred to ownership rather than the lumbering services provided on board by the sawmill boat proper. Rafted logs, often towed by a mean towboat charging the lowest ton/mile rate of all commodities, should be treated as a separate category when

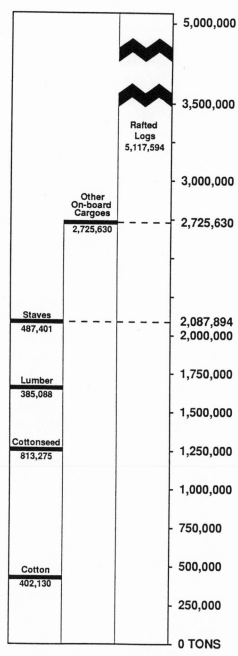

Figure 1. *River Trade by Major Commodity, 1890–1928*
(in tons)

evaluating river commerce. During the period 1890 to 1928, rafted logs amounted to more than 5 million tons, or 51.5 percent of the total tonnage. Freight transported on board steamboats or their barges accounted for slightly less than one-half of the rivers' commerce (Figure 2).[7]

Steamboats handled more than 4.8 million tons of freight during the thirty-eight years after 1890. The major on-board commodities were cotton, cottonseed, lumber, staves, grain, provisions, and a category listed as "miscellaneous," which generally referred to packaged goods other than foodstuffs. Provisions and miscellaneous freight were sometimes referred to as "upriver" or "return" cargoes. A few minor commodities such as hides, skins, livestock, logs, or hay were relatively unimportant in the freight business along the rivers. During the 1920s categories of grain, miscellaneous freight, and provisions were reported in greater detail and variety to include barged logs, coal, oil, gasoline, construction materials, sand, cement, and other bulk cargoes. Of all the commodities, cotton and cottonseed were reported for the longest time period.[8]

The first reliable reports on cotton shipments began in the 1878–79 season, when steamers brought 115,886 bales out of the Yazoo country. Eight years later, roustabouts handled a record 133,150 bales. Steamers transported almost 2.75 million bales in the Delta, but they carried more than a hundred thousand bales in only six seasons. The 37 bales reported in 1927 marked the virtual end of cotton and steamboats on the rivers. Available statistics indicated that cotton accounted for about 12 percent of the on-board freight. Although a relatively small percentage, cotton represented a significant portion of steamboat earnings.

Before the Parisot-Leathers war in the 1880s, steamboat clerks usually charged $1.50 to ship a bale of cotton from Yazoo City to Vicksburg. During that intensely competitive period, P. Line clerks sometimes charged 75¢ a bale, and during the early years of the twentieth century steamboats regularly charged 50¢ to 75¢ per bale. A decade later, steamboats charged 2.9¢ per ton/mile, or 75¢ a bale from Yazoo City to Vicksburg. Although cotton freight rates remained relatively stable, cotton shipments declined from an average of one hundred thousand bales a year from 1890 to 1900, to about fifty thousand per year in the next decade, and to twenty-five thousand annually in the third ten-year period before dwin-

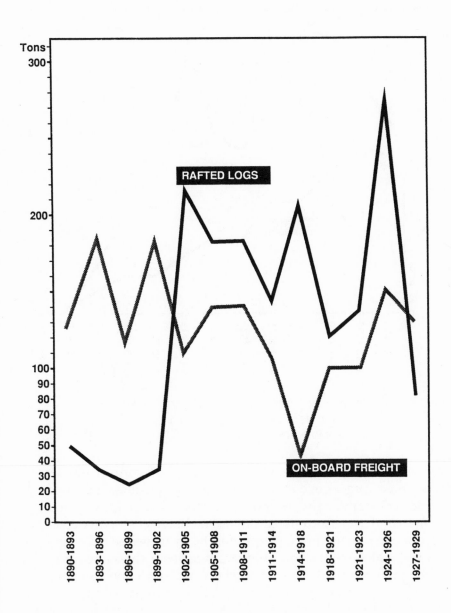

Figure 2. *Rafted Logs and All On-Board Freight, 1890–1929
(in thousands of tons, based on three-year averages)*
1890–1916 by shipping season, 1916–29 by calendar year

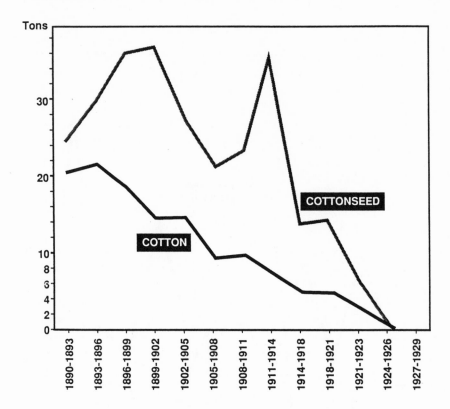

Figure 3. *Cotton and Cottonseed, 1890–1929*
(in thousands of tons, based on three-year averages)
1890–1916 by shipping season, 1916–29 by calendar year

dling to thirty-seven bales in 1927. Even as cotton shipments declined, cargoes of cottonseed and lumber products increased to such a degree that they supplanted cotton as the major commodity on steamboats. Cottonseed shipped on the river system exceeded cotton in tonnage by 50 percent for the entire period from 1878 to 1928, and since the ton/mile rate was about the same for each commodity, the fiber's seed ranked as the single most important cargo shipped on board steamers and their barges (Figure 3). Reported cottonseed tonnage after 1890 indicates that cottonseed amounted to almost one-fourth of the on-board commodities. The record tonnage was set in 1912–13, and for all practical purposes, cottonseed shipments ended ten years after the record year.[9]

While the commodities from cotton culture amounted to

slightly more than one-third of the rivers' on-board commerce after 1890, forest products of lumber and staves accounted for one-fourth of the on-board trade during the same period (Figure 4). Lumber totaled 378,000 tons and barrel staves measured a surprising 487,000 tons. Steamboatmen customarily charged 1.8¢ per ton/mile on the Tallahatchie and Coldwater rivers, 1.5¢ per ton/mile on the Yazoo and only 1¢ on the Sunflower River. The 1914–15 season was the end of barrel stave shipments, and lumber shipments ceased eleven years later.

As much as 36 percent of the total on-board commerce was made up of grain, provisions, and miscellaneous freight. Grain included livestock winter feed shipped within the river system as well as that sent upriver from Vicksburg. Perhaps the majority of the grain was a downriver commodity bound for Vicksburg elevators. Provisions, often referred to as "upriver" or "return" freight, included barrels of flour, meal, sugar, and coffee and were reported in tons (Figure 5). During one ten year period, 1909–19, the *Annual Reports* recorded not only the tons of provisions and miscellaneous freight, but also the number of packages. During that decade, steamboat clerks reported handling 700,000 packages of provisions and 1.4 million packages of miscellaneous freight, or a total of 2.1 million packages, each weighing an average of 200 pounds. That these impressive figures for the second decade of the twentieth century were recorded during the decline of river transportation suggest that the return freight for the P. Line must have been enormous.[10]

A dramatic increase in on-board freight in the 1920s reflected the gasoline-powered towboat upbound with loaded barges of coal, oil, or gasoline, bulk materials such as sand, gravel, cement, or brick, and in a few instances large cargoes of crossties or barges loaded with logs. The *Annual Reports* do not indicate that these towboats left with their barges loaded with Yazoo country agricultural produce. During the six years after 1928, all boats and barges transported slightly less than 35,000 tons of on-board freight and rafted about 5,000 tons of logs each year.[11]

Although Yazoo River steamboating did not decline rapidly until after World War I, river traffic experienced enormous changes in equipment and operating practices after 1890. During Captain Parisot's last season in control of the P. Line, he maintained a near monopoly over Yazoo shipping. The Corps of Engi-

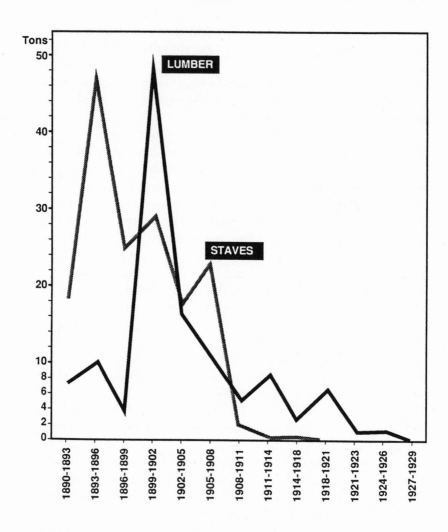

Figure 4. *Lumber and Staves, 1890–1929*
(in thousands of tons, based on three-year averages)
1890–1916 by shipping season, 1916–29 by calendar year

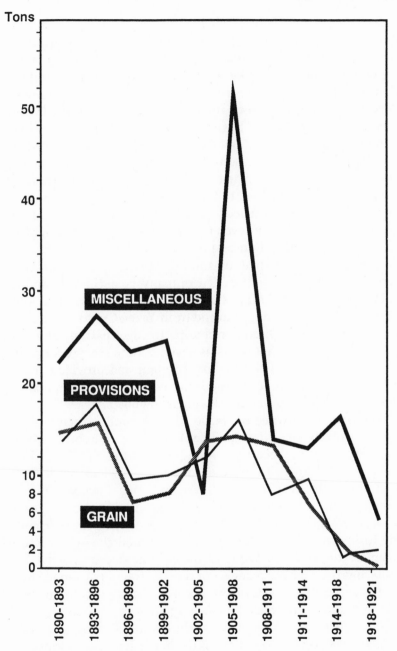

Figure 5. *Grain, Provisions, and Miscellaneous, 1890–1921*
(in thousands of tons, based on three-year averages)
1890–1916 by shipping season, 1916–21 by calendar year

neers reported that eight P. Line boats made 378 of the 433 trips on the river system and that three boats of the Sunflower River Packet Company, with Parisot on its Board òf Directors, made 55 trips on the Yazoo-Sunflower route. After absorbing the Sunflower Company, Parisot left the P. Line in control of F. M. Andrews of Vicksburg in 1890. Parisot's financial situation continued to collapse, but the steamboat business did not.

Indeed, the P. Line without Parisot's guiding hand enjoyed several prosperous cotton seasons. During the 1890–91 shipping year, twenty steamboats transported more than two hundred thousand tons, which included twenty-five thousand tons of cotton, thirty thousand tons of cottonseed, sixteen thousand tons of lumber staves, and almost sixty-seven thousand tons of return freight and towed about seventy thousand tons of logs. Of the twenty boats, the independently owned *Joe* and *Uncle Billy* towed logs on the Sunflower, the Yazoo City Oil Company boat *Gamma* and the Tchula-built *General Miles* busily hauled cottonseed and small shipments of return freight to and from Yazoo City, and the showboat *New Idea* presented her charms to eager patrons along the Yazoo and Tallahatchie rivers as seven P. Line steamers handled almost 80 percent of the on-board freight and provided accommodations for about seven thousand passengers. The remaining freight business was handled by eight towboats.[12]

Towboats, not owned by Yazoo River steamboatmen but originating in New Orleans, Natchez, Vicksburg, or another Mississippi River port, became a standard feature of Yazoo River shipping after 1890. In 1889–90 one such towboat with barges made one trip into the Sunflower, and two towboats reached Greenwood. Five towboats originating outside the waterways made a total of nine round trips on the Yazoo the next year, and in the following season eight towboats joined the seven P. Line steamers to serve the Yazoo Delta. By mid-decade, twelve towboats and their barges made 93 of the 786 round trips made by all boats on the Yazoo waterways, and ten years later, six towboats (out of twenty-three boats) made only 66 of more than 800 round trips on the river system. Because the *Annual Reports of the Chief of Engineers* after 1909 did not provide sufficient information to distinguish boats other than as gasoline- or steam-powered, the precise role of towboats has been blurred. But during the 1890s,

the presence of towboats did not seriously endanger the tradi-
tional role of the P. Line.[13]

Although an occasional towboat reached Greenwood, the P.
Line tended to concentrate on the Belzoni–Yazoo City–Vicksburg
trade and to neglect the upper rivers. Even when the railroads
provided services for planters along the upper waterways, W. F.
Ramay believed that the Yazoo River trade still offered a business
opportunity. He built the sternwheel steamer *Ferd R.* at Green-
wood in 1892 and entered the trade. The next year, the new boat hit
a snag and was towed to Captain Pugh's boatyard at Yazoo City.
She was originally only 70 feet long, but when rebuilt she measured 93.8 x 16.2 x 3 feet. When the *Ferd R.* returned to the Yazoo
River trade, she was owned by W. C. George, who had started the
Greenwood Transportation Company. Within a few months, the
Greenwood firm purchased the sixty-three-ton sternwheeler *E. A.
Pharr* to serve upper river shippers.[14]

Captain Pugh responded to the upriver competition by building three boats in two years. With machinery purchased from the
wrecked Tchula Lake boat *General Miles*, Pugh built a new hull
and gave her the name *Fifteen* when he sent her into the upper
Yazoo River. Less than twelve months later, Commodore Pugh
launched the *Yazonia* and the *Maggie*. At first, the *Yazonia*
steamed on the upper rivers, while the *Fifteen* was transferred to
the old P. Line at Vicksburg, and the *Maggie* steamed out of Yazoo
City under the command of Captain D. C. White. By mid-decade,
Pugh reestablished his old line, devised a logo with the letter "P"
superimposed on a "U," and ran the *Yazonia* and *Maggie* on the
upper rivers in competition with the Greenwood company. With
the PU Line and the Greenwood company competing for trade
around Greenwood, and the old P. Line operating on the lower
Yazoo and Sunflower rivers, Yazoo City shippers lacked adequate
steamboat services.[15]

Yazoo City businessmen called a meeting of people interested in
the steamboat business and invited Gus Meissonnier, who had
steamboating connections in Greenwood and Vicksburg, and F. M.
Andrews, president of the old P. Line, to discuss the possibility of a
new line at Yazoo City. Andrews suggested that the P. Line confine
its Vicksburg operations to the Sunflower trade, a new line at
Yazoo City be established to steam the middle reaches of the

Yazoo River from Belzoni to Campbellsville on the Sunflower River, and the Greenwood boats have the upper river trade. The lines would transfer through freight and barges at Belzoni and Campbellsville. The suggestion seemed sound, and willing investors formed a committee to seek additional subscribers, who organized the Yazoo City Transportation Company in 1897.[16]

Captain Pugh, the merchant George Quakemeyer, warehouseman Willie C. Craig, steamboatman Gus Meissonnier, cottonseed oil–man Steve Castleman, and six other Yazoo City investors purchased stock and participated in the organizational meeting. They elected Steve Castleman as president of the new company and Captain Pugh as vice-president and general manager. At the same time that the Yazoo City Company became operational, the Greenwood group received its corporate charter as the Greenwood Transportation Company. A month or so later, the company that had previously been regarded as the remnant of the P. Line went out of existence and was replaced by the Vicksburg and Yazoo River Packet Company running boats from Vicksburg in the Sunflower trade under the leadership of Joseph J. Powers. Three companies divided the trade once commanded by Commodore Parisot.[17]

If local lore is right, Steve Castleman fulfilled a long-standing ambition when he became president of the Yazoo City Transportation Company. As a young man he went to New Orleans but exhausted his funds before returning to his home in Belzoni. According to the story, he had only $2.25 when he reached Vicksburg on his return trip, and the steamboat fare from Vicksburg to Belzoni was $4.75. When refused passage at Vicksburg, he told the captain that he would beat the boat to Belzoni, and he began walking. For reasons that are unexplained, Castleman reached Belzoni before the steamboat, and he told the captain when they met: "I hope I will live to see the day when I can buy this boat, and you will still be captain so I can fire you." When the organization of Powers's line running on the Sunflower River signaled the death of the old P. Line, Castleman advertised the Yazoo City Transportation Company as the "successor" to Parisot's Yazoo and Tallahatchie Transportation Company. The P. Line was no more. Perhaps Castleman was satisfied.[18]

Castleman, representing the Yazoo City company, divided the trade with Joseph Powers of the Vicksburg company. Powers's boats remained in the Sunflower trade, while Castleman's boats

operated between Belzoni and Campbellsville, and the Greenwood company continued on the Tallahatchie and upper Yazoo
rivers. The Yazoo City line purchased the *Fifteen* and the *Rees
Pritchard* from the old P. Line in 1898, and the next year, with
Captain Pugh serving as president, added the *Maggie* and the
Hibernia before expanding to as many as six boats with the *Ashland City* and the *Rescue* by the end of the century. During the last
season of the nineteenth century, four Vicksburg boats made fifty-
three trips in the Sunflower trade, six steamers made more than
three hundred trips from their home port of Yazoo City, and three
Greenwood boats made seventy-five trips into the Tallahatchie
River. The division of trade was not absolute, and during the year
boats usually associated with one trade were sometimes reported
in another trade for several trips or under charter to another
company. In addition to the thirteen Yazoo boats, eight Mississippi River towboats made fifteen trips into the river system. The
river traffic had not dried up.[19]

The old ways were changing as the new century began. The P.
Line ended its corporate existence. The river trade was divided
among three lines. The P. Line elevator that had once been so
important to Vicksburg had "crumbled into a mass of time worn
and decayed timbers," and it was razed in 1902. George Irving,
onetime receiver for Parisot's properties and the current owner of
Vicksburg's "largest retail grocery store," was ill at his Campbellsville home, and he died three days after steaming to Vicksburg
aboard the *Wichita*. Despite changing times, Shum Parisot refused
to give up. In the third year of the new century, the aging steamboatman entered the Yazoo once more as Captain S. H. Parisot in
command of the sternwheel steamer *American*.[20]

Renewed interest in the Yazoo River commerce and Parisot's
return to steamboating stemmed from the Vicksburg District
Corps of Engineers' massive project to relocate the mouth of the
Yazoo River. The near isolation of Vicksburg on Lake Centennial
and the recurring bar at the mouth of the Yazoo River had plagued
steamboat interests for years. The Corps of Engineers planned to
correct both problems with a canal to divert the Yazoo River into
Lake Centennial. The Yazoo Diversion Canal was almost completed in December 1902, and Captain E. C. Carroll served as
chairman of a local committee to plan the ceremonial opening of
the canal in January. When the publisher of the *Vicksburg Amer-*

ican saw the *Rees Pritchard, Warren,* and *Elk* from the Yazoo tied up with the *Wichita* from the Sunflower and Captain Pugh's *Hallette* from the Mississippi River trade, he commented that the waterfront "looked like something doing to see the boats lined up there again." High waters broke through the last remaining obstacle between the Yazoo and Lake Centennial before Carroll's committee was quite prepared, but in January 1903, the committee officially and ceremoniously opened the Yazoo Diversion Canal.[21]

Interested investors, including Captain S. J. Searles, Joe McCullogh, and Major Lee Richardson, believed that the canal would offer new business opportunities in Delta commerce. They organized the Merchants and Planters Packet Company and contracted for a new sternwheel steamer that had been built on the Tennessee River in north Alabama. Named the *American,* the "gem" was 158 feet long and 27.6 feet in breadth. She was registered for "inland passenger" service and was measured at 190 tons. Company stockholders waited for her arrival.[22]

Captain Horace E. Bixby, noted for training river pilots, commanded the *American* on her trip down the Mississippi River from St. Louis. Captain Bixby nudged her against the Vicksburg landing on 28 April 1903, and four days later she began her maiden voyage up the Yazoo River with Captain S. H. Parisot in command. When Captain Parisot brought the *American* to the landing at Satartia, Mrs. Richardson sent a "magnificent bouquet with her compliments to the boat and Captain Parisot." Steaming upriver, Parisot stopped at P. Line Home. There the gracious Mary Ann Kinkead met the remarkable captain with beautiful flowers, cool, fresh milk, and a "basket of new vegetables." These two old friends who had endured so much met now in a scene reminiscent of so many such landings during better times a quarter of a century before. Leaving P. Line Home behind, Parisot took the *American* upriver and was welcomed at Yazoo City and at Greenwood. The new steamer apparently did not generate the business her owners expected, for although she made twelve trips during that season, six the next year, and ten the year after, she was eventually taken into the Mississippi River trade.[23]

If Captain Parisot's return to the Yazoo River aboard the sternwheel, steam-powered *American* reflected the old ways, the new ways were announced at the same time by the raucous, gasoline-fueled, internal combustion engine. The gasoline boats *Amy* and *May* entered the Yazoo in 1902, when the former made two trips up the Sunflower and the latter made only one. Twenty-one other gasoline boats entered the river system during the first decade of the twentieth century. The *Hester*, measuring ninety tons, was the largest in tonnage, but she was only fifty feet long. The *T. B. Butts* was the longest at eighty-four feet, but she was computed at seventeen tons. The *Kuroki* was the smallest at two tons, and the *Dolphin*, described as a "yacht," was only thirty feet long. Seventeen gasoline boats averaged about eighteen tons and almost fifty feet long. At first, the gasoline boats tended to be towboats entering the Yazoo River system from the Mississippi River with cargoes from Mississippi River ports aboard their barges. As age and accidents gradually diminished the number of steamers, gasoline boats began to fill all needs and had replaced all but the last, aged steamboats by the time of the 1927 flood.[24]

Three years after first appearing on the Yazoo River, eight gasoline boats towing barges from the Mississippi River competed with twelve steamboats owned by the three competing firms. In 1909, the last year the *Annual Report* listed boats by name, nine steamers, four gasoline boats, two tugs, and the little, three-ton propeller boat the *Admiral Schley* served local needs. The cotton season ending in 1915 marked a turning point, for during that shipping year fifteen gasoline-powered boats outnumbered the thirteen steam-powered boats. After another decade, gasoline boats made twice as many trips as did steamers. During the disastrous flood in 1927, gasoline boats made more than eleven hundred trips while steamers made about five hundred trips into the flooded waterways. The Corps of Engineers rarely reported as many as a thousand trips annually during the next few years, and the number of trips made by steamboats gradually declined until the last steamer was reported as running in 1934. The internal combustion engine replacing the steam power plant was not the only change on the Yazoo River system in the early twentieth century.[25]

When the steamboatmen met in 1897 to organize the Yazoo City Transportation Company, they undoubtedly expected the short haul to become more important than the long haul. With each company responsible for a defined trade area, the onetime long haul from Vicksburg into the Tallahatchie River above Green-wood was for all practical purposes eliminated or turned over to Mississippi River towboats or to the railroads. The steamboats running in the twentieth century developed the short haul be-tween river ports and plantation landings into a productive trans-portation system. Indeed, during the first two decades of the twentieth century, boats engaged in short hauls transported some of the record tonnage for the river system.

During the last year of the golden age, the Corps of Engineers reported that steamboats made 433 round trips, and about 25 percent of these were from Vicksburg to the head of navigation, which was often as far up as Sharkey's landing. Three years later, about 30 percent of 429 trips ran from Vicksburg far up the Talla-hatchie, but at the same time 36 percent of the trips originated in Yazoo City and terminated at a landing between Belzoni and the Sunflower River. At the turn of the century as few as 5 percent of 520 trips were reported as running between Vicksburg and Sharkey's landing, while only 92 ran the length of the Yazoo from Vicksburg to Greenwood. Just a few years later (1904–5) riverboats made only 17 round trips between Vicksburg and Greenwood, while almost 48 percent of all reported round trips were made from Greenwood to "local points."[26]

The *Annual Reports of the Chief of Engineers* adopted a new report form in 1910 and began recording the average length of haul by commodity. At that time, the average haul was less than 65 miles for boats operating out of Greenwood, while Yazoo City boats averaged about 125 miles per round trip. Some of the Yazoo City boats continued to run to Vicksburg loaded with cotton and cottonseed on the downstream run and with provisions and pack-aged goods as return freight. Forest products and logs usually constituted the bulk of short hauls of less than 50 miles. After 1915, the *Annual Reports* indicated that boats on the Tallahatchie averaged about 45 miles, which was approximately the distance between Greenwood and Minter City. Boats on the Yazoo averaged about 85 miles per haul in 1915, but that distance decreased to 40 miles in 1920 and to less than 30 miles in 1925. By then, steam-boats had been all but replaced by gasoline boats. And just two years later, even the gasoline boats no longer transported the historic commodities of cotton, cottonseed, lumber, or staves.

The century-long history of steamboats on the Yazoo River and its tributaries had come to an end.[27]

River transportation on the Yazoo River system ended much as it began: with a few independently owned boats entering from the Mississippi River. Between the beginning of powered river commerce in the 1820s until its virtual end in the 1920s, steamboats played an important role in the development of the Yazoo–Mississippi River Delta. Yazoo steamboating was characterized during its first quarter of a century by itinerant Mississippi River steamers entering the waterways for one or two trips and maybe returning the next season. But as individual boats, they seldom became an integral part of the Delta. Only when young men who had grown up along the rivers completed their apprenticeships and by the 1850s began to command their own boats to serve their rivers, their neighbors, and their towns did steamboats become part of the whole Delta fabric. The work of these early local entrepreneurs was interrupted by four years of war, when more than forty steamers, both large and small, tried to aid the Confederacy only to become part of the wartime debris choking the Yazoo waterways. Steamboatmen began rebuilding after the war, and local rivermen quickly regained control of their waterways. River people such as John and Milton Dent, Thomas and Christine Metzler, and especially Shum Parisot turned an almost chaotic and highly competitive situation into an orderly transportation system. Captain Parisot went further and built a benevolent monopoly, which provided safe and reliable service at landings from Vicksburg to Sharkey's. Parisot's P. Line, organized in 1870 and continuing under his influence until 1890, constituted the golden age of Yazoo steamboating.

Parisot's failure to break out of the Yazoo into the Mississippi River trade undoubtedly contributed to his financial ruin and his retirement from the P. Line in 1890. Steamboating did not collapse then, nor did it end with the nineteenth century. Indeed, steamboats enjoyed about twenty-five prosperous years after Parisot left the P. Line. Railroads caused rivermen to change their operating patterns but not to go out of business. Drawing a direct causal relationship between railroads and the end of river transportation does not recognize the business ability of rivermen. Perhaps the increased use of trucks and an improved road system following World War I administered the coup de grace to riverboats by taking over even the short-haul business. During the forty years building up to the golden age, and through the two decades presided over by Commodore Parisot and the P. Line, and even through the forty years of the long decline, steamboats served the Yazoo country. Steamers provided the Delta waterways with pleasure and profit, with relative elegance and mundane regularity, with excitement, but seldom with boredom. Most of all, steamboats provided generations of Delta planters, farmers, merchants, townspeople, and working people with a way to the outside world.

Shum Parisot was the dominant personality in Yazoo River steamboating history. The aged commodore and his wife, Mary, lived in near poverty as they passed their forty-first wedding anniversary in August 1917. Both were in failing health, and a few days after Thanksgiving, Mary S. Parisot died. Commodore Parisot, remaining in his home under the care of Lula Aden, wrote his will soon after Mary's funeral and explained carefully that since he and his wife had no children he inherited their home under the laws of Mississippi. Having established his title to the house, the captain directed that "all of my property, both real and personal, consisting of my residence at 600 Locust Street . . . and the contents thereof," should go to Lula Aden on the condition that she would "take care of and support me during the remainder of my life."[28] Captain S. H. Parisot died in Vicksburg at 6:00 on Saturday morning, 29 December 1917. A verse written by Annie Kinkead Dent thirty years earlier continued to reflect the affection held for the Commodore of the Yazoo when she wrote that she hoped it would be remembered that she and her friends "loved the P. Line best."[29]

Appendix A

STEAMBOATS

NAME	RIG	YEARS ON THE YAZOO	TONS	DIMENSIONS (in feet, l x w x d)
A. B. Shaw	SW	1847	67	
Acadia	SW	1861–63	343	188 x 35 x 7
Addie E. Faison	StW	1889–94	241.5	135 x 30.6 x 4.9
Addie T.	StW	1906–8	97	112.6 x 24.8 x 3.8
Admiral Schley	SS	1906–9	31	51.4 x 17.9 x 11.6
Afton	SW	1852–55	287	
Afton, Jr.	SW	1858	155	
Aqnes	SW	1846	170	
Alarm	StW	1887–93	189.09	142 x 26 x 4.3
Albert Gallatin	SW	1840	94	
Alda	StW	1902–4	73	121 x 21.2 x 4
Alert	StW	1880–84	27.55	70.4 x 14.4 x 2.6
Alice	SW	1883–89	24.35	60 x 15 x 3
Alice B. Miller	StW	1908–10		130 x 27 x 4
Alice Maria	SW	1835–36	72	
Algonquin	SW	1841	221	
Alonzo Child	SW	1861–62	493	222 x 36 x 6.5
Alpha	StW	1874		110 x 20
Alys Gray	StW	1921		
American	StW	1903–6	190	158 x 27.6 x 4.2
Angelina M.	SS	1903		
Anna	SW	1860	110	135 x 25
Annie Lauri	StW	1898	199.81	138 x 27 x 4.8

Abbreviations: SW = Sidewheel; StW = Sternwheel; SS = Steam screw.

NAME	RIG	YEARS ON THE YAZOO	TONS	DIMENSIONS (in feet, l x w x d)
Argo	StW	1858–62	99	136 x 21 x 4
Arkansas, CSS	SS	1862		165 x 35 x 18
Arkansas City	SS	1879	70.89	99 x 18 x 4
Arrowline	SW	1871–72	80.3	
Ashland City	StW	1898–1900	94.55	120 x 20 x 3.9
Atalanta	StW	1840	180	
Atalanta	SW	1856–58,60	141	
Atlanta	Stw	1896–98	85.03	93 x 16.4 3.7
B. F. Franks		1872–77		
B. H. Hurt		1872–74		80 x 20 x 4
Badger State	SW	1858–59	127	
Banjo	SW	1859–60	105	
Baron De Kalb, USS		1862–63	521	
Beaver	SW	1832		
Bee	SW	1851	153	
Belle		1868		
Belle of Arkansas	SW	1843–44	224	
Belle of Ouachita	SW	1845	103	
Belle Yazoo	SW	1869–76	349.03	162 x 30 x 5
Belmont	SW	1841–47	115	
Ben Adams	SW	1846–47	158	
Ben Lee	StW	1852–54	122	
Ben McCulloch	StW	1861–63	80	100 x 22 x 3.9
Benton, USS	SW	1863	512	
Bertha C.		1894–1901		
Beta	StW	1876–88	78.15	116 x 22 x 3.5
Bicknell		1859		
Big-A-Plenty	StW	1900–1901	54	87 x 20 x 4
Big Black	SW	1838	81	
Big Horn	StW	1868	313.33	154 x 33.5 x 4.5
Big Sunflower	StW	1870–75		128 x 28 x 4
Bill Nigh	StW	1890		
Birdie Bailey	StW	1886–97	109.7	111 x 22 x 3.5
Black Hawk, USS	SW	1863	902	285 x 38 x 6.5
Black Hawk	SS	1908	34	80 x 15 x 5.8
Blanks Cornwell	StW	1888–96	232.4	140 x 28 x 4.6
Bloomer	SW	1852	79	
Bluella	StW	1873	74.75	86.2 x 21.2 x 3.4
Blue Wing	SW	1865	158.15	150 x 31 x 5.7

NAME	RIG	YEARS ON THE YAZOO	TONS	DIMENSIONS (in feet, l x w x d)
Bluff City	SW	1858–59	252	
Bonito	SW	1834	138	
Brandywine	SW	1832		
Bride	SW	1850	295	
Bridgewater	SW	1838	160	
Brownsville	SW	1846	99	
Bunker Hill	SW	1836–40	301	
C. B. Bryon	StW	1903	189	142 x 26 x 4.3
C. H. Woods	StW	1898–99	70.83	110 x 22 x 3.2
C. J. Reynolds	StW	1904–6	71	112 x 22.1 x 2.6
C. P. Huntington	StW	1870–77	147	131 x 26 x 3
Cairo, USS		1863	515	175 x 50 x 7
Cairo Belle	StW	1866	365	
Calumet	SW	1866–71	305.16	151 x 26 x 5
Capitol	SW	1861–62	448	224 x 32 x 6
Carondolet, USS		1863	512	176.5 x 52 x 6.5
Carrie Converse	StW	1870	241.05	160 x 33 x 4
Carrie Hogan	StW	1877–81	119.4	136.8 x 28.6 x 4
Carrie Williams	SS	1873	59.74	
Ceres	SW	1836	58	
Champion No. 4	SW	1863	115	
Charles H. Tompkins	StW	1880	356	181 x 25 x 3.5
Charles Rebstock	StW	1883–84	98.28	95.7 x 20.4 x 3.5
Charleston	SW	1835	84	
Charlotte	SW	1846–47	250	
Charm	SW	1860–61	223	
Chattahoochee	StW	1892		155 x 31 x 5
Cherokee	StW	1883–84	474.86	210 x 38.8 x 6.6
Chicago		1844–45		
Chickasaw	SW	1838	149	
Chillicothe, USS	SW	1863	395	159 x 46.5 x 6.8
Chocchuma	SW	1838	120	
Choctaw	SW	1834–36		
Choctaw, USS	SW	1863	1,000	245 x 28 x 7
Choctaw	StW	1899–1905	223	127 x 24 x 4
Choctaw (rebuilt)	StW	1905–16	99	124 x 24 x 2.3
Choctaw	StW	1917–22		121 x 27.8 x 4
Cincinnati, USS		1863	512	
Citizen	StW	1863	233	

NAME	RIG	YEARS ON THE YAZOO	TONS	DIMENSIONS (in feet, l x w x d)
City of Cairo	StW	1856	199	
City of Greenwood	StW	1899–1904		130 x 28 x 3.5
City of Knoxville	StW	1901–4	147	130 x 18 x 3
City of Yazoo	StW	1879–84	630.38	200 x 38 x 7
Clara S.	StW	1877–84	199	
Clarksville	StW	1877	443.2	168 x 34 x 5
Cleopatra	SW	1833	118	
Clermont	SW	1844	111	
Col. T. H. Judson	SW	1858–61	191	140 x 28 x 5.2
Columbia	StW	1899	75	116 x 24 x 3
Compromise	SW	1858	270	
Concord	SW	1840		
Condor		1838		
Cora No. 2	SW	1853–54	375	
Corrine	SW	1847	183	
Cotton Plant	SW	1843	122	
Cotton Plant	SW	1859–63	59	
Cotton Plant	SW	1860–63	180	158 x 31 x 6.5
Countess	SW	1866–71	195.41	155 x 30.2 x 4
Countess (rebuilt)	SW			140 x 30 x 5
Creole	SW	1831–32	171	
Creole	StW	1856		(one boiler)
Crescent	StW	1898–1900	159.14	144 x 28 x 5
Crown Point	StW	1890–95	159.14	123 x 25 x 4.2
Cruiser	StW	1897	240.06	152 x 30 x 5
Cumanchee	SW	1838	169	
Cumberland	SW	1848	121	
Cumberland	StW	1866	232	154 x 33 x 5
D. B. Mosby	SW	1850–53	164	
D. O. Fogel		1889		
D. S. Stacy	SW	1852	376	
Dahlia	SS	1863	50	
Dart	SS	1873	13.74	43 x 9 x 1
David Stinson	StW	1878		
Deer Creek	StW	1874–80	83	90 x 25 x 4
Delia No. 2		1874–75		
Des Arc	StW	1893–95	40.88	95 x 18 x 3
De Smet	SW	1880–84	485.61	188.4 x 34 x 5
Detroit	SW	1838	136	

NAME	RIG	YEARS ON THE YAZOO	TONS	DIMENSIONS (in feet, l x w x d)
Dew Drop	SW	1858–63	184	150 X 26 X 4.5
Diligent	SW	1863	140	
Dime	SW	1846–48	61	
Dime	SS	1872	57.78	48.4 X 9.2 X 4
Dixie	SW	1860–62	106	130.8 X 24.4 X 4.2
Dixie	SS	1901	33	52.6 X 12 X 4
Dove	StW	1843	34	
Dove	SW	1854	237	
Duck River	SW	1847	132	
Duke of Orleans	SW	1846	301	
E. A. Pharr	StW	1895–99	63.61	90 X 29.9 X 4.2
E. C. Carroll, Jr.	StW	1878–84		155 X 35 X 4.5
E. C. Wood	StW	1897		
Economist	StW	1871	199.85	128 X 27 X 3.3
Eddie	StW	1866–68	59.09	
Ed Durant	StW	1895–96	153.49	113.6 X 29.6 X 4.6
Edendale		1842		
Ed Foster	StW	1887		100 X 26.5 X 4
Edna	StW	1902–7	50	75 X 18 X 3
Edna	StW	1904–7	78	70 X 21.4 X 3
Edward J. Gay	SW	1862–63	824	277 X 39 X 8.5
Effort	SW	1843–44	54	
Electric	StW	1898–99	34.57	77.6 X 20 X 2.8
Elk	SW	1847	84	
Elk	StW	1899–1901	111.22	153 X 22 X 4
Ella Belle	StW	1870–72		
Emma	StW	1865–76		121 X 24.5 X 4.5
Emma No. 2	StW	1866	372.89	156.7 X 33.7 X 5
Emma Bett	StW	1860–63	79	
Emma Francis	StW	1898	48	60 X 14 X 2
Enterprise	SW	1845–46	106	
Enterprise	SW	1858		172 X 26.5 X 8.5
Era No. 8	SW	1869–70	162.68	121.9 X 25.3 X 4
Era No. 10	StW	1870		136 X 30.8 X 5
Erin	SW	1838	88	
Euteau	StW	1915–20		
Eva Alma	StW	1899		111.2 X 16.6 X 3.1
Evergreen		See New Evergreen		
Exit	SW	1847	158	

NAME	RIG	YEARS ON THE YAZOO	TONS	DIMENSIONS (in feet, l x w x d)
F. Barksdale	StW	1884–88	216.67	155 X 30.5 X 5.4
F. K., Jr.	StW	1855	61	
F. Weyerhauser	StW	1902–5	216	140 X 31 X 4.5
Fairfield	SS	1875	62.91	
Fair Play	SW	1860–62	162	139 X 27 X 4.7
Fairplay	StW	1879		
Favorite	SS	1868		
Fawn	StW	1906–9	46	95 X 18.5 X 3.3
Ferd Kennett	SW	1861–63	591	238 X 40.5 X 6.5
Ferd R.	StW	1893–99	45.5	93.8 X 16.2 X 3
Fifteen	StW	1893–97	75	103 X 18 X 3.5
Fountain City	StW	1907–8	65	99.5 X 23.5 X 4.3
Frank Beck, Jr.	StW	1873–75		90 X 21 X 3.5
Freestone	StW	1863–65	150	
Fern	SS	1863	50	
Forest Rose, USS	StW	1863	260	155 X 32.2 X 4.7
Gamma	StW	1888–94	44.32	84 X 18.4 X 4.3
Ganges	SW	1849	155	
Gasconade	StW	1873–74	49.95	
Gazelle	SW	1838	82	
General Byran	SW	1845	172	
Gen. Earl Van Dorn	SW	1862	524	182 X 28.3 X 10.7
General Miles	StW	1881	75	103 X 18 X 3
General Morgan	SW	1840	165	
General Polk	SW	1861–62	390	280 X 35 X 8
Gen. Price, USS	SW	1863	483	182 X 30 X 9.2
General R. H. Stokes	SW	1853	140	
General Worth	SW	1853	125	
George Baker	StW	1878–79	69.94	90.7 X 18 X 3
George Campbell	SW	1847–51	159	
Georgetown	SW	1853	395	
Gladiator	SW	1837–38	99	
Gladiator	SW	1851	236	
Golden Age	SW	1862–63	250	180 X 32 X 6.5
Golden Era	StW	1883–89	35.25	69.1 X 13.2 X 3.3
Governor Morehead	SW	1844	98	122 X 20 X 4.2
Granger	StW	1878–79	44.31	96 X 20 X 3.6
Greenback	StW	1870	63.94	
Greenwood	SW	1844–45	198	

NAME	RIG	YEARS ON THE YAZOO	TONS	DIMENSIONS (in feet, l x w x d)
Grenada	SW	1851–52	217	140 x 28 x 6
Greyhound	StW	1889		
Guide		1850s		
Gus Fowler	StW	1898–99	309.62	160 x 29.5 x 5.6
H. D. Mears	SW	1862–63	338	214 x 34 x 5.5
H. L. Brockman	StW	1903–5	75	91 x 22.6 x 3.8
H. M. Townsend	StW	1893–95	97.5	116.7 x 18 x 3.1
Hail Columbia	SW	1852	279	
Hallette	SW	1902–4	196	161 x 30.5 x 4.5
Hambleton	SW	1867		
Hannibal	SW	1838	81	
Happy Harry		1884		
Hard Cash	StW	1883		170 x 35 x 5
Hard Times	SW	1845–50	291	
Harry Bluff	SW	1838		
Harry Higbee	StW	1902	93	113.6 x 22.2 x 3.7
Hartford City	SW	1862–63	150	
Hatchie Eagle	SW	1845	116	
Haunt	StW	1921		
Headlight	StW	1877–87	99.37	140 x 24 x 3.5
Helen	SW	1843–46	169	
Helen Meade	StW	1886–87	82.37	112 x 20 x 4.2
Henry Clay	SW	1843	310	
Henry Marx	StW	1898–99	257.35	138 x 30 x 4.5
Henry Sheldon	StW	1907–9	220	159 x 29 x 3.9
Herald		1831		
Hibernia	StW	1893–99	157.06	135 x 25 x 4
Hill City	StW	1885		95 x 22 x 4
Hinds	SW	1838–39	130	
Home	SW	1855–60	183	150 x 25 x 5
Home	SW	1877–78		155 x 35 x 4.5
Hope	SW	1855–63	193	145 x 26 x 4.5
Hope	SW	1866–68	218	128 x 34 x 5
Hope	StW	1878–83		107 x 20 x 3.5
Houston Combs	StW	1893	95.96	98 x 22 x 3
Huron	SW	1831	183	
I. H. Sargent	StW	1894	85.46	116.2 x 22.4 x 4.3
Idaho	StW	1865–67	62	99.4 x 17 x 3.4
Ike Bonham	StW	1886–94	78.52	93.4 x 18 x 3.6

NAME	RIG	YEARS ON THE YAZOO	TONS	DIMENSIONS (in feet, l x w x d)
Imogene	StW	1905–8	51	77.5 x 17 x 4.2
Indian	SW	1838	60	
Iola	SW	1846	84	
Ione	SW	1835–36		
Isabella	SW	1854–55	248	
Issaquena	SW	1886	306.08	190.7 x 28 x 4.7
Ivy	SW	1862–63	454	191 x 28 x 9
J. A. Towns	StW	1908	97	101.5 x 25 x 3
J. B. O'Brian	SS	1893-97	44.49	70.8 x 15.2 x 7
J. C. Atlee	StW	1909	87	101 x 19.4 x 3.8
J. F. Pargoud	SW	1862–63	523	243 x 38 x 8
J. H. Williams	StW	1884–85		
J. L. McLean		1854	271	167.9 x 24 x 7
J. M. Sharp	SW	1859–64	218	147 x 29 x 6.5
J. W. Cheesman	StW	1863	215	165 x 33 x 5.5
Jack Osborn	StW	1903–6	125	120 x 30 x 5
James Jacobs	SW	1855		
Jeff Davis	SW	1848–51	107	
Jennie Campbell	StW	1895	225.06	144 x 26.5 x 4
Jimmie B.	StW	1889		97.3 x 20 x 2.3
Joan of Arc	SW	1841	343	
Joe (Little Joe)	SS	1893–96	18.07	44.5 x 10 x 4
Joe Seay	StW	1890–1901	27.74	75 x 16 x 6
John Bell	StW	1863	209	
John Drennon	SW	1848	131	
John F. Allen	StW	1888–93	133.9	130 x 24.2 x 4
John L. Lowery	StW	1895	54.15	108 x 16 x 3.6
John M. Abbott	StW	1893–94	97	92 x 20 x 3.6
John M. Chambers	StW	1878		174 x 32 x 4.7
John R. Meigs	StW	1879–97		172 x 38 x 5
John Strader	SW	1853–54	235	137 x 28.3 x 5.8
John Walsh	SW	1862–63	809	275 x 38 x 8
John Wesley	SW	1846–49	133	
Josephine Lovinza	SS	1897–98	95	113.6 x 22.2 x 3.7
Josephine Spengler	StW	1878–80	104.5	106.5 x 35 x 3.7
Josie D. Harkins	StW	1888	73.13	110 x 19.5 x 3.3
Josie Sively	StW	1899–1901	46	88 x 20.3 x 3.1
Joy Patton	StW	1897	63.04	100 x 21.3 x 5.4
Judah Touro	SW	1855	332	

NAME	RIG	YEARS ON THE YAZOO	TONS	DIMENSIONS (in feet, l x w x d)
Julia	SW	1851–52	99	
Kate	SS	1868	22	
Kate Dixon	StW	1878–79	96	
Kate P. Kountz	StW	1880		
Katie Robbins	StW	1884–90	162.52	141 x 28 x 4.9
Katie Simon		1884		
Kennedy	StW	1904	140	121 x 24.4 x 3.9
Kenwood, USS	SW	1863	232	154 x 33 x 5
Keoto	StW	1868		
Key West No. 3	StW	1863	207	156 x 32 x 4.5
L.L.B.	StW	1896–97	6.54	36.6 x 16.7 x 2.3
Lacon	SW	1845–46	118	
Lady Washington	SW	1842		
Lake City	StW	1885–93	44	75 x 16.6 x 4.6
Lake Palmyra	StW	1896–1901	141	123.5 x 26 x 4.8
Lake Washington	StW	1885–86		
Lancaster	SW	1835–36	130	
Lancaster, USS	SW	1862	257	170 x 30 x 55
Lancaster	StW	1893	156.09	135.6 x 23.5 x 3.8
Laurel	SW	1846–47	148	
Laurens	StW	1896		
Lavinia Logan	StW	1863	144	
Lawyer		1863		
Lebanon	StW	1863	225	
Lebanon No. 2	StW	1863	254	
Leflore	SW	1834–36	106	
Leflore	StW	1878–84	137.3	129.6 x 27 x 4
Leona	SW	1858	232	150 x 20 x 5.6
Lewis Whitman	SW	1858	319	178 x 29 x 6.5
Lida Norvell	StW	1874	88.45	103.7 x 13 x 3.7
Linden, USS	StW	1863	177	
Little P.	StW	1878–79		
Little Red	SW	1838	201	
Little Rufus	StW	1907–9	131	130.9 x 29.5 x 5
Little Sallie	StW	1860	71	98 x 23 x 3.5
Little Wabash	StW	1909		
Livingston	SW	1862	680	180 x 40 x 9.5
Lizzie	StW	1871–75	429	165 x 35 x 5
Lizzie Bayliss	SW	1878		117 x 21 x 3

NAME	RIG	YEARS ON THE YAZOO	TONS	DIMENSIONS (in feet, l x w x d)
Lone Star	SW	1860	126	112 x 26 x 4.7
Lottawanna	StW	1871–73	479.22	155 x 35 x 5
Louisville, USS		1863	326	176.8 x 52 x 6.6
Lucile	StW	1912		98.4 x 22.9 x 3.1
Lucy Keirn	SW	1870–71	191.74	162 x 28 x 4.5
Lucy Long	StW	1845–46	82	
Lucy Robinson	SW	1853–54	239	121 x 26.7 x 5.6
Lumberman	StW	1879–81		
M. B. Hamer	SW	1854	271	167.9 x 24 x 7
Mabel Cameaux	StW	1904		178 x 36 x 6.5
Madison	SW	1848	322	
Magenta	SW	1862	768	265 x 40 x 8.5
Maggie	StW	1895–1907	50	85 x 19 x 3.5
Magnolia	SW	1862–63	824	275 x 40 x 8.5
Maid of Kentucky	SW	1841–43	192	
Maid of Osage	SW	1845–46	63	
Major Aubrey	SW	1855	79	
Mammie B.		1877		
Mammoth Cave	SW	1851–52	96	
Manchester	SW	1836	105	
Manitou	SW	1863	286	
Marcella	SW	1870	436.99	180 x 19 x 3.5
Marie J.	StW	1907–9	76	100 x 20 x 4.4
Mariner	StW	1863	212	
Marmora, USS	StW	1863	207	155 x 33.4 x 4.8
Martin Walt		1866–67	64	
Mary C.	StW	1917–21		65 x 16.5 x 3.2
Mary E. Keene	SW	1862–63	659	225 x 38 x 8.5
Mary H. Miller	StW	1909–10	97	112.6 x 24.8 x 3.8
Mary Joyce	StW	1896–99	34.46	65 x 14 x 2.4
Mary Miller	StW	1871	411	
Mary T.	SS	1897		
May Flower	StW	1898	19.07	64.3 x 15.6 x 6.7
Memphis	SW	1838	355	
Memphis	StW	1897–98	110.28	111 x 26.6 x 4
Meteor	SW	1845–46	165	
Mike Davis	StW	1878	110.72	105.3 x 18 x 3
Mildred	StW	1897–98	19.96	54.5 x 11 x 3.2
Mima	StW	1895–98	62.67	66 x 17 x 3.2

NAME	RIG	YEARS ON THE YAZOO	TONS	DIMENSIONS (in feet, l x w x d)
Minie	StW	1873	40	83.2 x 18 x 3.3
Missouri	SW	1830–31	110	
Missouri Fulton	SW	1848	120	
Mobile	SW	1862–63	282	
Modoc	StW	1904–6	27	64 x 14 x 2.5
Molly Thomas		1870		
Monarch, USS	SW	1862	406	
Monarch	SS	1907–9	43	71.2 x 14.3 x 3.4
Monroe	SW	1851–52	183	
Morningstar	StW	1897–1900	46.5	95 x 20.4 x 2.4
Mound City, USS		1863	512	175.5 x 52 x 6.5
Mountain Girl	StW	1889–1900		115 x 24 x 3
Muscle No. 2	SW	1849	168	
Myrtle	SW	1866–68	183	137 x 20.6 x 4
Naiad		1870–71		
Nancy H.	StW	1917–21		
Naomi		1868		
Natchez (No. 5)	SW	1862–63	800	290 x 38 x 8.5
Navigator	SW	1835–36	69	
Nellie Hudson	StW	1888–90		141.3 x 25 x 3.4
Nellie Thomas	StW	1871	45.85	
Nettie Grant		1918	10	60.3 x 11.2 x 1.7
Neva	SW	1845	141	
New Era	StW	1883		
New Evergreen	StW	1884–90	22.62	68 x 16 x 2.2
New Idea	StW	1888–89		125 x 26 x 4
New National	SW	1862–64	379	184 x 33 x 6.7
New Richmond Belle		1876		
Newsboy	StW	1866–69	72.48	
Nile	SW	1835–36		
Norma	SW	1842	188	
North Alabama	SW	1841	341	
Novelty	StW	1895–99	49.95	107.5 x 24 x 3.2
O. G. Wagoner	StW	1875–95		130.5 x 36 x 4.8
Obena	SW	1834–35	151	
Old Rip	StW	1901	78	82.8 x 20.8 x 3
Olive Branch		1838		
Orange		1878		
Orion	SW	1838	65	

NAME	RIG	YEARS ON THE YAZOO	TONS	DIMENSIONS (in feet, l x w x d)
Oronoko	SW	1838	367	
Osage	SW	1844	129	
Osage	StW	1904–9	98	100 x 19.8 x 3.8
Osceola	SW	1850	125	125 x 23 x 4.7
Ostego		1838		
Otuay		1838		
Ouchita	SW	1834	160	
P. C. Wallis	SW	1855–56	230	166 x 32 x 5.5
Palmetto		1869–71		
Panola	SW	1840	136	
Panola	SW	1845	120	
Panther	SS	1921		
Pathfinder	SW	1842–43	137	
Patrick Henry	SW	1837–38	93	
Patrick Henry	SW	1847–50	298	120 x 30 x 6.1
Paul Jones	SW	1861	353	172 x 34 x 6.5
Paul Pry	StW	1842	34	
Peerless	StW	1906–8	50	100 x 20 x 4
Peri	StW	1904	71	102 x 25.5 x 4
Petrel, USS	StW	1863–64	226	
Peytona	SW	1862–63	653	268 x 38 x 8.5
Phil Armour	StW	1886–87		149 x 29 x 4.3
Pittsburg, USS		1863	512	176.5 x 52 x 6.5
Plain City	SW	1868	210	135 x 24 x 4
Planter	SW	1855	182	156 x 38 x 6.5
Planter	SW	1860	343	156 x 38 x 6.5
Pochahontas	SW	1863	163	180 x 32
Poland	StW	1865	161	
Pontchartrain	SW	1835–36	132	
Portsmouth	SW	1836	97	
Prairie Bird, USS	SW	1863	171	158 x 30 x 4.7
Prima Donna	StW	1863	304	151 x 37.3 x 6
Prince	SW	1860–61	223	
Prince of Wales	SW	1862–63	572	248 x 40 x 7
R. E. Hill	StW	1866	103	128 x 22 x 4
R. J. Lackland	SW	1862–63	675	275 x 40 x 7
R. L. Cobb	StW	1887–89	204.56	145.1 x 28.5 x 3
R. W. Adams	SW	1858	399	260 x 36 x 5.5
Racket	StW	1892		99 x 16.2 x 3.6

NAME	RIG	YEARS ON THE YAZOO	TONS	DIMENSIONS (in feet, l x w x d)
Rainey		1896		
Ranger	StW	1858–59	86	
Rattler, USS	StW	1862–63	165	
Rebstock	See Charles Rebstock			
Rees Pritchard	StW	1896–1904	196.2	150.3 x 31 x 3.3
Reindeer	SW	1833	98	
Reliance	SW	1845–46	156	129.3 x 26 x 5
Republic	SW	1862–63	699	249 x 40 x 7.5
Rescue	StW	1898–99	135.9	126 x 24.3 x 3.7
Resolute	StW	1898	207.98	139.6 x 29 x 3.9
Richland	SW	1846–47	82	
Richmond	SW	1836	16	
Richmond Belle	See New Richmond Belle			
Rodolph		1845		
Roebuck	SW	1857–60	164	147 x 23 x 5
Roma Wheeler	StW	1869–70	67	80 x 14 x 4
Romeo	SW	1838	109	
Romeo, USS	StW	1862–63	175	154.1 x 31.1 x 4
Rose K.	StW	1915–16		
Rover	StW	1897	57.07	100 x 31.5 x 5
Ruth	StW	1898–1900	319.4	160 x 31.5 x 5
Ruth	StW	1900–1902	60	97.2 x 18 x 3.7
S. Bayard	StW	1863	150	
S. H. Parisot	StW	1882–83	563.57	225 x 40.5 x 7.5
S. S. Prentiss	SW	1853–54	272	180 x 30 x 6
St. James	SW	1851	347	207.9 x 29.3 x 5.9
St. Landry	SW	1845–46	240	148 x 29 x 6
St. Lawrence	SW	1836	111	
St. Louis	StW	1863	191	
St. Mary	SW	1862–63	40	89.6 x 15 x 5
Sallie Anderson	SW	1846	62	
Sallie Carney	StW	1883–85	80.9	96 x 24 x 3
Sallie Robinson	SW	1856–58	267	160 x 33 x 5.5
Sam A. Conner	StW	1906–9	63	98.5 x 16 x 2.6
Sam Atlee	StW	1900	234	133.3 x 26.3 x 4
Sarah	SW	1851	138	137.8 x 22.7 x 4.7
Scotland	SW	1862–63	567	165 x 31 x 5.5
Selma	SW	1836	355	
Selma	SW	1873–74	600	180 x 37.5 x 7

NAME	RIG	YEARS ON THE YAZOO	TONS	DIMENSIONS (in feet, l x w x d)
Seminole	StW	1877	420	157.6 x 44 x 5
Shakespeare	SW	1836–38	227	
Shawnee	StW	1900–1901	21	50 x 10 x 3
Signal, USS	StW	1862–63	190	
Silverthorn	StW	1883–86	209	
Silver Wave	SW	1863	800	
Sovereign, USS	StW	1863	245	159 x 35 x 5
Sportsman		1858		
Star of the West	SW	1862–63	1,172	
Steamer B	StW	1905	15	
Steamer C	StW	1905	10	
Stella	SW	1860		165 x 28
Stella	StW	1904–6	83	101 x 25 x 3
Stoneware	StW	1900–1901	104.4	100 x 17 x 3
Submarine No. 11		1866–68		
Submarine No. 12		1866–68		
Sully	SW	1868	280.80	
Summerville	SW	1844	358	
Sunflower	SW	1838		
Sunflower	StW	1878–84	140	
Sunflower Belle	StW	1874–78		
Susie B.	StW	1883	18.59	62 x 14 x 2.5
T. P. Leathers	SW	1854	435	230 x 32.8 x 6.7
Tallahatchie	SW	1848–52	163	
Tallahatchie	StW	1875–78		
Tallahatchie	StW	1890		
Talma	SW	1832	136	
Tchula	SW	1835–38		
Tchula	SW	1840–41	204	
Tempest	SS	1907–24	24	74.4 x 13.2 x 6
Texana	SW	1854–55	348	179 x 32 x 6.1
Thirty-Fifth Parallel	SW	1862–63	419	
Thistle	SW	1863	50	
Thomas B. Florence	StW	1879–80		96 x 20 x 4
Thomas B. Hendricks	StW	1896–1900	81.86	108 x 22.5 x 4.2
Thomas Powell	StW	1869–71	109.3	101.4 x 20.2 x 3.8
Timmie Baker	StW	1881–82	78	100 x 21 x 3
Trade Palace	SS	1868	295.47	154 x 29.5 x 5
Trader	StW	1871–73		81 x 20

NAME	RIG	YEARS ON THE YAZOO	TONS	DIMENSIONS (in feet, l x w x d)
Traveler	StW	1873		
Travis Wright	StW	1873	202.69	129 x 31.7 x 4.6
Trenton	StW	1871	260.78	130 x 32.2 x 4.2
Tributary	SS	1885–86	93.78	83 x 18.6 x 3
Troy	StW	1846	92	
Tuscarora		1836		
Tuscumbia	SW	1851	281	172 x 26.2 x 6.5
Tuskina		1836–38		
Tyler, USS	SW	1863	575	180 x 45.3 x 7.7
U.S. Aid	StW	1855–58	125	140 x 25 x 4.5
Uncle Billie	StW	1894	79.81	88 x 17.7 x 3.9
Unicorn	SW	1854–55	188	
Vanguard	SS	1906–7		81 x 17.2 x 9
Vernie Mac	StW	1903–4	122	127 x 24.7 x 4.9
Veteran	SW	1835	86	
Vicksburg	StW	1874–76		90 x 21 x 3
Violet	SW	1850–52		
Virago	SW	1839	50	
Virginia K.		1870–73		
Volant	SW	1840–45	113	
Volant	SW	1852–53	136	
Volunteer	StW	1863	210	125.1 x 33 x 4.5
W. C. Young	SW	1858	199	140 x 28 x 5.5
W. G. Campbell	SW	1851–53	168	
W. H. Mercer		1846		
W. M. Lawrence		1860		
W. N. Sherman	SW	1855	194	130 x 30 x 5.5
W. P. Swiney	SW	1853–56	199	170 x 39 x 6
Wabash Valley	SW	1845–46	99	
Wagoner	StW	1846–47	43	
Walnut Hills	SW	1841–42	190	
Walter Scott	SW	1831–35	193	
Wanderer	SW	1832–35	186	
Warren	StW	1903–4	144	134 x 26 x 4
Warren Belle	SW	1866	142.23	144 x 25 x 5.4
Wash Honshell	StW	1897	134.99	157 x 28.6 x 4
Water Maiden	StW	1897–98	23.13	69 x 12 x 2.6
Wave	SW	1845–46	78	
Westwood	SW	1846	249	163.5 x 20.6 x 7

NAME	RIG	YEARS ON THE YAZOO	TONS	DIMENSIONS (in feet, l x w x d)
White Oak	SS	1895–96	31.32	69 x 13 x 6.4
White River	StW	1856	71	
Whiteville	SW	1846	102	
White Wing	SW	1845	100	
Wichita	StW	1901–4	46	88 x 20.3 x 3.1
William Armstrong	StW	1846	89	
William H. Wood	SS	1908	44	77.2 x 16.2 x 7.6
Willie J.	StW	1872	75.36	100.6 x 18 x 2.6
Wilmington		1840–41		
Woodsman	SW	1834	84	
Yalobusha	SW	1835–36		
Yalobusha	SW	1845–46	116	115 x 24 x 5
Yazonia	StW	1894–98	62.84	95 x 19.8 x 3.5
Yazoo	SW	1834–36	150	
Yazoo	SW	1842–43	304	151 x 28 x 6.8
Yazoo	SW	1860–61	371	178 x 33.5 x 6.5
Yazoo	StW	1873–83	270.91	143.5 x 32.2 x 4.7
Yazoo Belle	SW	1845–46	122	113 x 25 x 4.8
Yazoo Belle	SW	1855–58	138	134 x 28 x 4
Yazoo City	SW	1843–46	229	146 x 28 x 6
Yazoo Planter	StW	1841	82	
Yazoo Valley	StW	1876–80	299	180 x 36 x 5.5
Yellowstone	SW	1832–35	144	130 x 19 x 6

Appendix B
WRECK HEAPS ON THE RIVERS

NAME	YEAR	REPORTED LOCATION
Acadia	1863	On the Yazoo River near the mouth of the Yalobusha River
Addie E. Faison	1890	On the Yazoo River four miles below the Big Sunflower River
Afton	1855	Belcher's Bar south of Yazoo City
Alonzo Child	1863	Scuttled at Snyder's Bluff
Argo	1863	Burned up the Sunflower River
B. H. Franks	1872	Unspecified location on the Yazoo River
Baron De Kalb	1863	Near the Confederate Navy Yard at Yazoo City
Bee	1851	Parker's Bar south of Yazoo City
Belmont	1842	On the Tallahatchie forty miles below Panola
Ben McCulloch	1863	Burned in Tchula Lake
Bill Nigh	1890	Belle Prairie Landing on the Yazoo River
Birdie Bailey	1897	Burtonia Landing on the Yazoo River
Blanks Cornwell	1896	Dew Drop Landing on the Yazoo River
Bluff City	1859	Near Snyder's Bluff
C. P. Huntington	1877	Near Roseneath Landing on the Yazoo River
Cairo	1862	Sank on the lower Yazoo River
Calumet	1871	Glass's Bayou in Vicksburg
Capitol	1863	Scuttled at Liverpool Landing
Carrie Hogan	1881	Above Yazoo City on the Yazoo River
Choctaw	1916	Near Palo Alto Landing on the Yazoo River
Cotton Plant (180 tons)	1863	On the Tallahatchie River near Greenwood

NAME	YEAR	REPORTED LOCATION
Cotton Plant (59 tons)	1863	Scuttled on Lake George
Dew Drop	1863	Burned on the Quiver River
E. A. Pharr	1900	Thirty miles above Riverside on the Coldwater River
Eddie	1867	Grassy Mound Landing on the Sunflower River
Edward J. Gay	1863	On the Yazoo near the mouth of the Yalobusha River
Ella Belle	1872	Burned in Steele's Bayou
Emma Bett	1863	On the Sunflower River
Emma Francis	1903	Near Shepardstown on the Yazoo River
Erma	1913	On the Yazoo River below Belzoni
F. Barksdale	1888	Burned opposite Hendrick's Landing on the Yazoo River
Ferd Kennett	1863	On the Yazoo River near Greenwood
Ferd R.	1899	On the Yazoo River near Greenwood
Fifteen	1897	Near the Head of Honey Island on the Yazoo River
Frank Beck, Jr.	1875	On Steele's Bayou
Freestone	1865	Below Piney Creek on the Yazoo River
General Earl Van Dorn	1862	Exploded at the Liverpool raft
General Miles	1892	Near Mulberry Landing on the Yazoo River
General Polk	1862	Burned at the Liverpool raft
Gladiator	1838	Near Liverpool Landing on the Yazoo River
Golden Age	1863	Scuttled and burned at Southworth's Bar on the Yazoo River
Guide	1852	Near the Head of Honey Island
H. D. Mears	1863	Near Garvin's Ferry on the Sunflower River
Hallette	1905	Yazoo City
Hartford City	1863	Near Greenwood
Helen	1845	Near Satartia Landing
Hill City	1885	Sank on the Big Sunflower River
Hope	1863	Burned near Greenwood up the Tallahatchie River
Hope	1868	Near Eagle Bend Landing on the Yazoo River
Idaho	1867	Near the old mouth on the Yazoo River
Ike Bonham	1888	At Pecan Point on the Tallahatchie River

NAME	YEAR	REPORTED LOCATION
Ivy	1863	Scuttled at Liverpool Landing on the Yazoo River
J. A. Townes	1909	Eagle Bend on the Yazoo River
J. F. Pargoud	1863	Near Yazoo City
J. H. Williams	1885	On the Yazoo River near Greenwood
J. M. Sharp	1863	On the Yalobusha River near Greenwood
Jack Osborn	1906	Between Greenwood and Belzoni
James Jacobs	1858	Tuscahoma Landing on the Yalobusha River
Jeff Davis	1850	Below Satartia (probably raised)
Joe Seay	1905	South of Yazoo City
John F. Allen	1896	On the Yazoo River near the mouth of the Big Sunflower River
John Walsh	1863	Scuttled and burned at Southworth's Bar
Josie Sively	1901	On the Big Sunflower River
Katie Robbins	1980	On the Yazoo River near Little Deer Creek
Lacon	1847	Oxbows on the Tallahatchie River
Lady Washington	1842	Hard Times Landing on the Yazoo River
Lake City	1893	On the Tallahatchie River near Minter City
Leflore	1884	Belle Yazoo Landing on the Yazoo River
Livingston	1863	At Liverpool Landing
Lucille	1912	Above Van Land Landing on the Yazoo River
Magenta	1863	Near Yazoo City
Maggie	1903	Wolf Lake
Magnolia	1863	Near Yazoo City
Martin Walt	1866	On the Yazoo River near the mouth of Tchula Lake
Mary E. Keene	1863	At French Bend on the Yazoo River
Mary H. Miller	1910	Near Yazoo City
Mobile	1863	Near the Confederate Navy Yard at Yazoo City
Monarch	1909	On Tchula Lake
Muscle No. 2	1849	One hundred yards above the mouth of the Little Sunflower River on the Yazoo River
Myrtle	1866	On the Yazoo River above the mouth of Tchula Lake; may have been raised
Naiad	1870	Near Bailey's Landing on the Yazoo River

NAME	YEAR	REPORTED LOCATION
Natchez	1863	Below Belzoni on the Yazoo River
Nellie Hudson	1890	On the Big Sunflower River
Nettie Grant	1918	Jarman's Bridge on the Tallahatchie River
New Evergreen	1890	Brown's Landing near Graball on the Tallahatchie River
New Richmond Belle	1876	Pecan Point on the Tallahatchie River
Novelty	1899	Near Vicksburg
Panther	1916	On the Yazoo River near Redwood
Paul Pry	1842	One mile above the mouth of the Big Sunflower on the Yazoo River
Petrel, USS	1864	Captured and burned near Yazoo City
Peytona	1863	Above Yazoo City near Koalunsa Landing
Poland	1865	On the Yazoo River near the mouth of the Big Sunflower River
Prince of Wales	1863	Above Yazoo City
R. E. Hill	1866	At French Bayou on the Yazoo River
R. J. Lackland	1863	Scuttled and burned at Southworth's Bar
Rainey	1896	At Turner Place on the Tallahatchie River
Rees Pritchard	1904	Near Yazoo City
Republic	1863	Near the Confederate Navy Yard at Yazoo City
Rescue	1899	Near Longwood Landing on the Yazoo River
Roma Wheeler	1870	On the Sunflower River
Rover	1897	Near Van Land Landing on the Yazoo River
Sallie Carney	1885	Above Greenwood on the Tallahatchie River
Scotland	1863	Scuttled and burned at Southworth's Bar
Shakespeare	1838	McCormack's Bar on the Yazoo River
Silverthorn	1886	Near Vicksburg
Star of the West	1863	On the Tallahatchie River near Fort Pemberton
Tallahatchie	1890	Cassidy Bayou
Texana	1854	Chickasaw Bayou
Thirty-Fifth Parallel	1863	On the Tallahatchie River
U.S. Aid	1856	Below Tchula on Tchula Lake
Unicorn	1855	Salem Landing below Yazoo City
Violet	1852	One mile below Grenada on the Yalobusha River
Virago	1839	On the Yazoo River near Satartia

NAME	YEAR	REPORTED LOCATION
Volant	1845	On the Yazoo River
Volant	1853	Near Cardiff Landing south of Yazoo City
Wagoner	1847	Near Grenada on the Yalobusha River
William Armstrong	1846	Near Marcella Landing on Tchula Lake
W. N. Sherman	1855	Four miles below Satartia
Willie J.	1875	At Lodi Landing on the Yazoo River
Wilmington	1841	On the Yazoo River opposite Satartia Landing
Yazonia	1899	Near Glendora on the Tallahatchie River

Appendix C
YAZOO–TALLAHATCHIE
RIVER LANDINGS

The following list of steamboat landings was compiled from the Yazoo River Map (1875), the Yazoo-Tallahatchie River Map (1879), and the Tchula Lake Map (1882) with the aid of the two Vicksburg directories published in 1877 and 1879. A small number of additional place names and locations were found on maps in the National Archives, in the annual reports of the chief of engineers, and from newspaper references. Estimated mileage from Vicksburg and the owners/operators were taken from the 1879 directory. The three maps used in this study provided the surmised location of section, range, and township, as well as the left or right bank location, which is determined by facing downstream. Twentieth century changes in the river (Pecan Point Cut-off, Hard Cash Cut-off, and others) are not indicated in the list; the landings in such cases were on the unimproved meander of the waterway.

TALLAHATCHIE RIVER

LANDING	MILE	OWNER/ OPERATOR	BANK*	SECTION	TOWN- SHIP	RANGE
Turner Landing/Ferry			R	NE¼, 7	26N	1E
Oxbows			–	S½, 33	26N	1E
Locopolis			L	SE½, 6	24N	1E
Jarman Landing/Ferry			R	SE¼, 6	24N	1E
Sharkey's (Head of Navigation)	374	T. J. James & Co.	L	NE¼, 35	24N	1W
Cassidy Bayou Landing	373	J. S. Robinson	R	NW¼, 35	24N	1W
Arbin (Strathmore)	371	H. C. Staten	R	SE¼, 3	23N	1W
Swan Lake Landing	370½	J. W. Powell	R	SE¼, 10	23N	1W
Staten	370	H. C. Staten	L	NE¼, 10	23N	1W

*Right or left bank is determined by facing downstream.

TALLAHATCHIE RIVER

LANDING	MILE	OWNER/ OPERATOR	BANK*	SECTION	TOWN- SHIP	RANGE
Craig's	368½		R	NE¼, 10	23N	1W
Swan Lake Ferry			R	SW¼, 14	23N	1W
Twilight	368	B. W. Sturdivant	L	SW¼, 14	23N	1W
Graball	367	J. W. Powell	L	SW½, 14	23N	1W
Brown's Store	365½	Patrick Brown	L	NE¼, 22	23N	1W
Whitehead	364		R	SW¼, 22	23N	1W
Glendora	364	W. D. Graham	R	SW¼, 27	23N	1W
Bonnet (Bonnie) Lake	362	N. J. McMullen	L	NE¼, 27	23N	1W
Black Bayou Landing	361	R. L. Jones & Son	R	NE¼, 34	23N	1W
McCaleb's	358		L	E½, 26	23N	1W
Pecan Point, or Jones' Landing	357	R. L. Jones	R	NE¼, 32	23N	1W
Turner's	355		L	NW¼, 32	23N	1W
Belle View	353	J. J. Farrow	L	NE¼, 32	23N	1E
Shegogg	352	H. B. Knox				
Ray's	346	J. Ray	L	NW¼, 32	23N	1E
Russell's			L	SE¼, 33	23N	1E
Blythe's	344	John Blythe	L	SW¼, 34	23N	1E
Walter's, or Ashley's	343½	Jeff. McLemore	L	S½, 3	22N	1E
Lone Star	341	Jeff. McLemore	R	NE¼, 10	22N	1E
Sykes'	342	J. N. Knowles	L	NE¼, 10	22N	1E
Hibernia	339	William Bew				
Bailey's	339	S. S. Bailey	R	center, 15	22N	1E
Lamkin's	337½	D. W. Lamkin	L	NE¼, 21	22N	1E
Phillip's			L	N½, 21	22N	1E
Bennett's	337	T. C. Coopwood	L	NE¼, 20	22N	1E
Sisloff Junction			R	SW¼, 18	22N	1E
Moss'	337	J. A. Towns				
Palo Alto	331	J. A. Towns	L	SW¼, 22	22N	1E
Minter City, or Walnut Place	330	Jones & Sawyer	R	N½, 28	22N	1W
Red Cross	329	J. A. Towns	R	SE¼, 32	22N	1W
Shannondale	328	Mrs. Shannondale	R	W½, 4	21N	1W
Marsh Prairie	326	Frank Hawkins	R	SE¼, 9	21N	1W
Eutaw Bend	325	J. A. Towns	L	SE¼, 10	21N	1W
Beverly	324½	Dr. Dardin	R	SW¼, 11	21N	1W
Sunny Side	324	Dr. Portwood	R	SE¼, 11	21N	1W
Holly Grove	320½	J. McLemore	R	W½, 1	21N	1W

TALLAHATCHIE RIVER

LANDING	MILE	OWNER/ OPERATOR	BANK*	SECTION	TOWN- SHIP	RANGE
Archula	319	D. N. Quinn	R	NE¼, 36	22N	1W
Omega	318	J. A. Towns	L	NE¼, 6	22N	1W
Beulah	316	J. A. Towns	L	NE¼, 31	22N	1E
Ruby			L	SW¼, 32	22N	1E
Hazard			L	NE¼, 5	22N	1E
Sandy Ridge	314	R. S. McLemore	L	SW¼, 5	21N	1E
New Hope	312	Stephen Johnson	R	SW¼, 18	21N	1E
Dry Bayou Landing	311	S. Patterney	R	NW¼, 19	21N	1E
Melrose	310	Dr. C. P. Stancil	R	SE¼, 19	21N	1E
Stancil's			R	SW¼, 20	21N	1E
Money			L	SE¼, 20	21N	1E
Loch Lomond	306½		L	NE¼, 29	21N	1E
Ewing's	306	Dr. Ewing	R	NE¼, 29	21N	1E
Woodstock	305	H. D. Money	L	SE¼, 29	21N	1E
Yuba Dam Landing	304		R	SW¼, 31	21N	1E
Wildwood	302	G. A. McLean & Co.	L	SW¼, 6	20N	1E
Rosedale	300	W. A. Barr				
Shellmond	299	W. S. Barry, W. A. Barr, M. S. McLean, W. T. Bew	R	SE¼, 11	20N	1W
Barry's	298	Mrs. W. S. Barry	R	SW¼, 14	20N	1W
Parish's	296	R. P. Parish	R	SE¼, 23	20N	1W
Terry's			R	NE¼, 25	20N	1W
Sally Mound Landing	293	W. D. Spivey	L	NE¼, 24	20N	1W
Glen Burr	293	G. A. McLean	R	W½, 19	20N	1E
Mark Love's Landing, or Overcup	291		L	SW¼, 18	20N	1E
Portwood, or Oasis Landing	290		L	NE¼, 18	20N	1E
Bareneau's	289	M. Bareneau	L	NW¼, 16	20N	1E
Craig's Store, or Craigside			L	SE¼, 16	20N	1E
Union Landing	286½	A. Moss	L	NE¼, 21	20N	1E
St. Joseph	286		L	W½, 21	20N	1E
Tindall's	285	M. Tindall	L	SE¼, 20	20N	1E
Race Track Landing	284	W. & T. Walton	R	SE¼, 30	20N	1E
Last Resort	282	Dr. J. H. Lucas	R	NW¼, 6	19N	1E
Fort Pemberton			R	NW¼, 7	19N	1E

Tallahatchie River

LANDING	MILE	OWNER/ OPERATOR	BANK*	SECTION	TOWN- SHIP	RANGE
Pebble Bluff	279½	J. Z. George	R	SE¼, 16	19N	1E
Farmer's Home			L	NE¼, 6	19N	1E
Ashley Farm (present Greenwood)	279	A. A. Stoddard				
Ashwood			L	center, 4	19N	1E
Bushatchie	274	W. A. Gillespie	L	SE¼, 34	20N	1E
George's	275	George & Sproule	R	SW¼, 34	20N	1E
Confluence of Tallahatchie River and the Yalobusha River						

Yazoo River

LANDING	MILE	OWNER/ OPERATOR	BANK*	SECTION	TOWN- SHIP	RANGE
Point Leflore			L	center, 34	20N	1E
Greenwood	270		L			
Henry's	270	Dr. Henry	L	SE¼, 9	19N	1E
Phoenix Mills	269½	D. A. Outlaw	L	SW¼, 9	19N	1E
St. Cloud's	269¼		R	SW¼, 9	19N	1E
Stronghold Landing	269	B. F. Chambers	L	SE¼, 8	19N	1E
Zoar Landing	269		L	SW¼, 8	19N	1E
Bluff Springs	268	Henry Sisloff	L	SE¼, 7	19N	1E
Brooklyn	267½	Mrs. M. J. Searles	L	NE¼, 7	19N	1E
Jim Young's Landing			R	NW¼, 7	19N	1E
Montjoy's Ferry	267	Gideon Montjoy	R	NW¼, 7	19N	1E
Gerson's	265	Benj. Gerson				
Fort Loring, or McLemore's	264	McLemore & Co.	R	NW¼, 24	19N	1W
Delta			L	NE¼, 24	19N	1W
Shongaloe			R	SE½, 24	19N	1W
Double Oaks	263	T. J. Edmonson	L	center, 24	19N	1W
Glen Mary	261½	B. J. Humphreys	R	SW¼, 24	19N	1W
Grand View	259	T. J. Edmonson	R	NE¼, 25	19N	1W
Pleasant View	257	E. Scott	L	SE¼, 19	19N	1E
Water Front	255	John Erskine	L	NE¼, 30	19N	1E
Magenta	253½	Mrs. Mary Murdock	L	NE¼, 30	19N	1E
French Bend	253	W. D. McLeod				
Rising Sun	252	Allen Nugent & Co.	L	SW¼, 32	19N	1E

YAZOO RIVER

LANDING	MILE	OWNER/ OPERATOR	BANK*	SECTION	TOWN- SHIP	RANGE
Roebuck Landing			R	SW¼, 32	19N	1E
Rose Bower	250½	A. G. Smith	L	NE¼, 31	19N	1E
Ingelside	250	Kate Murdock	R	SE¼, 31	19N	1E
Douglass			L	SW¼, 32	19N	1E
Roebuck Landing	249½	Aaron & Co.	R	S½, 6	18N	1E
Oakwood	249	Aaron & Co.	R	SW¼, 7	18N	1E
Sedgefield	247½	Robert Hicks	R	SW¼, 17	18N	1E
Robinson's	247	Jerry Robinson	L	NE¼, 20	18N	1E
Sidon No. 1	245½	W. E. Poindexter	L	NE¼, 20	18N	1E
Sidon No. 2	245¾	C. B. Holmes, W. A. McCarthy, B. Prince	L	E½, 20	18N	1E
Sidon No. 3	246	A. Casper	L	SE¼, 20	18N	1E
Newton Landing	245	B. E. Prince	L	SW¼, 26	18N	1W
Phillipston	240	B. E. Prince	L	NE¼, 34	18N	1W
Shell Bluff	238	W. H. Morgan	R	SE¼, 29	18N	1W
Pickens'			R	SE¼, 32	18N	1W
Sheppardston	234½	Morgan & Caldwell	R	SW¼, 5	17N	1W
Hazel Dell			R	SE¼, 5	17N	1W
Valley Forge	234	Turkey & Martin	R	SW¼, 4	17N	1W
Mayday	232	Prince Estate	R	SE¼, 4	17N	1W
Eden			L	NE¼, 15	17N	1W
Egypt	229	B. S. Ricks	L	NE¼, 15	17N	1W
Lower Egypt	228	Mrs. H. E. Sides	L	SE¼, 15	17N	1W
Rose Bank	227	Rice & Crow	R	SE¼, 15	17N	1W
Ward's (Head of Honey Island)	225½	Abe Archer	L	SW¼, 22	17N	1W
C. T. White	225					
McAfee's Landing and Ferry			L	NW¼, 27	17N	1W
Shipp's	222	John Shipp	R	SW¼, 21	17N	1W
Eagle Lake Landing	220	Jane Elmore	R	SW¼, 29	17N	1W
Montgomery Place, or Smith Brothers	219	Smith Brothers	L	NW¼, 30	17N	1W
Henry Hall's	218	W. P. Oslin	R	NW¼, 30	17N	1W
West Over	215½	W. H. Garnet	R	NW¼, 1	16N	2W
Markham's Ferry			L	NW¼, 1	16N	2W

Yazoo River

LANDING	MILE	OWNER/ OPERATOR	BANK*	SECTION	TOWN- SHIP	RANGE
Silent Shade	214	Mrs. B. F. Barkou	L	SW¼, 1	16N	2W
West Point, or Huntsfield	213	H. Hunt	R	NE¼, 2	16N	2W
Wakes Valley			R	SW¼, 2	16N	2W
Perkin's	211		L	NE¼, 14	16N	2W
Random Shot	209	C. L. Davis	L	N½, 23	16N	2W
Randal's	204	Perkins, Waring, and Co.				
Jim's Island Landing			R	NW¼, 16	16N	2W
Lousy Level	201	D. G. Pepper	L	SW¼, 16	16N	2W
Famolsa Landing			L	SE¼, 21	16N	2W
Winter Quarters	199	D. G. Pepper	L	NE¼, 28	16N	2W
Wasp Lake Landing	197	Winn & Sons	R	SE¼, 29	16N	2W
Mahrud			L	center, 33	16N	2W
Welch's Camp			L	center, 33	16N	2W
Sheltonia			L	S½, 32	16N	2W
Young's			L	SE¼, 31	16N	2W
Whiskey Slough	194	Thomas Estis	R	SW¼, 31	16N	2W
Hope On	191	J. L. Godkin				
Fairview			R	NE½, 1	15N	3W
Belzoni	189	W. C. Morris	R	NW¼, 2	15N	3W
Burtonia	188	Taylor, McMurtrie, and Co.	R	NE¼, 10	15N	3W
Callao, or Norris'	188		L	NE¼, 10	15N	3W
Gun Bayou Landing	187		L	NE¼, 15	15N	3W
Island Side	187	W. McMurtrie & Co.				
Maxwell's	186½	James Mathews	R	NW¼, 15	15N	3W
Tuscola	186	Powers & Bowles	R	SW¼, 15	15N	3W
Bridges Landing			L	NW¼, 22	15N	3W
Freedman's Bureau	184	W. Richardson	R	SW¼, 16	15N	3W
Blue Sack	182½	J. C. Prewill	R	NW¼, 21	15N	3W
Springwood	182	Judge Robert Bowman	R	NW¼, 21	15N	3W
Morganza	182½	Owen Brown	L	SW¼, 21	15N	3W
Goat Hill Landing			L	SE¼, 21	15N	3W
Dew Drop Landing	180	Pink Garrett	L	NW¼, 27	15N	3W
Riverside	177	A. A. Parisot	R	NW¼, 27	15N	3W

Yazoo River

LANDING	MILE	OWNER/ OPERATOR	BANK*	SECTION	TOWN-SHIP	RANGE
Lusk's	179½	Robert Lusk				
Silver Creek			R	SE¼, 34	15N	3W
Silver City	174¾		R	SE¼, 34	15N	3W
Palmetto Home	174	R. V. Powers	R	SE¼, 34	15N	3W
Griffin's	174¼	Thomas R. Griffin	L	SE¼, 34	15N	3W
Millport	172	Alex. Montgomery	R	NW¼, 2	14N	3W
Point Pleasant, or Pleasant Point	170	John H. McKee	R	NE¼, 2	14N	3W
Holly Mound	170	John H. McKee	R	NW¼, 1	14N	3W
Wilderness	166	H. Burrus	L	SE¼, 1	14N	3W
Bermuda	168	Alex. Moss	R	SE¼, 1	14N	3W
Dickson (Dixon)	167	J. M. Dickson	R	SE¼, 6	15N	2W
Martin's	164½	J. C. Martin	R	NE¼, 6	15N	2W
Lambert's, or Swisher & May's	164½		L	SE¼, 31	15N	2W
Stones', or Yazoo Point	163½		R	NW¼, 5	14N	2W
(Mouth of Tchula Lake)						
Fangle Retreat	161	James Raney	R	SW¼, 5	14N	2W
Jenkins'	162	M. Jenkins	L	SW¼, 5	14N	2W
Gum Grove	159½	P. G. Cocks	L	NW¼, 8	14N	2W
Roseneath			L	SW¼, 8	14N	2W
Fort Place	158	W. B. Ricks	R	NW¼, 17	14N	2W
Hendricks'	157	D. W. Hendricks	R	NE¼, 20	14N	2W
Lodi	155½	I. H. Hunter	R	NW¼, 21	14N	2W
Casebow	155½	Mrs. Hibbard	L	NE¼, 21	14N	2W
Hidi			R	NW¼, 22	14N	2W
Warmack's or Pluto Landing	153½	Wm. Warmack Store Jno. Warmack Ferry	L	SW¼, 23	14N	2W
Bee (B.) Lake Landing	152½	I. R. Tucker	L	SW¼, 23	14N	2W
Bailey's, or Mrs. Simmons' Landing	151	Mrs. Simmons	L	NW¼, 26	14N	2W
Altera	150	Dr. C. N. Brown	R	SE¼, 27	14N	2W
Golden's	149	Eli Golden	R	SE¼, 27	14N	2W
Esmeralda	148	Eli Golden	R	SW¼, 35	14N	2W

Yazoo River

LANDING	MILE	OWNER/ OPERATOR	BANK*	SECTION	TOWN- SHIP	RANGE
H. Golden's Landing	147	Hilliard Golden	R	SW¼, 35	14N	2W
Chew's	145	Samuel Smith	L	SW¼, 36	14N	2W
Parker's Bayou Landing	144½		L	NW¼, 31	14N	2W
C. S. Wylies', or Cape Horn	144	S. C. Parisot	R	NW¼, 31	14N	2W
Cooper's	143	Arthur Green	L	SE¼, 31	14N	2W
Sheppard's			L	SW¼, 12	13N	2W
Vand Land Landing	141½	W. S. Reid	R	SW¼, 12	13N	2W
Ingersols'	140	O. W. and B. W. Phillips	L	SE¼, 11	13N	2W
Dover			L	SE¼, 11	13N	2W
Beech Grove	139	R. L. Bates	L	NW¼, 11	13N	2W
Montgomery's	137	George Montgomery				
Haywood Phillips' W. H. Phillips'	136½		L	SW¼, 3	13N	2W
Belle Prairie Landing	135½	B. S. Ricks	R	NW¼, 3	13N	2W
Wilson's	134	John Wilson	L	SW¼, 3	13N	2W
Crump's Upper Landing	133½	G. P. Crump	R	NE¼, 8	13N	2W
Crump's Lower Landing	132½	G. P. Crump	R	NE¼, 17	13N	2W
Hillman's	132	M. Hillman	R	SE¼, 16	13N	2W
Eureka	131½	Ricard & Gilruth	R	NE¼, 21	13N	2W
Excelsior	131	S. H. Kellogg	L	NE¼, 21	13N	2W
Ashwood	129½	R. D. Hines	L	SE¼, 21	13N	2W
Koalunsa	129	M. R. Payne	R	NE¼, 28	13N	2W
Washburn's	124	Dr. A. W. Washburn				
Monterey	123	M. R. Payne				
Downing's	121½	Downing & Payne	R	SE¼, 32	13N	2W
Home Park	121	M. R. Payne	R	NE¼, 5	12N	2W
Boston Place	121	Rev. R. Abbey	L	NE¼, 5	12N	2W
Linden	119	Clark Bros. Store	R	SE¼, 7	12N	2W
Lintonia	119	J. W. Chaplin & Son	L	SE¼, 7	12N	2W
Wolf Lake Landing			R	NE¼, 13	12N	2W
Hagan's	117½	H. C. Tyler	R	SE¼, 13	12N	2W

YAZOO RIVER

LANDING	MILE	OWNER/ OPERATOR	BANK*	SECTION	TOWN-SHIP	RANGE
Gassaway Landing and Ferry	117	T. C. Gassaway	R	NE¼, 24	12N	2W
Dunn's	114	A. C. Dunn	L	NE¼, 30	12N	3W
McGruder's			L	NE¼, 30	12N	3W
Inchuka	113	George Woodbury	R	NE¼, 25	12N	3W
Tokeba Bayou Landing	112¼		R	SW¼, 25	12N	3W
Elmwood	111½	N. H. Ingram	R	NE¼, 36	12N	3W
Goosey's Ferry	110	Peter Goosey				
Yazoo City	110		L			
Confederate Navy Yard	110		L	SW½, 32	12N	2W
Holt's	109	Mrs. A. S. Holt	L	NE¼, 6	11N	2W
Longwood	109	J. N. Ratcliff	R	NW¼, 6	11N	2W
Short Creek Landing	108		L	SE¼, 1	11N	3W
Wilton's	108	H. M. Dixon	R	SE¼, 1	11N	3W
Dubuisson's	106¼	C. J. Dubuisson	L	SE¼, 1	11N	3W
Session's	106½	Dr. W. Y. Gadberry	L	SE¼, 1	11N	3W
Goosey's		P. C. Goosey	R	NE¼, 11	11N	3W
Palo Alto	105	A. Kincaide	R	NE¼, 10	11N	3W
Rialto	104	D. T. Saffaran	R	NE¼, 10	11N	3W
Rough and Ready	103	D. T. Saffaran	R	SE¼, 16	11N	3W
Joe's Walk	101	Peter Barnes	L	NW¼, 21	11N	3W
Willow Dale	101	John Davey	R	NW¼, 21	11N	3W
Paul's, or Tarsus	101	Otho S. Paul	R	SE¼, 20	11N	3W
Success	100½	S. H. Parisot and R. Kinkead	L	SW¼, 21	11N	3W
Sherrard's Old Landing	99	Parisot and Kinkead	L	NE¼, 29	11N	3W
Ratcliff's	98½	Parisot and Kinkead	L	NW¼, 29	11N	3W
Oak Valley	100	Mrs. L. C. Barksdale	R	NW¼, 29	11N	3W
Limerick, or Kinkead's	97½	Parisot and Kinkead	L	NE¼, 31	11N	3W
Twelve Mile Bayou	97¼		L	NW¼, 31	11N	3W

Yazoo River

LANDING	MILE	OWNER/ OPERATOR	BANK*	SECTION	TOWN- SHIP	RANGE
Haw Bluff	97	Parisot and Kinkead	L	NW¼, 31	11N	3W
Avoca	96	Parisot and Kinkead	L	SW¼, 36	11N	4W
Gandercleugh	95	Dr. W. L. Wilson	R	SW¼, 35	11N	4W
Gandercleugh	94	H. Tinker & Sons	R	NW¼, 2	10N	4W
Pleasant Green Landing	93½	John Newberry	L	SW¼, 2	10N	4W
Eagle Bend Landing	92	J. T. Jennings	L	NW¼, 11	10N	4W
Melrose	92	Dr. J. W. Maybin	R	NE¼, 10	10N	4W
Potato Hill Bayou			R	SE¼, 10	10N	4W
Braden's	90	Samuel Braden	R	SE¼, 14	10N	4W
Salem	90	Robert G. Johnson	L	NE¼, 14	10N	4W
Stella	88	S. L. Barksdale	R	SW¼, 13	10N	4W
Wilson & Screws	85	R. Wilson	L	NW¼, 18	10N	3W
Llanda	85	R. Wilson	L	NW¼, 17	10N	3W
O'Neal's Creek Landing	84½	Robert Goody	L	NW¼, 17	10N	3W
Liverpool	84	Wellington Smith	L	SW¼, 16	10N	3W
Anderson Creek Landing	84		L	NW¼, 20	10N	3W
Gale's	82½	Robert Gale	L	SE¼, 20	10N	3W
Holly Bend	82	V. M. Cannon	R	SW¼, 20	10N	3W
Kincade's	80	E. Kincade	R	NE¼, 20	10N	3W
Sestos	79½	J. J. Fouche	L	NE¼, 31	10N	3W
Richard's Bayou Landing			L	NW¼, 31	10N	3W
Adybos	79	Thomas Gayle	R	SE¼, 30	10N	3W
Satartia	78½		L	NW¼, 31	10N	3W
Miles'			L	SE¼, 36	10N	4W
Templeton's	77	P. P. Bailey	R	NW¼, 36	10N	4W
Ewing's, or Anna Dale	76	Mrs. M. J. Hogan	L	NW¼, 35	10N	4W
Woodstock	74	Charles O. Willis	R	SW¼, 27	10N	4W
Hopewell	72	William R. Spears	L	SE¼, 28	10N	4W
Lake George Landing			R	SE¼, 32	10N	4W
Harbin's	71	John Harbin	R	NE¼, 32	10N	4W
Upper Hard Times	70½	P. M. Doherty	L	NW¼, 33	10N	4W
Hard Times	70	R. Wilson	L	NW¼, 33	10N	4W

YAZOO RIVER

LANDING	MILE	OWNER/ OPERATOR	BANK*	SECTION	TOWN-SHIP	RANGE
Lake Dick Landing	69	J. D. Partee	L	NE¼, 5	9N	4W
L'Argent			R	NW¼, 36	10N	5W
Big Sunflower Landing	65		R	SW¼, 36	10N	5W
Madison's Woodyard	63½		L	NE¼, 34	10N	5W
Nelson's Place	62		R	NE¼, 27	10N	5W
Spanish Fort Landing	61	William Clark	R	SW¼, 22	10N	5W
Trucks' Woodyard	59	A. Trucks	R	NW¼, 28	10N	5W
Least's	56	Samuel Least	R	NW¼, 33	10N	5W
Shell Mound			R	NW¼, 9	9N	5W
Eldorado, or Volentine's	53		L	SW¼, 15	9N	5W
Little Sunflower	50		R	SW¼, 16	9N	5W
Collins' Bayou Landing			L	SW¼, 5	18N	5E
Purvis'	43	T. P. Bruce	L	NE¼, 5	18N	5E
Adam's	44	M. McCarthy	L	SW¼, 6	18N	5E
Greasy Bayou Landing			R	SE¼, 36	9N	6W
Ball Ground Creek			L	SE¼, 36	9N	6W
Little Deer Creek			R	NE¼, 10	18N	4E
Haynes' Bluff	35	James Wilson	L	NW¼, 26	18N	4E
Fox's	33⅓	A. Waltemeyer	L	NE¼, 27	18N	4E
Chicora, or Paxton's	33½	K. Marshall	R	NW¼, 27	18N	4E
Snyder's Bluff	32		L	SE¼, 34	18N	4E
Ross'	31	William Ross	R	NW¼, 34	18N	4E
Skillikalia Bayou			L	SW¼, 34	18N	4E
Barnes Bayou Landing			L	SE¼, 33	18N	4E
Ross'		J. N. Ross	R	SE¼, 33	18N	4E
Beasley's			R	SE¼, 33	18N	4E
Anthony's Ferry			L	NE½, 4	17N	4E
Cardiff	30		L	NE¼, 4	17N	4E
McCarthy's	30	A. McCarthy		NW¼, 4	17N	4E
Redwood	29	J. B. Blake	L	NE¼, 7	17N	4E
Ally [?] Thompson			L	SE¼, 5	17N	4E
Gaskin's	27	Banson Blake	L	center, 6	17N	4E
Tucker's			R	SE¼, 7	17N	4E
Taylor's	25	Joe Taylor	R	NE¼, 18	17N	4E
Chickasaw Bayou Landing	24	Thomas Marshall	L	SW¼, 18	17N	4E

Yazoo River

LANDING	MILE	OWNER/ OPERATOR	BANK*	SECTION	TOWN- SHIP	RANGE
Mrs. Lake's Landing			L	NE¼, 11	17N	3E
Boats' Slough Landing	21½		L	NE¼, 10	17N	3E
Steele's Bayou Landing	19		R	SW¼, 14	17N	3E
Crook's Point	18½	Michael Ryan	L	SE¼, 4	17N	3E
McKee's	16	John McKee	R	E½, 19	17N	3E
Locust Grove	15	John Taylor	L	S½, 5	17N	3E
Dalney's		John Clark	L	N½, 30	17N	3E
White House	13	John Williams	L	NW¼, 17	17N	3E
Mouth of Yazoo River	9			Sec. 2	16N	2E

Tchula Lake

LANDING	MILE	OWNER/ OPERATOR	BANK*	SECTION	TOWN- SHIP	RANGE
Head of Honey Island				SW¼, 22	17N	1W
Marksville (Marks' Store)	229½		L	SE¼, 27	17N	1W
Archerletti	229½	Abe Archer	L	SE¼, 34	17N	1W
Walton Bend	229	Dr. Percy	L	NE¼, 2	16N	1W
Ashton	228	W. L. Keirn	L	NW¼, 2	16N	1W
Clifford's	226		L	NW¼, 1	16N	1W
Crescent Landing	226	W. L. Keirn	R	NE¼, 1	16N	1W
Baldwin's			L	SW¼, 31	17N	1E
Keirn			L	SW¼, 5	16N	1E
Linden	220	W. L. Keirn	R	NE¼, 12	16N	1W
Keirn & Jones Landing	218	W. L. Keirn	R	SW¼, 13	16N	1W
Ware's	216½	Mrs. Ware				
Oregon	215	Frank Wyatt	L	NE¼, 19	16N	1E
Lynchfield			R	SE¼, 19	16N	1E
Horseshoe Bend Landing			L	SW¼, 20	16N	1E
Oswego	211	J. J. Hooker	R	SE¼, 30	16N	1E
Jno. Albino Landing	210	John M. Stewart	L	NE¼, 31	16N	1E
Tchula City	208	Jones Bros. Store, Han's Store	L	SE¼, 5	15N	1E
Gwin Landing			L	SW¼, 8	15N	1E
Derryberry	206		L	NW¼, 7	15N	1E

TCHULA LAKE

LANDING	MILE	OWNER/ OPERATOR	BANK*	SECTION	TOWN- SHIP	RANGE
Holly Bank	202	Mrs. Cooper	R	SW¼, 36	16N	1W
Graves'	201	Thomas Graves	R	SW¼, 36	16N	1W
Tallequah	200	Mrs. Cooper	L	NE¼, 15	15N	1W
Belmont	199		R	NE¼, 15	15N	1W
German Bend	196					
Hooker's Woodyard		J. J. Hooker	R	SE¼, 8	15N	1W
Marcella	196	Ed Richardson	R	W½, 16	15N	1W
Marcella Quarters			R	SE¼, 16	15N	1W
Choctow Landing	195	J. J. Hooker	L	SW¼, 15	15N	1W
Thorton Place	195	Ed Richardson	L	NW¼, 22	15N	1W
Morgan's	195	J. W. Morgan				
Black Creek Landing	194	Gen. W. R. Miles	L	NW¼, 26	15N	1W
Mileston			L	NW¼, 35	15N	1W
Pleasant Ridge	192	Gen. W. R. Miles	L	NW¼, 34	15N	1W
Goodhope	189	Gen. W. R. Miles	L	SE¼, 28	15N	1W
Omega	189	Gen. W. R. Miles	L	SE¼, 28	15N	1W
Marcella Quarters	188	Ed Richardson	R	SE¼, 20	15N	1W
Watson's	185		R	SE¼, 24	15N	2W
Phoenix	183		R	NE¼, 36	15N	2W
Dunbarton	182	Dunn Bros. Store	L	SE¼, 25	15N	2W
Quafaloma	182	Gen. W. R. Miles	L	SW¼, 31	15N	2W
Eagle Bank	178	Swisher Estate	L	SE¼, 26	15N	2W
Manchester	175	Swisher Estate	R	SE¼, 23	15N	2W
Richardson Bend Landing	173½	P. James	R	SE¼, 27	15N	2W
Arcola			L	SE¼, 35	15N	2W
Stonewall Landing	172	Peter James	L	SW¼, 2	14N	2W
Bucksnort	169	D. G. Cocks	L	NE¼, 32	15N	2W
Mouth of Tchula Lake				SW¼, 32	15N	2W

Appendix D
COMMERCIAL STATISTICS

YEAR	COTTON (bales)	COTTON (tons)	COTTONSEED (tons)
1878–79	115,886	28,972	
1879–80	108,952	27,191	10,000
1880–81	93,381	23,345	6,500
1881–82	89,000	22,250	4,900
1882–83	112,400	28,100	7,500
1883–84	88,500	22,125	12,867
1884–85	87,200	21,800	13,354
1885–86	88,300	22,075	42,380
1886–87	133,150	33,287	13,500
1887–88	68,500	17,125	30,000
1888–89	72,054	18,014	54,000
1889–90	75,904	18,975	17,633
1890–91	80,500	20,125	22,000
1891–92	101,472	25,368	30,277
1892–93	67,696	16,919	22,445
1893–94	90,200	22,550	30,355
1894–95	94,904	23,725	32,132
1895–96	77,200	19,300	28,931
1896–97	103,600	25,900	44,449
1897–98	60,396	15,099	40,706
1898–99	62,812	15,703	22,984
1899–1900	56,940	14,235	39,470
1900–1901	49,500	12,375	19,325
1901–1902	77,460	19,368	50,883
1902–1903	61,584	15,396	29,373
1903–1904	73,024	18,256	33,934

continued

YEAR	COTTON (bales)	COTTON (tons)	COTTONSEED (tons)
1904–1905	49,088	12,272	19,339
1905–1906	25,592	6,398	23,904
1906–1907	35,240	8,810	17,497
1907–1908	57,816	14,454	23,887
1908–1909	44,900	11,225	14,069
1909–10	45,963	11,441	27,148
1910–11	31,488	7,872	29,495
1911–12	34,056	8,514	25,726
1912–13	29,867	7,467	60,861
1913–14	33,184	8,296	21,536
1914–15	32,061	8,014	14,364
1916	24,140	6,035	16,162
1917	13,880	3,470	12,549
1918	23,197	5,797	17,077
1919	24,302	6,075	15,876
1920	14,774	3,693	12,830
1921	5,066	1,289	7,443
1922	11,589	2,897	5,688
1923	14,563	3,641	—
1924	200	50	423
1925	333	83	—
1926	30	8	—
1927	37	10	—
1928	—	—	—

YEAR	LUMBER (tons)	STAVES (tons)	RAFTED LOGS (tons)
1890–91	5,944	13,814	36,510
1891–92	6,867	14,741	61,308
1892–93	6,822	25,775	57,500
1893–94	10,632	37,050	40,960
1894–95	16,215	42,932	33,475
1895–96	3,572	62,762	37,000
1896–97	3,924	27,730	46,200
1897–98	1,070	26,239	22,000
1898–99	6,010	19,204	13,000
1899–1900	117,320	25,562	18,794
1900–1901	27,154	24,899	29,800
1901–1902	18,054	38,487	61,786
1902–1903	15,514	29,835	395,400
1903–1904	24,412	18,120	163,248
1904–1905	12,474	4,312	100,720
1905–1906	12,181	26,707	212,627
1906–1907	11,646	15,887	205,237
1907–1908	10,754	25,630	142,900
1908–1909	5,219	3,138	210,662
1909–10	8,629	2,250	173,840
1910–11	2,180	—	173,104
1911–12	3,096	727	179,917
1912–13	14,436	—	114,670
1913–14	7,035	—	146,699
1914–15	2,625	1,600	175,125
1916	3,211	—	252,829
1917	1,530	—	204,923
1918	15,514	—	155,391
1919	3,760	—	133,925
1920	1,745	—	85,859
1921	1,184	—	104,847
1922	1,734	—	188,807
1923	156	—	128,131
1924	460	—	177,334
1925	1,164	—	393,078
1926	1,745	—	264,433
1927	—	—	109,424
1928	—	—	66,131

YEAR	GRAIN (tons)	PROVISIONS (tons)	MISCELLANEOUS (tons)	PASSENGERS
1890–91	15,880	13,220	20,013	7,205
1891–92	18,265	16,073	28,469	5,826
1892–93	7,907	11,997	17,718	5,730
1893–94	20,380	16,770	23,373	4,550
1894–95	20,060	18,125	25,523	5,000
1895–96	7,218	17,720	32,305	5,497
1896–97	7,580	18,381	29,953	7,837
1897–98	7,240	2,856	10,878	2,661
1898–99	6,253	7,265	10,302	5,031
1899–1900	6,485	4,745	22,827	4,320
1900–1901	3,900	7,678	16,314	5,890
1901–1902	13,800	16,400	44,791	14,022
1902–1903	25,953	19,106	3,978	14,602
1903–1904	4,161	8,294	11,128	5,815
1904–1905	9,842	7,316	8,638	—
1905–1906	22,297	25,126	10,465	—
1906–1907	11,062	13,751	118,289	3,132
1907–1908	10,485	7,636	27,338	5,723
1908–1909	11,174	8,084	20,907	3,972
1909–10	14,786	7,386	15,966	4,935
1910–11	12,622	7,394	4,008	3,500
1911–12	16,821	16,630	15,790	—
1912–13	2,951	7,068	13,386	1,100
1913–14	2,985	3,029	9,266	2,346
1914–15	1,963	1,050	22,567	400
1915–16	2,798	1,898	22,081	—
1917	234	953	4,530	50
1918	516	21	9,690	—
1919	569	5,672	5,484	—

YEAR	SUNFLOWER	YAZOO	TALLAHATCHIE-COLDWATER	TOTAL
1890–91	31,984	74,322	53,706	160,012
1891–92	47,054	102,069	60,419	209,542
1892–93	43,299	80,643	48,371	172,313
1893–94	30,320	123,542	92,817	246,679
1894–95	24,534	125,118	70,939	220,591
1895–96	38,868	127,571	43,572	210,011
1896–97	35,112	147,311	22,434	204,857
1897–98	8,931	82,089	34,170	125,190
1898–99	19,356	60,610	22,132	102,098
1899–1900	53,222	155,463	45,550	254,235
1900–1901	34,473	79,525	33,864	147,862
1901–1902	70,418	134,648	62,191	267,257
1902–1903	186,313	326,383	16,402	529,098
1903–1904	121,181	161,882	15,965	299,028
1904–1905	39,874	109,212	25,336	174,422
1905–1906	188,792	68,400	88,353	345,545
1906–1907	145,160	228,537	29,359	403,056
1907–1908	142,180	73,201	25,432	240,813
1908–1909	63,058	176,220	130,163	369,441
1909–10	79,888	153,080	50,276	283,244
1910–11	92,488	200,940	40,642	334,070
1911–12	51,341	208,078	41,623	301,042
1912–13	30,591	128,917	46,841	206,349
1913–14	92,024	100,586	66,695	259,305
1914–15	98,141	110,365	22,747	231,253
1916	69,938	142,514	60,658	273,110
1917	61,407	110,400	38,158	209,965
1918	18,583	118,873	33,258	170,714
1919	41,188	124,345	68,528	234,061
1920	65,472	189,039	22,444	276,955
1921	33,182	118,452	5,291	156,925
1922	55,516	218,819	3,423	277,758
1923	73,310	217,010	5,627	295,947
1924	59,673	193,943	—	253,616
1925	143,810	402,438	—	546,248
1926	179,175	314,443	—	493,618
1927	75,268	234,449	—	309,717
1928	24,285	110,886	—	135,171
TOTAL	2,669,409	5,834,323	1,427,386	9,931,118

Notes

Preface

1. Robert William Fogel, *Railroads and American Economic Growth: Essays in Economic History* (Baltimore: Johns Hopkins Press, 1964), 110, 219.

Chapter 1

1. *Natchez*, 13 February 1830.

2. See announcements and advertisements in the *Vicksburg Register*, September 1831–March 1832.

3. "Source Material for Mississippi History, Humphreys County, Mississippi," Federal Writers Project, Works Progress Administration, 1936 (typescript), State Department of Archives and History, Jackson, Mississippi, emphasis added.

4. *Ariel* (Natchez, Mississippi), 19 December 1825, 23 January 1826; *Courier de la Louisiana* (New Orleans), 2, 6 February 1826; see below, Appendix A, for a list of known steamboats on the Yazoo River.

5. J. B. Wilson, *Handbook of Yazoo County, Mississippi* (N.p.: N.p., 1884), 50.

6. Harriet DeCell, "The Yazoo River," in Richard A. Bartlett, ed., *Rolling Rivers: An Encyclopedia of America's Rivers* (New York: McGraw-Hill, 1984), 299–302; see below, Chapter 10, for changes in the river system.

7. Harriet DeCell and JoAnne Prichard, *Yazoo: Its Legends and Legacies* (Yazoo City, Miss.: Yazoo Delta Press, 1976), 27–33; Arthur H. DeRosier, Jr., *The Removal of the Choctaw Indians* (New York: Harper Torchbooks, 1972), chaps. 4–8.

8. DeCell and Prichard, *Yazoo*, 51–57, for maps showing early settlement patterns and land grants in Yazoo County.

9. Ibid., 98; DeRosier, *Removal of the Choctaw Indians*, 143–44.

10. "Map Showing Site of Proposed Crossing of the Yazoo River, State of Mississippi, by the Georgia Pacific Railway, 1887," Cartographic Division, Record Group 77, National Archives, Washington, D.C.

11. For a complete list of steamboat landings see below, Appendix C.

12. Louis C. Hunter, *Steamboats on the Western Rivers: An Economic and Cultural History* (Cambridge, Mass.: Harvard University Press, 1949), 61–120.

13. See Appendix A; William M. Lytle and Forrest R. Holdcamper, *Merchant Steam Vessels of the United States, 1807–1868, "The Lytle List"*

(Mystic, Conn.: Steamship Historical Society of America, Publication 6, 1952), provides information regarding year, tonnage, and place of building for the antebellum boats.

14. *Statutes at Large*, vol. 1, chap. 11, sec. 3, pp. 55–56 describes the process: "Deduct from the length three-fifths of the breadth, multiply the remainder by the breadth, and the product by the depth, dividing the product of the whole by ninety-five, the quotient shall be deemed the true contents or tonnage of such ship or vessel." Changes in the late nineteenth century excluded areas holding boilers, engines, and machinery. Antebellum boats described by tonnage, characterized by sidewheel design and technology and dominating the Yazoo trade until the 1850s, form a distinct category of steamboats. After the Civil War, packets and towboats using sternwheel design and technology became a second category of boats. These postwar boats were also distinguished from their antebellum predecessors by different operational and service components.

15. *Yazoo City Whig*, 9 June 1843; *Vicksburg Whig*, 3 March 1858; *Yazoo City Herald*, 22 April 1887; Lytle and Holdcamper, *Merchant Steam Vessels*, 50, 149.

16. "New Orleans Inspection Certificates, 1854–1855," Bureau of Marine Inspection and Navigation, Record Group 41, National Archives, Washington, D.C., *General Stokes*, no. 6 (1854), and *W. P. Swiney*, no. 35 (1855); *Yazoo Democrat*, 22 June, 5 October 1853; *Yazoo City Whig*, 23 December 1853, 3 February, 6 October 1854–12 January 1855; *Vicksburg Tri-Weekly Whig*, May–September 1853, January–May 1854.

17. "New Orleans Certificates," RG 41, NA, *T. P. Leathers*, no. 46 (1854); *Yazoo City Whig*, 17 February 1854; Frederick Way, Jr., *Way's Packet Directory, 1848–1983* (Athens: Ohio University Press, 1983), 442.

18. Hunter, *Steamboats*, 61–89.

19. Ibid., 80–82.

20. Ibid.; *Vicksburg Whig*, 19 June, 10 November 1860.

21. Hunter, *Steamboats*, 90.

22. *Yazoo Democrat*, 20 July 1853; *Vicksburg Whig*, 30 November 1858, 17 November 1860.

23. Hunter, *Steamboats*, 155, 159–67.

24. *Ibid.*, 250.

25. Ibid., 136–42.

26. Compiled from steamboat arrival and departure notices published in Vicksburg and Yazoo City newspapers, 1830–60.

27. Compiled from 1838 newspapers, including extant issues of the *Vicksburg Sentinel*, the *Vicksburg Daily Register*, the *Vicksburg Register*, and the *Yazoo Banner*.

28. *Vicksburg Daily Register*, 3 January, 9, 12, 20 February, 5 March 1838; *Greenwood Reporter*, 25 February, 18 March 1845; for the subsequent career of the *Enterprise* see Lytle and Holdcamper, *Merchant Steam Vessels*, 58, 226.

29. Compiled from arrival and departure notices and advertisements in Vicksburg, Yazoo City, and Greenwood newspapers.

Chapter 2

1. Compiled from arrival and departure notices in the *Vicksburg Whig*, 1850–60; *Yazoo City Whig*, 1853–55; *Yazoo Democrat*, 1850–55; and *Yazoo Democrat*, 1859–61.

2. *Vicksburg Tri-Weekly Whig,* October 1851–January 1852; Lytle and Holdcamper, *Merchant Steam Vessels,* 104; Way, *Way's Packet Directory,* 260.

3. *Vicksburg Tri-Weekly Whig,* 16 June 1855; Way, *Way's Packet Directory,* 305; "New Orleans Certificates," RG 41, NA, *Major Aubrey,* no. 40 (1855), describes the steamer as having fourteen staterooms with two berths in each.

4. *Vicksburg Whig,* 18, 22 December 1858; Lytle and Holdcamper, *Merchant Steam Vessels,* 15; Way, *Way's Packet Directory,* 36; "New Orleans Certificates," RG 41, NA, indicates that the *General R. H. Stokes, Sarah, Afton, John Strader, W. P. Swiney, Home,* and *Lewis Whitman* were licensed in the New Orleans–Yazoo River trade.

5. *Yazoo Democrat,* December 1852–January 1853; Way, *Way's Packet Directory,* 118; "New Orleans Certificates," RG 41, NA, *D. S. Stacy,* no. 2 (1855).

6. *Yazoo City Whig,* 9 February–11 May 1855; *Vicksburg Tri-Weekly Whig,* 6 September–24 November 1855; for a description see *Vicksburg Whig,* 1 February 1856, and Way, *Way's Packet Directory,* 360.

7. *Vicksburg Whig,* January–December 1858 and 5 December 1860; Way, *Way's Packet Directory,* 105.

8. "New Orleans Certificates," RG 41, NA, *Grenada,* no. 1 (1854); Way, *Way's Packet Directory,* 200; Lytle and Holdcamper, *Merchant Steam Vessels,* 235, documents the collision with the *Mammoth Cave.*

9. Way, *Way's Packet Directory,* 10, 189; *Yazoo Democrat,* 18 June 1851, 1 January 1853.

10. *Vicksburg Whig,* January–April 1858.

11. *Yazoo City Whig,* 17 February 1854; "New Orleans Certificates," RG 41, NA, *T. P. Leathers,* no. 46 (1854).

12. *Vicksburg Whig,* 26 January, 3 April 1858; "New Orleans Certificates," RG 41, NA, *Lewis Whitman,* no. 70 (1855).

13. *Vicksburg Sentinel,* 5 February 1850; *Vicksburg Whig,* 12 September 1855, 26 May 1860.

14. For activities of the *Volant,* see the *Yazoo Democrat,* 23 November 1853, and the *Vicksburg Tri-Weekly Whig,* September 1852–November 1853; for the *General R. H. Stokes,* see *Yazoo Democrat,* 22 June–December 1853, and *Vicksburg Tri-Weekly Whig,* May–September 1853; for the *John Strader,* see *Yazoo City Whig,* December 1853–February 1854; for the *Creole* of unknown tonnage, see *Vicksburg Whig,* 19 April 1856, and for the *Roebuck,* ibid., March–December 1858.

15. For the *Belmont,* see *Yazoo City Whig,* September 1841–May 1842; on 12 May 1842 the newspaper reported that she sank on the Little Tallahatchie River about forty miles below Panola. The *Lacon* was reported in the *Yazoo City Whig,* October 1845–February 1846; for the *Laurel,* see *Vicksburg Whig,* February–May 1847; for the *Jeff Davis,* see *Yazoo Democrat,* January 1848–November 1850, and *Vicksburg Whig,* 10 September 1851; the *Sarah* was reported in the *Yazoo Democrat,* May–August 1851; for the *Afton,* see *Yazoo Democrat,* June 1852–4 May 1855, and *Vicksburg Tri-Weekly Whig,* 1 May 1855; "New Orleans Certificates," RG 41, NA, *Afton,* no. 26 (1854); ibid., *Lewis Whitman,* no. 70 (1855); the *J. M. Sharp* was described in the *Yazoo Democrat,* 22 October 1859; see below, Chapters 3 and 4, for the Confederate career of the *J. M. Sharp.*

16. Undated newspaper clipping in Captain E. C. Carroll Papers, Old Court House Museum, Vicksburg, Mississippi.

17. Ledbetter's recollections were reported in the *Yazoo City Herald,* 12

January 1912; *Vicksburg Whig,* January 1858–December 1860, reported the *Argo* as leaving Vicksburg for the Sunflower River almost every week except during the summer months.

18. U.S. Sixth Census, 1840, Manuscript Population Schedules, Warren County, Mississippi, 252.

19. U.S. Fifth Census, 1830, Manuscript Population Schedules, Yazoo County, Mississippi, 293; ibid., Sixth Census, 1840, 329; ibid, Seventh Census, 1850, 521, 526; DeCell and Prichard, *Yazoo,* 108, 140, 260; Frank E. Smith, *The Yazoo River* (New York: Rinehart & Company, 1954), 67–68; *Vicksburg Evening Post,* 16 April 1934; *Waterways Journal,* 14 December 1960.

20. U.S. Seventh Census, 1850, Manuscript Population Schedules, Yazoo County, 521.

21. *Yazoo Democrat,* 14 June 1854. After the Civil War other boats made record runs, but none were reported as equaling the 1854 record from Vicksburg to Yazoo City by the *S. S. Prentiss.* The *Lucy Keirn,* running in the early 1870s, made the two-hundred-mile round trip between Greenwood and Sharkey's landing on the Tallahatchie River in twenty hours and fifty minutes for an average speed of slightly less than ten miles per hour. The *Home* averaged ten miles per hour in a run from Vicksburg to Black Bayou, a landing twelve miles below Sharkey's, and a few years later the *F. Barksdale* made the trip from Vicksburg to Sharkey's landing in ten minutes less than the *Home.* During the famous race between the *Rob't E. Lee* and the *Natchez* on the lower Mississippi River, both boats averaged about seventeen miles per hour. For comments on speed, see Hunter, *Steamboats,* 22–25, and Mark Twain, *Life on the Mississippi* (New York: Heritage Press, 1944), 110–12.

22. *Vicksburg Whig,* 1858, esp. 9 January, 24 April, 3, 10 July, and 19 October.

23. Ibid., 31 August, 30 November, 21 December 1858.

24. Ibid., 21 December 1858.

25. Ibid., 14 September, 19 October 1858; *Yazoo Democrat,* 26 February 1859.

26. *Yazoo Democrat,* 3 September 1859.

27. For the *Roebuck,* see *Yazoo Democrat,* 24 March 1860, *Vicksburg Whig,* 21 September, 30 October 1860; for the *Dixie,* see ibid., 15, 26 September, 2, 6, 13 October, 30 November 1860; Way, *Way's Packet Directory,* 130.

28. *Yazoo Banner,* March 1841; *Yazoo City Whig,* January–December 1841 and January–March 1845; *Vicksburg Sentinel,* January 1848; *Vicksburg Whig,* January–December 1860.

29. *Vicksburg Daily Whig,* 13 February 1840.

30. Ibid.; *Yazoo City Herald-Democrat,* 16 February 1877; *Yazoo Valley Flag,* 21 December 1882; *Yazoo City Herald,* 11 November 1898.

31. *Vicksburg Register,* 16 December 1831; *Yazoo City Whig,* 12 September 1845; *Vicksburg Daily Whig,* 13 December 1855; *Yazoo Democrat,* 5 November 1859; *Vicksburg Whig,* 30 November 1858.

32. *Vicksburg Weekly Whig,* 1 November 1845; *Yazoo City Whig,* 3, 24 November 1854. Carl Carmer, *Stars Fell on Alabama,* American Century Series (New York: Hill and Wang, 1961), 236, reported that the "*Ben Lee,* sternwheeler," was abandoned in "a bayou up the Warrior [River], a few miles from Mobile."

33. Compiled from arrival and departure notices and advertisements in the *Yazoo Democrat,* January–December 1852.

34. *Vicksburg Whig,* 7, 10 July, 2 August 1860.

35. Ibid., 16 October 1858.

36. *Vicksburg Register*, 15, 22 October 1835; *Vicksburg Daily Whig*, January 1838; Lytle and Holdcamper, *Merchant Steam Vessels*, 76.

37. See Appendix B for a list of wrecks.

38. *Vicksburg Weekly Whig*, 9 May 1855, reported the wreck of the *W. N. Sherman*, but the machinery may have been salvaged and placed on a new hull; see Way, *Way's Packet Directory*, 489; the *U.S. Aid* was reported wrecked in the *Vicksburg Tri-Weekly Whig*, 29 January 1856 but was noted as running again, ibid., 16 December 1856, and with a new hull on 17 June 1858; for the *Bluff City*, see *Yazoo Democrat*, 3 December 1859; the *Yazoo City Herald*, 22 April 1887, contained a list of wreck heaps judged by Parisot and Ledbetter to be obstructions to navigation.

39. *Yazoo Democrat*, 17 October, 6 November 1850; *Vicksburg Tri-Weekly Sentinel*, 15 September 1849; *Vicksburg Whig*, 2 February 1858; *Yazoo City Whig*, 29 January 1847; and *Yazoo Democrat*, May–September 1852.

40. *Yazoo Democrat*, 23 March 1853; *Vicksburg Daily Whig*, 13 December 1855; *Yazoo City Whig*, 4 May 1855; Lytle and Holdcamper, *Merchant Steam Vessels*, 68; *Yazoo City Herald*, 22 April 1887, reported that the *Texana* was a wreck heap obstructing navigation.

41. Smith, *Yazoo*, xvi; DeCell and Prichard, *Yazoo*, 22.

42. *Vicksburg Whig*, 11 October 1860; Way, *Way's Packet Directory*, 374; "Papers Pertaining to Vessels of, or Involved with the Confederate States of America," War Department Collection of Confederate Records, *Planter*, File P-15, Enclosure 19, Record Group 109 (Microcopy M 909), National Archives, Washington, D.C. (hereafter cited as "Vessel Papers"); *Vicksburg Whig*, 5 December 1860, and for the *Anna* and *Prince*, ibid., October–December 1860; "Vessel Papers," *Anna*, File A-18, and Enclosures dated 14, 23 November 1862, and 25 September 1863, RG 109, NA.

43. *Vicksburg Whig*, 17 November 1860.

44. Compiled from *Vicksburg Whig*, September–December 1860; *Yazoo Democrat*, 30 July 1859, 7 July 1860.

45. Compiled from the *Vicksburg Whig* and *Yazoo Democrat*, 1860–61; "Vessel Papers," *Yazoo*, File Y-2, Enclosures 9–11, RG 109, NA.

Chapter 3

1. Kate S. Carney, Diary, 15 April, 3 May 1861, Southern Historical Collection, University of North Carolina, Chapel Hill; Samuel Usher Dilley, Satartia, Mississippi, to Mr. Smith, 1 May 1861, Dilley Letters, Private Collection, in DeCell and Prichard, *Yazoo*, 287; Dilley to George and Sarah, 14 May 1861, ibid., 288; Claude E. Fike, ed., "Diary of James Oliver Hazard Perry Sessions of Rokeba [sic] Plantation, on the Yazoo," *Journal of Mississippi History* 39 (August 1977): 239–54.

2. Compiled from *New Orleans Daily Picayune*, September 1861–March 1862.

3. "Vessel Papers," *Yazoo*, Y-2, Enclosures 9–11, RG 109, NA; H. Allen Gosnell, *Guns on the Western Waters: The Story of the River Gunboats in the Civil War* (Baton Rouge: Louisiana State University Press, 1949), 83–100; Shelby Foote, *The Civil War: A Narrative*, 3 vols. (New York: Random House, 1958), 1:546–49; J. Thomas Scharf, *History of the Confederate States Navy from its Organization to the Surrender of Its Last Vessel* (New York: Rogers & Sherwood, 1887), 239–302; William N. Still, *Iron Afloat: The Story of the*

Confederate Armorclads (Nashville: Vanderbilt University Press, 1971), 41–61.

4. The distance between the mouth of the Yazoo River and Vicksburg has most often been given as twelve miles, which probably originated with Scharf, *Confederate Navy*, 309. River distances were estimates at best, and the distances reckoned by Sherman H. Parisot, Thomas G. Ledbetter, and other Yazoo River pilots appear to have been most accurate; these were published by Abel C. Tuttle in *Business Directory of Vicksburg, Jackson, Meridian . . . Landings, Distances, Etc., Yazoo and Tallahatchie Rivers, Tchula Lake. . . .* (Vicksburg: Rogers & Groome Book and Job Printers, 1879), 80–92.

5. Foote, *Civil War*, 1:548.

6. Boat tonnages were compiled from Lytle and Holdcamper, *Merchant Steam Vessels*, and Way, *Way's Packet Directory*. All of the boats included in the Yazoo Fleet are listed in at least two and most often several contemporary documents; the *General Clark* and the *Argosey*, each mentioned only once in documents, have not been included as part of the Yazoo Fleet.

7. Way, *Way's Packet Directory*, 16.

8. Frederick Way, Jr., "Wrecks of Thirty Packets on Yazoo May Serve in Future Scrap Drives," *Waterways Journal*, 28 December 1963, pp. 9–12.

9. For the *Prince of Wales* see the F. L. Wooldridge Collection, Memphis Room, Memphis and Shelby County Public Library and Information Center, Memphis, Tennessee.

10. Way, *Way's Packet Directory*, 303–4.

11. Leathers Family Papers, File 17, Department of Archives and Manuscripts, Louisiana State University Library, Baton Rouge.

12. Way, *Way's Packet Directory*, 337–39.

13. Scharf, *Confederate Navy*, 244–45.

14. Gosnell, *Guns on the Western Waters*, 70–100; Scharf, *Confederate Navy*, 239–63; Way, *Way's Packet Directory*, 10, 412–13.

15. In addition to Gosnell, *Guns on the Western Waters*, and Scharf, *Confederate Navy*, see Foote, *Civil War*, vols. 1 and 2, and Still, *Iron Afloat*.

16. James L. Roark, *Masters without Slaves: Southern Planters in the Civil War and Reconstruction* (New York: Norton, 1977), 45, raises the question of self-interest.

17. See Lawrence N. Powell and Michael S. Wayne, "Self-Interest and the Decline of Confederate Nationalism," in Harry P. Owens and James J. Cooke, eds., *The Old South in the Crucible of War* (Jackson: University Press of Mississippi, 1983), 45; and David M. Potter, *The South in the Sectional Conflict* (Baton Rouge: Louisiana State University Press, 1968), 34–83, for self-interest and nationalism.

18. Isaac N. Brown, "The Confederate Gun-Boat *Arkansas*," in Robert U. Johnson and Clarence C. Buel, eds., *Battles and Leaders of the Civil War*, 4 vols. (New York: Century Company, 1887–88), 3: 572–80; Charles W. Read, "Reminiscences of the Confederate States Navy," *Southern Historical Society Papers* 1 (May 1876): 331–62; George W. Gift, "The Story of the *Arkansas*," *Southern Historical Society Papers* 12 (January–May 1884): 48–54, 115–19, 163–70; Still, *Iron Afloat*, 62–78; Charles M. Getchell, Jr., "Defender of Inland Waters: The Military Career of Isaac Newton Brown, Commander, Confederate States Navy, 1861–1865" (M.A. thesis: University of Mississippi, 1978).

19. Read, "Reminiscences," 350–51; Isaac N. Brown to Daniel Ruggles, 9

June 1862, in *The War of the Rebellion: A Compilation of the Official Records of the Union and Confederate Armies*, 128 vols. (Washington, D.C.: Government Printing Office, 1880–1901), Ser. 1, vol. 15, p. 752 (hereafter cited as *OR; Official Records of the Union and Confederate Navies in the War of the Rebellion*, 27 vols. (Washington, D.C.: Government Printing Office, 1894–1917), Ser. 1 (hereafter cited as *ORN*).

20. "Vessel Papers," *Dew Drop*, File D-8, and Enclosures; *Dixie*, File D-12, and Enclosures; *Fair Play*, File F-1, Enclosure 12; *Argo*, File A-23 and Enclosures, RG 109, NA. Joshua Wiley owned a half-interest in the *Fair Play* and received his portion of the $25,000 paid by the Confederate government after his boat was captured. He also owned the *Argo*, and after his death his heirs sought compensation from the United States government by claiming that Wiley was "a Union citizen and loyal man." See "Vessel Papers," *Argo*, File A-23, Enclosure 17, RG 109, NA; M. M. Quaife, ed., *Absalom Grimes: Confederate Mail Runner* (New Haven: Yale University Press, 1926), 122.

21. "Vessel Papers," *Mary E. Keene*, File M-32, Enclosure 7; *Magnolia*, File M-5, Enclosures 16, 18; *Thirty-Fifth Parallel*, File P-2, Enclosure 16; *Fair Play*, File F-1 and Enclosures; *Hartford City*, File H-4, Enclosure 2; *Ben McCulloch*, File B-29¼, Enclosure 6, RG 109, NA; see Brown, "Confederate Gun-Boat *Arkansas*," for a picture of the *Capitol* working beside the *Arkansas*.

22. Read, "Reminiscences," 349–50; Brown to Ruggles, 9 June 1862, *OR*, Ser. 1, vol. 15, pp. 752, 762–63.

23. Brown to Ruggles, 4 June 1862, *OR*, Ser. 1, vol. 15, pp. 749–50.

24. Alfred W. Ellet to E. M. Stanton, 28 June 1862, ibid., 750; "Log of the Ram *Lancaster*," *ORN*, Ser. 1, vol. 23, pp. 4, 242–43, contains the only reference found to the *General Clark*; Read, "Reminiscences," 351, describes Pinkney's actions as "cowardly."

25. Stephen R. Mallory to Jefferson Davis, 16 August 1862, *ORN*, Ser. 1, vol. 2, p. 242.

26. Brown, "Confederate Gun-Boat *Arkansas*," 572–80; Still, *Iron Afloat*, 62–78.

27. Report of S. L. Phelps to Flag Officer C. H. Davis, 23 August 1862, *ORN*, Ser. 1, vol. 23, pp. 296–97; Alfred W. Ellet to E. M. Stanton, 26 August 1862, reported Phelp's findings as "where the enemy have a number of fine gunboats secreted" (ibid., 301).

28. "Vessel Papers," *Capitol*, File C-65, Enclosure 3, RG 109, NA.

29. Ibid., *Paul Jones*, File P-6 and Enclosures; *Charm*, File C-6 and Enclosures; the *Charm* and *Paul Jones* were discovered by skin divers in 1962, see Way, *Way's Packet Directory*, 81, 364; General M. L. Smith to Major Waddy, 19 October 1862, "Vessel Papers," *Charm*, File C-6, Enclosure 18, RG 109, NA, recommended the *Dixie, Hope*, or *Dew Drop* as suitable for the salt run up the Red River. Both the *Hope* and *Dew Drop* remained on the Yazoo River; the *Dixie* was not again reported in the "Vessel Papers."

30. Report of William F. Lynch, Flag Officer, CSN, 9 October 1862, *ORN*, Ser. 1, vol. 23, pp. 706–7; *Atlas to Accompany the Official Records of the Union and Confederate Armies* (Washington, D.C.: Government Printing Office, 1891–95), Plates XXVII-2, and XXXVII-4; Tuttle, *Business Directory*, provides the mileage figures.

31. "Vessel Papers," *Hartford City*, File H-4, Enclosure 3; *Hope*, File H-9, Enclosure 13; *Peytona*, File P-9, Enclosures 12–17, RG 109, NA.

32. Ibid., *Alonzo Child*, File A-11, and Enclosures.

33. Ibid., *Capitol*, File C-65, Enclosure 3.

34. Thomas B. Reed to General Martin L. Smith, 10 December 1862, *OR*, Ser. 1, vol. 17, pt. 2, pp. 792–93.

35. The Union movements are not the major subject of this chapter; for a general account of the expeditions, see Foote, *Civil War*, 2: 52–79, 186–220; and Edwin C. Bearss, *Decision in Mississippi* (Jackson: Mississippi Commission on the War between the States, 1962).

Chapter 4

1. Reed to Major L. Mims, 2 December 1862, *OR*, Ser. 1, vol. 17, pt. 2, p. 777; Reed to General Martin L. Smith, 10, 23 December 1862, ibid., 792–93, 802.

2. Jno. G. Devereux to Reed, 25 December 1862, ibid., 805; Wirt Adams to General Louis Hebert, 15 January 1863, ibid., 836.

3. Summarized from "Vessel Papers," RG 109, NA.

4. Ibid., *Emma Bett*, File E-17, Enclosure 9; *Ben McCulloch*, File B-29¼, Enclosure 7; *Dew Drop*, File D-8, Enclosure 13; *Hope*, File H-9, Enclosures 4–10; *Cotton Plant*, File C-27½, Enclosures 16–28.

5. Ibid., *Edward J. Gay*, File E-25, Enclosures 13–16; *Ferd Kennett*, File F-4, Enclosure 9.

6. For the Yazoo Pass Expedition see Bearss, *Decision in Mississippi*, 142–210; and Foote, *Civil War*, 2: 201–6.

7. William E. Loring to John C. Pemberton, 21 February 1863, *OR*, Ser. 1, vol. 24, pt. 3, p. 638; "Vessel Papers," *Cotton Plant*, File C-27½, Enclosures 23–28, RG 109, NA; Quaife, *Absalom Grimes*, 129–33.

8. "Vessel Papers," *Prince of Wales*, File P-17, Enclosure 6, RG 109, NA, contains the information on the *J. F. Pargoud*; *John Walsh*, File J-16 and Enclosures, contain no information regarding Confederate purchase; "Map of Greenwood and Vicinity, 1863," Office of the Chief of Engineers, Cartographic Division, Record Group 77, National Archives, Washington, D.C., erroneously shows the *John Walsh* near the *Star of the West* and the *J. F. Pargoud* sunk on the Yazoo below Fort Pemberton; for the *Star of the West*, see Report of Watson Smith, 10 March 1863, *ORN*, Ser. 1, vol. 24, p. 266; Bearss, *Decision in Mississippi*, 169–70.

9. Brown to Pemberton, 10 March 1863, *ORN*, Ser. 1, vol. 24, p. 421; "Vessel Papers," *Thirty-Fifth Parallel*, File P-2, Enclosure 15, RG 109, NA.

10. Watson Smith to David D. Porter, 3 March 1863, *ORN*, Ser. 1, vol. 24, p. 266.

11. "Vessel Papers," *Thirty-Fifth Parallel*, File P-2, Enclosure 15, RG 109, NA.

12. Brown to Smith, 2 March 1863, ibid., *Natchez*, File N-1, Enclosure 72.

13. In addition to the thousand bales of cotton, the *Ferd Kennett* transported the Thirty-fifth Mississippi and "two artillery companies and their horses and guns, two wagons and twelve mules" (quoted in Bearss, *Decision in Mississippi*, 209, n. 34); "Yazoo River Claims Papers, February 1863–April 1864," Records of Field Offices, Mississippi, Treasury Department, Record Group 365, National Archives, Washington, D.C., contains twenty-nine claims from the Yazoo River, eight of which involved cotton impressed by Brown and Leathers. The Confederate government paid ten cents per pound for the cotton.

14. "Vessel Papers," *Magnolia*, File M-5, Enclosures 1, 15; *Natchez*, File N-1, Enclosures 31, 36, 37; *Mary E. Keene*, File M-32, Enclosure 3, indicated

that she was paid as a cotton-clad for sixty-two days from 17 February through 19 April 1863; *Magenta*, File M-3, Enclosures 6, 7, RG 109, NA; see also Way, *Way's Packet Directory,* 302, 303, 312, 337.

15. Summarized from "Vessel Papers," *Natchez,* File N-1; *Mary E. Keene,* File M-32; *Magenta,* File M-3; *Magnolia,* File M-5, RG 109, NA.

16. Brown to Pemberton, 17 April 1863, ibid., *Magenta,* File M-3, Enclosure 11.

17. Ibid., *Natchez,* File N-1, Enclosures 31, 36, 37, 39.

18. Brown to Pemberton, 10 March 1863, *OR,* Ser. 1, vol. 24, pt. 1, p. 421.

19. Pemberton to Joseph E. Johnston, 14 March 1863, ibid., pt. 3, p. 669; W. H. Tunnard, *A Southern Record: The History of the Third Regiment of Louisiana Infantry* (Baton Rouge, 1866; Facsimile ed. with preface and notes by Edwin C. Bearss, Dayton, Ohio: Morningside Bookshop, 1970), 220, 232.

20. Foote, *Civil War,* 2: 206–11; Gosnell, *Guns on Western Waters,* 145–76; David D. Porter, *Incidents and Anecdotes of the Civil War* (New York: D. Appleton and Company, 1885), 136–73.

21. Report of Samuel W. Ferguson, 20 March 1863, *OR,* Ser. 1, vol. 24, pt. 1, p. 465; Winfield S. Featherston to John C. Pemberton, 20 March 1863, ibid., 457; "Vessel Papers," *J. M. Sharp,* File J-58, Enclosure 5; *Emma Bett,* File E-17, Enclosure 9, RG 109, NA.

22. Report of Winfield S. Featherston, *OR,* Ser. 1, vol. 24, pt. 1, pp. 458–561; Featherston to Pemberton, 23 March 1863, ibid., 457–58; "Vessel Papers," *Acadia,* File A-I, and Enclosures, RG 109, NA.

23. Pemberton to Loring, 19 March 1863, *ORN,* Ser. 1, vol. 24, p. 497, and *OR,* Ser. 1, vol. 24, pt. 3, p. 677; Loring to Pemberton, 20 March 1863, and C. L. Stevenson to Pemberton, 19 March 1863, *OR,* Ser. 1, vol. 24, pt. 3, pp. 678, 680.

24. Pemberton to Stevenson, 23 March 1863, *OR,* Ser. 1, vol. 24, pt. 3, p. 687.

25. Foote, *Civil War,* 2: 205.

26. Tunnard, *Southern Record,* 220–22; Report of S. D. Lee, 30 March 1863, *OR,* Ser. 1, vol. 24, pt. 1, pp. 461–65.

27. "Vessel Papers," *Dew Drop,* File D-8, Enclosures 17, 68, RG 109, NA, indicate that payments included funds for wages, fuel, stores, expenses, and damages.

28. Frederick Steele to U. S. Grant, 10 April 1863, *OR,* Ser. 1, vol. 24, pt. 1, pp. 501–2.

29. "Report of the Expedition to Greenville, Black Bayou, and Deer Creek," 7–10 April 1863, ibid.

30. C. L. Stevenson to R. W. Memminger, 2 April 1863, ibid., pt. 3, p. 710; Pemberton to Brown, 9 April 1863, ibid., pt. 1, p. 504; Pemberton to Loring, 10 April 1863, ibid., 732; S. D. Lee to J. J. Reeve, 12 April 1863, ibid., pt. 1, pp. 505–6; Stevenson to Memminger, 14 April 1863, ibid., 503–4; Pemberton to Loring, 7 April 1863, *ORN,* Ser. 1, vol. 24, p. 716.

31. Brown to Pemberton, 17 April 1863, "Vessel Papers," *Magenta,* File M-3, Enclosure 11, RG 109, NA.

32. Ibid., *Mary E. Keene,* File M-32, Enclosure 20, receipt for payment dated 10 September 1863, "For Services rendered in the defense of the Yazoo River as cotton clad from February 17th to April 19th inclusive, $21,700.00."

33. Ibid., *Golden Age,* File G-30, Enclosure 10; *Emma Bett,* File E-17, Enclosure 9; *Hope,* File H-9, Enclosures 13, 14; see also Stephen D. Lee to J. J. Reeve, 12 April 1863, *OR,* Ser. 1, vol. 24, pt. 1, pp. 505–6.

34. Report of Edmund W. Pettus, "Sunflower Expedition," 8 April 1863,

OR, Ser. 1, vol. 24, pt. 3, pp. 725–26; "Vessel Papers," *Dew Drop,* File D-8, Enclosures 13, 14; *H. D. Mears,* File H-13 and Enclosures, RG 109, NA; the *H. D. Mears* had forty-two staterooms, and her officers' quarters and main cabin were lighted with "Johnson's Self Generating Gas" (Way, *Way's Packet Directory,* 203).

35. "Vessel Papers," *Acadia,* File A-1, Enclosures 6–8, RG 109, NA. The *Acadia* burned 466 cords of wood valued at $2,330 between 4 June and 15 July 1863 (ibid., Enclosure 6).

36. Walker to David D. Porter, 19 May 1863, *ORN,* Ser. 1, vol. 25, p. 10.

37. Compiled from "Vessel Papers," *J. F. Pargoud,* File J-37, *Magenta,* File M-3, *Magnolia,* File M-5, *Mary E. Keene,* File M-32, *Peytona,* File P-6, and *R. J. Lackland,* File R-84, RG 109, NA.

38. The *Republic* has mistakenly been said to have been converted into an ironclad; see *ORN,* Ser. 1, vol. 25, p. 10, and Scharf, *Confederate Navy,* 340. Instead, she was dismantled; see "Yazoo Claims Papers," Claims of De Haven and Shirley, and enclosed affidavits of Isaac N. Brown, John W. Cannon, G. Edie, and other steamboat captains, RG 365, NA; "Vessel Papers," *Republic,* File 6, Enclosure 11, RG 109, NA, documented the $25,000 payment dated 21 May 1863. The *Ivy* was erroneously reported as "burned on the Yazoo River 1863 to avoid capture" in *ORN,* Ser. 2, vol. 1, p. 256.

39. Brown to Joseph E. Johnston, 28 May 1863, *ORN,* Ser. 1, vol. 25, p. 136; "Vessel Papers," *John Walsh,* File J-16; *Scotland,* File S-11, *Golden Age,* File G-30, *R. J. Lackland,* File R-84, RG 109, NA. The boats remaining on the upper Yazoo included the *Acadia, Ben McCulloch, Cotton Plant* (180 tons), *Edward J. Gay, Ferd Kennett, Hartford City, Hope, J. F. Pargoud, Magenta, Magnolia, Mary E. Keene, Peytona,* and *Prince of Wales.* Steamers on the Sunflower River system included the *Argo, Cotton Plant* (59 tons), *Dew Drop, Emma Bett, H. D. Mears,* and *J. M. Sharp.*

40. Walker to David Porter, 1 June 1863, *ORN,* Ser. 1, vol. 25, pp. 10–13, 133–36; "Log of the U.S.S. *Forest Rose,*" Old Army and Navy Records, Record Group 45, National Archives, Washington, D.C. William T. Sherman reported that the expedition found the *Dew Drop, Sharp, Argo,* and *Argosey* in the Sunflower River. Sherman's report contained the only reference to the *Argosey,* and because of the lack of supporting evidence, I have not included her as part of the Yazoo Fleet; see Sherman to Grant, 2 June 1863, *ORN,* Ser. 1, vol. 25, p. 136.

41. Walker to Porter, 1 June 1863, *ORN,* Ser. 1, vol. 25, pp. 133–36.

42. "Vessel Papers," *Dew Drop,* File 8, Enclosure 25, RG 109, NA.

43. Walker to Porter, 1 June 1863, *ORN,* Ser. 1, vol. 25, pp. 133–36.

44. Johnston to Brown, 1 June 1863, ibid., 117.

45. "Vessel Papers," *Mary E. Keene,* File M-32, Enclosure 1, RG 109, NA.

46. Ibid., *Ben McCulloch,* File B-29¼, Enclosure 5; *Hope,* File H-9, Enclosures 2, 15, 16 (the *Hope* was moored at Yazoo City for two days while her crew shelled corn); "Yazoo Claims Papers," *Ben McCulloch* File, RG 365, NA.

47. Brown to Johnston, 10 July 1863, *OR,* Ser. 1, vol. 24, pt. 3, p. 1000; Benj. S. Ewell to Brown, 14 July 1863, ibid., 1003.

48. "Vessel Papers," *Mary E. Keene,* File M-32, Enclosure 1; *Magnolia,* File M-5, Enclosure 15; *Magenta,* File M-3, Enclosure 6, RG 109, NA.

49. Ibid., *Ferd Kennett,* File F-4, Enclosure 20.

50. John G. Walker to David D. Porter, 22 July 1863, *ORN,* Ser. 1, vol. 25, pp. 280–83.

51. The seven boats were the *Magenta, Magnolia, J. F. Pargoud, Peytona,* and *Prince of Wales,* all near Yazoo City, and the *Ferd Kennett* and *Edward J. Gay* near Greenwood. The capture of the *St. Mary* was reported in Walker to Porter, 22 July 1863, *ORN,* Ser. 1, vol. 25, p. 283, and in Herron to John A. Rawlins, 25 July 1863, *OR,* Ser. 1, vol. 24, pt. 2, p. 668. The *Acadia, Hope, Hartford City,* and *Cotton Plant* were sunk near Greenwood by the end of the month.

52. John S. Mellon to Major W. H. Davison, 2 November 1863, and E. A. Banks to A. M. Barbour, 2 November 1863, in "Vessel Papers," *J. M. Sharp,* File S-74, Enclosure 4, RG 109, NA.

53. Report of Elias K. Owen, 15 February 1864, *ORN,* Ser. 1, vol. 25, pp. 755–56.

54. General Leonidas Polk to General S. Cooper, 23 April 1864, *ORN,* Ser. 1, vol. 26, p. 260; for Union reports see ibid., 249–59.

55. Potter, *The South in the Sectional Conflict,* 58.

56. John Brooks of the *Edward J. Gay,* William F. Corkery of the *Mary E. Keene,* and Ed Carter of the *Thirty-Fifth Parallel* served as appraisers. All boats except the *John Walsh* were reported in "Vessel Papers," *R. J. Lackland,* File R-84, Enclosure 8, RG 109, NA.

57. Ibid., *Magenta,* File M-3, Enclosure 7.

58. Ibid., *Edward J. Gay,* File E-25, Enclosure 21, appraised for $150,000; *Ferd Kennett,* File F-4, Enclosure 20, appraised for $150,000; *J. F. Pargoud,* File J-37, appraised for $200,000; *Magenta,* File M-3, Enclosure 6, appraised for $250,000; *Magnolia,* File M-5, Enclosure 15, appraised for $180,000; *Mary E. Keene,* File M-32, Enclosure 1, appraised for $240,000; *Peytona,* File P-9, Enclosures 10, 11, appraised for $150,000.

59. Ibid., *Magenta,* File M-3, Enclosure 6; *Dew Drop,* File D-8, Enclosure 25; *Peytona,* File P-9, Enclosures 10, 11; "Yazoo Claims Papers," *Magenta* File, and *Ben McCulloch* File, RG 365, NA. The *Ben McCulloch* was appraised at $42,500 on 16 December 1863.

60. See below, Chapter 9.

Chapter 5

1. John K. Bettersworth, ed., *Mississippi in the Confederacy: As They Saw It* (Baton Rouge: Louisiana State University Press, 1961), 149–59.

2. J. J. Cornwell (USN) to Rear Admiral S. P. Lee (USN), 20 June 1865, *ORN,* Ser. 1, vol. 27, p. 276.

3. Roark, *Masters without Slaves,* 42–44, recounts James Lusk Alcorn's cotton trading in the war-torn Delta; Way, *Way's Packet Directory,* 375; and E. Merton Coulter, *The Confederate States of America, 1861–1865* (Baton Rouge: Louisiana State University Press, 1950), 242, provide cotton prices; for the *Poland* and Captain Blackburn see George Bacon (USN) to Rear Admiral S. P. Lee, 8 February 1865, *ORN,* Ser. 1, vol. 27, p. 18.

4. John J. Cornwell to Lee, 20 June 1865, *ORN,* Ser. 1, vol. 27, p. 276.

5. "Yazoo Claims Papers," *Magenta* File, "A true copy of the contract, 9 October 1863," RG 365, NA; Josiah Gorgas to Colonel J. M. Kennard, Demopolis, Alabama, 29 April 1863, File 3, Leathers Family Papers; Leathers's claim was initially approved by the local committee of the Southern Claims Commission but was disallowed in the final hearings. See Frank W. Klingberg, *The Southern Claims Commission* (Berkeley and Los Angeles: University of California Press, 1955), 57–72. Leathers's last known efforts to secure pay-

ments from the Federal government appeared in Senate Bill 41, 8 August 1893, and Senate Bill 2074, 7 June 1894, in File 16, Leathers Family Papers.

6. Way, *Way's Packet Directory*, 337–39, 395–98.

7. Ibid., 140, 172, 234–35.

8. Ibid., 217, 451; *Vicksburg Daily Times*, February–April 1869.

9. The surname was variously spelled as "Parrasott," "Parrasot," or "Parasott" until after the Civil War, when "Parisot" became the standard spelling. The earliest known reference to "Shum" Parisot appeared in the *Vicksburg Daily Times*, 14 December 1866.

10. The italicized adjectives were taken from comments published in Vicksburg, Yazoo City, and Greenwood newspapers from 1866 to 1890.

11. *Vicksburg Daily Herald*, 19 October 1865; "Enrollment Certificates," *Calumet* no. 5085, Bureau of Marine Inspection and Navigation, Record Group 41, National Archives, Washington, D.C. Steamboats were inspected and new certificates issued annually, but the same number, measurements, and tonnage remained as on the date of issue. Way, *Way's Packet Directory*, 69; Yazoo County Deed Records, Book 4, 21 February, 24 June 1868, in Office of the Clerk of the Chancery Court, Yazoo County Courthouse, Yazoo City, Mississippi; *Vicksburg Daily Times and Republican*, 27 July 1871; Ledger, pp. 38–39, in Box 2, Rees V. Downs Collection, Memphis Room, Memphis and Shelby County Public Library and Information Center, Memphis, Tennessee.

12. Compiled from *Vicksburg Daily Herald* and *Vicksburg Daily Times*, January–December 1868; tonnage figures are from Lytle and Holdcamper, *Merchant Steam Vessel*, and Way, *Way's Packet Directory*.

13. *Vicksburg Daily Times*, 10 January, 22 February 1868.

14. U.S. Congress, Department of War, *Annual Report of the Chief of Engineers*, (Washington, D.C.: Government Printing Office, 1875), 367; all references to these annual reports will be cited as *Annual Report, Chief of Engineers*, year.

15. *Vicksburg Daily Times*, 28 October 1869. The *Belle Yazoo* was named for Carrie Hogan McKee *(Yazoo City Daily Herald*, 21 June 1979).

16. "Enrollment Certificates," *Lucy Keirn*, no number, RG 41, NA, offers a good example of rapidly changing ownership patterns. Four certificates for the *Lucy Keirn* show the owners as follows: November 1870, S. H. Parisot, C. M. Kain, and E. J. Shaw, each owning one-third interests; May 1871, C. M. Kain owned two-thirds and Parisot held his one-third interest; September 1871, Parisot, Kain, and Thomas Ledbetter each owned one-third; January 1873, Parisot, Kain, and Ledbetter still owned equal shares. See also Ledger, pp. 114–15, Downs Collection; William H. Tippett Collection, 3 vols., mimeographed, built 1870: vol. 1, p. 10, Memphis Room, Memphis and Shelby County Public Library and Information Center, Memphis, Tennessee.

17. Carroll Papers, Old Court House Museum, Vicksburg, contain a letter on Parisot Line stationery, and the letterhead shows a wharfboat scene with four steamboats, each with the letter "P" between the chimneys; see also *Vicksburg Daily Times*, 27 July, 25 August, 20 October 1871; "Enrollment Certificates," *Big Sunflower*, no. 2977, *Frank Beck, Jr.*, no number, RG 41, NA. The *Frank Beck, Jr.*, was jointly owned by Metzler and Captain Charles Pare, who later married the widow of Milton P. Dent. For a description of the *Frank Beck, Jr.*, see *Vicksburg Daily Times*, 6 May 1873.

18. *Vicksburg Daily Times*, 27 August 1874.

19. Compiled from *Vicksburg Daily Times* and *Vicksburg Herald*, August 1874–April 1875; dimensions are from Way, *Way's Packet Directory*. The

Emma took a gin stand to Montjoy and Hymen on the Tallahatchie River in September, but she made few other trips (Bill of Lading, John F. Johnson Papers, in private collection held by John W. Brannon, Oxford, Mississippi, and used with his permission).

20. *Vicksburg Daily Times,* 13 April 1875.

21. Undated newspaper clipping, Carroll Papers.

22. *St. Louis Times,* 8 July 1877, clipping in Carroll Papers.

23. Yazoo County Marriage Records, 8 August 1876, in Office of the Clerk of the Chancery Court, Yazoo County Courthouse, Yazoo City, Mississippi; S. H. Parisot's will, filed 15 January 1918, Warren County Will Book C, Office of the Clerk of the Chancery Court, Warren County Courthouse, Vicksburg, Mississippi, indicates that they had no children; S. H. Parisot to Mrs. Leathers, 27 September 1876, Carroll Papers.

24. *Louisville Courier-Journal,* 11 August, 1 October 1876; Charles Preston Fishbaugh, *From Paddle Wheels to Propellers* (Indianapolis: Indiana Historical Society, 1970), 73; "Enrollment Certificates," *Yazoo Valley,* no. 27611, RG 41, NA; Tippett Collection, built 1876, vol. 2, p. 11; undated newspaper clipping, Carroll Papers.

25. "Articles of Agreement," in *John Tobin et al.* v. *S. H. Parisot,* Case 10228, and *John Tobin et al.* v. *S. H. Parisot,* Case 10414, General Case Files, 1836–1911, United States Fifth Circuit Court, Eastern District of Louisiana, Record Group 21, National Archives Branch, Fort Worth, Texas.

26. "Articles of Agreement," ibid.; a bill of sale by which Parisot transferred ownership of the *Yazoo Valley* to Leathers, 3 April 1877, is in File 6, Leathers Family Papers.

27. See below, Chapter 10, and Appendix D for commercial statistics.

28. Compiled from arrival and departure notices and advertisements in Vicksburg, Greenwood, and Yazoo City newspapers; reference to Carroll's son from an undated newspaper clipping, Carroll Papers.

29. "Enrollment Certificates," *City of Yazoo,* no. 125759, RG 41, NA; Tippett Papers, Built 1879, vol. 3, p. 8; undated newspaper clipping, Carroll Papers; *Louisville Courier-Journal,* 27 September 1879; advertisements for the *City of Yazoo, New Orleans Daily Picayune,* 19 July 1880.

30. *Greenwood* (Mississippi) *Oriental,* 7 December 1877.

31. Compiled from *Vicksburg Daily Herald* and (Greenwood, Mississippi) *Yazoo Valley Flag,* 1878.

32. "Enrollment Certificates," *C. P. Huntington,* no number, RG 41, NA; Way, *Way's Packet Directory,* 66; Tippett Collection, lost 1877, vol. 3, p. 2; *Yazoo Valley Flag,* 6 December 1878.

33. *Yazoo Sentinel,* 7 January 1886; *Yazoo City Herald,* 9 November 1883, regarded the P. Line as "the best monopoly ever known."

34. Parish Records, Christ Episcopal Church, Vicksburg, Mississippi; clipping from *Vicksburg Daily Herald,* 21 July 1880, Carroll Papers.

35. Clipping from *New Orleans Daily Picayune,* 19 July 1880, Carroll Papers; "Memorandum of Agreement," 17 July 1880, *Tobin* v. *Parisot,* 10414.

36. Compiled from U.S. Census, Manuscript Population Schedules, Yazoo County, 1840–80; steamboat landings from Tuttle, *Business Directory . . . 1879;* for P. Line Home, see Jack T. Wynn, "Cultural Resources Survey of Rocky Bayou Project, Yazoo County Mississippi, Conducted for Vicksburg District, U.S. Army, Corps of Engineers" (Starksville, Miss.: Archaeological Research, 1980), Appendix B; the landholdings are summarized in deed of S. H. Parisot to Samuel L. Wooldridge, 4 January 1884, Deed Records, Book AF,

pp. 29–33, in Office of the Clerk of the Chancery Court, Yazoo County Courthouse, Yazoo City, Mississippi.

37. *Yazoo City Herald*, 24 July 1880; *New Orleans Daily Picayune*, 20 July 1880.

38. "Enrollment Certificates," *City of Yazoo*, no. 125759, RG 41, NA; *Louisville Courier-Journal*, 27 September 1879; undated newspaper clipping, Carroll Papers.

39. *New Orleans Daily Picayune*, 18 July 1880.

40. Deposition of Murray F. Smith, 16 November 1883, *Tobin* v. *Parisot*, 10414.

41. Ibid.

42. "Memorandum of Agreement," 17 July 1880, *Tobin* v. *Parisot*, 10414. The memorandum did not include the wharfboat, boat store, or P. Line offices, although the "Note of Evidence on trial of application for injunction" included a list of documents submitted by both parties. Many of the documents were not retained in the files, but listed as included in the evidence submitted by Parisot was "original bill of sale of 22 September 1881 by S. H. Parisot of all his steamboat interests."

43. Clipping from *Vicksburg Daily Herald*, 21 July 1880, Carroll Papers.

Chapter 6

1. "Memorandum of Agreement," 17 July 1880, *Tobin* v. *Parisot*, 10414. According to Murray Smith's deposition in the case file, Floweree used his stock in the Vicksburg Ice Company as collateral for his $20,000 commitment, and Campbell secured his $20,000 note by using one of his Yazoo County plantations as collateral; for the disposition of Campbell's estate, see below, Chapter 7.

2. Corporate Charter of the Mississippi and Yazoo River Packet Company, 30 August 1880, in the Office of the Clerk of the Court, Madison Parish Courthouse, Tallulah, Louisiana. The relationship between Ed and Charles Carroll is unknown, but the facts of their last names, that both were connected with insurance companies in St. Louis, and that the St. Louis newspapers provided good press releases for Captain Carroll of Vicksburg are suggestive.

3. Deposition of Murray F. Smith, 16 November 1883, *Tobin* v. *Parisot*, 10414. Smith was mistaken about Mississippi corporate law, for a competing company was chartered under Mississippi law on 12 August 1880; see Charter of Incorporation of the Yazoo River Merchants and Planters Transportation Company, in Corporate Division, Secretary of State, State of Mississippi, Jackson, Mississippi; see also Mississippi, *Laws of the State of Mississippi Passed at the Regular Session of the Legislature Held at the City of Jackson, 3 January 1882–9 March 1882* (Jackson: J. L. Brown, State Printers, 1882), chap. 26, pp. 50–51, and notations.

4. Corporate Charter of the Mississippi and Yazoo River Packet Company.

5. "Note of Evidence on trial of application for injunction, 22 November 1883," *Tobin* v. *Parisot*, 10414; Deposition of Murray F. Smith, ibid.

6. *Vicksburg Daily Herald*, 21 July 1880.

7. Compiled from newspaper clippings in Carroll Papers.

8. "Enrollment Certificates," *De Smet*, no. 6744, RG 41, NA; Way, *Way's Packet Directory*, 125–26; Ledger, pp. 48–49, Downs Collection; *Vicksburg Herald*, 27 October 1880; *Yazoo Valley Flag*, 2 December 1880.

9. *Yazoo Valley Flag*, 8 September 1881; "Enrollment Certificates,"

Josephine Spengler, no. 76060, RG 41, NA, reported measurements of 106 x 35 x 3.7 feet; *Yazoo Valley Flag*, 5 August 1880.

10. Charter of Incorporation of the Yazoo River Merchants and Planters Transportation Company, organized 12 August 1880, and approved by the secretary of state 18 September 1881; see also *Yazoo Valley Flag*, 21 October 1880; the editor accused the captain of the *Tompkins* of blowing his steamboat whistle louder than anyone else on the river (ibid., 22 December 1880).

11. The usual charge was $2.50 for a bale of cotton loaded in Greenwood, but the Merchants and Planters Company charged only $1.25; see *Yazoo Valley Flag*, 10 February, 26 May, 8 September, 21 October 1881, 9 February 1882; *Murray F. Smith* v. *Steamboat Charles H. Tompkins* in a newspaper clipping dated 19 May 1881, Carroll Papers; the *Josephine Spengler* was condemned and sold at auction for $2,800, which was "a little more than one-third of the amount paid for her by the M & P Line" (*Yazoo Valley Flag*, 3 February 1881).

12. *Yazoo Valley Flag*, 15 February 1883, reporting on the local Farmers Union, noted that "a union of this kind is essential to the well being of the farmers, and every county in the state ought to have an organization of the kind." The motto of the newspaper was "Devoted to the Interests of Leflore and Sunflower Counties."

13. *Yazoo Valley Flag*, 30 November 1882; unidentified newspaper clippings, Carroll Papers.

14. E. C. Carroll to Editor, *Flag*, 14 December 1882, Carroll Papers.

15. *New Orleans Daily Picayune*, 18 November 1882, reported the Yazoo River rates, and on 25 November those for the Arkansas River trade; *Yazoo Valley Flag*, 30 November 1882.

16. *Yazoo Valley Flag*, 30 November 1882.

17. Carroll to *Flag*, 14 December 1882, Carroll Papers; *Yazoo Valley Flag*, 21 December 1882.

18. Unidentified newspaper clippings, Carroll Papers; *St. Louis Post-Dispatch*, [?] January 1883, ibid.

19. *New Orleans Daily Picayune* (copied from *Vicksburg Commercial*), 19 July 1880, 16 November 1883; Deposition of Murray F. Smith, 16 November 1883, *Tobin* v. *Parisot*, 10414; *Vicksburg Daily Herald*, 30 December 1917.

20. Deposition of John C. Howard of the Howard Ship Yards, Jeffersonville, Indiana, 14 December 1882, and S. H. Parisot to Howard & Co., 27 May 1882, *Tobin* v. *Parisot*, 10228. The original letter from Parisot, according to Howard, served in lieu of a contract, but it had been lost in Howard's office. "Enrollment Certificates," *S. H. Parisot*, RG 41, NA, was dated 18 October 1882.

21. Deposition of Richard H. Woolfolk, 1 December 1883, and a "True Copy of the Articles of Incorporation of the New Orleans and Bend Packet Company," in *Tobin* v. *Parisot*, 10228.

22. *New Orleans Daily Picayune*, 30, 31 October 1882; Way, *Way's Packet Directory*, 407; "Enrollment Certificates," *S. H. Parisot*; Fishbaugh, *From Paddle Wheels to Propellers*, 201, reports that the hull cost $41,000.

23. *New Orleans Daily Picayune*, 19 November, 30 October 1882.

24. Ibid., 17 January 1883; *Vicksburg Herald*, 9 March 1883, in Carroll Papers.

25. Deposition of Murray F. Smith, 16 November 1883, *Tobin* v. *Parisot*, 10414.

26. *New Orleans Daily Picayune*, 7 March 1883; *Vicksburg Herald*, 9 March 1883; unidentified newspaper clipping, 9 March 1883, Carroll Papers.

27. *Tobin* v. *Parisot*, 10228, was a case in equity seeking $95,000 in damages; *Tobin* v. *Parisot*, 10414, sought a writ of injunction to keep Parisot from steaming on the Mississippi in violation of the Articles of Agreement.

28. *New Orleans Daily Picayune*, 1, 2, 10, and 13 February 1883; the "unpleasantness" was reported in the *Yazoo Valley Flag*, 8 February 1883.

29. Advertisements in the *Yazoo City Herald* and the *Yazoo Valley Flag*, January 1883; *Yazoo Valley Flag*, 8, 15 February, 20 October 1883; the *Susie B.* is identified as a pressboat in Way, *Way's Packet Directory*, 438, and reported on the Yazoo by the *Yazoo Valley Flag*, 15 February 1883.

30. *New Orleans Daily Picayune*, 7, 8, 9, 10, 23, and 27 March 1883.

31. Deposition of Murray F. Smith, 16 November 1883, *Tobin* v. *Parisot*, 10414; Amendment to the Corporate Charter of the Mississippi and Yazoo River Packet Company, Delta, Louisiana, 30 May 1883, on file in the Corporate Records Division, Office of the Secretary of State of Louisiana, Baton Rouge. This amendment to the charter listed the stockholders and their stock as follows: E. C. Carroll (250), C. C. Floweree (225), M. F. Smith (125), S. H. Parisot (225), Frank Beck, Jr. (50), [Charles C.] Carroll and Powell (100), C. M. Klein (150), W. K. Ingersol (125).

32. Exceptions filed by W. S. Benedict, attorney for the defendant Parisot, 21 April 1883, *Tobin* v. *Parisot*, 10228; see advertisements and river news columns in the *New Orleans Daily Picayune* and the *Vicksburg Herald*, April–September 1883.

33. Deposition of Murray F. Smith, 16 November 1883, *Tobin* v. *Parisot*, 10414; *Yazoo Valley Flag*, 10 November, 27 October 1883.

34. *New Orleans Daily Picayune* (copied from *Vicksburg Herald*), 10 October, 5 November 1883; *Yazoo Valley Flag*, 27 October 1883.

35. Compiled from *New Orleans Daily Picayune*, *Vicksburg Herald*, and *Yazoo City Herald*, September–December 1883.

36. Way, *Way's Packet Directory*, 141, 234–35, 338–39.

37. *New Orleans Daily Picayune*, 10, 14, 24, 25 October, 4, 5, 7 November, 8, 29 December 1883; *Yazoo Valley Flag*, 20, 27 October 1883, 9 February 1884; "Enrollment Certificates," *Hard Cash*, no. 95456, RG 41, NA, reported her measurements as 170 x 35 x 5 feet; Tippett Collection, built 1877, vol. 2, p. 2, described the *Clara S.* as "Light draft and fast," with measurements of 107 x 20 x 3.5 feet; Way, *Way's Packet Directory*, 154, recorded the *Era No. 10* as 136 x 30.8 x 5 feet.

38. Compiled from *New Orleans Daily Picayune* and *Yazoo City Herald*, September–November 1883; for the arrival of the *S. H. Parisot* in Yazoo City, see *Yazoo City Herald*, 15 November 1883, and *New Orleans Daily Picayune*, 16 November 1883.

39. *New Orleans Daily Picayune*, 16 November 1883, 16 January 1884.

40. Ibid., 7, 8 November 1883; *Yazoo Valley Flag*, 1 November 1883.

41. *New Orleans Daily Picayune*, 21, 22 December 1883.

42. Ibid., 19 November 1883.

43. "Enrollment Certificates," *Cherokee*, no. 125173, RG 41, NA, dated 1 December 1883, named the Mississippi and Yazoo River Packet Company as owner; *Yazoo City Herald*, 30 November 1883; *New Orleans Daily Picayune*, December 1883.

44. *Tobin* v. *Parisot*, 10414, contains the injunction with the U.S. marshal's endorsement dated 29 January 1884; the injunction was published, in part, in the *Yazoo City Herald*, 15 February 1884.

45. *Vicksburg Herald*, 2 February 1884; *New Orleans Daily Picayune*, 4

February 1884. Perhaps Leathers learned of Carroll's bluster a day or so earlier, for on 3 February 1884, the *Picayune* reported that Captain Leathers was ill with an "inflammation of the bowels."

46. Compiled from the *Yazoo City Herald* and the *New Orleans Daily Picayune*, January–February 1884.

47. *New Orleans Daily Picayune*, 5 February 1884.

48. Ibid., 6 April 1884; "Motion to discontinue," *Tobin* v. *Parisot*, 10228.

49. *Yazoo City Herald*, 11 April 1884; *Yazoo Valley Flag*, 12 April, 3 May, and 20 September 1884.

50. Works Progress Administration, Federal Writers Project, "Source Materials for Mississippi History, Yazoo County, Mississippi, State Department of Archives and History, Jackson, Mississippi, "Transportation," 47.

Chapter 7

1. Twain, *Life on the Mississippi*, 105; Way, *Way's Packet Directory*, "Preface," n.p.; Jane Curry, *The River's in My Blood: Riverboat Pilots Tell Their Story* (Lincoln: University of Nebraska Press, 1983), 117.

2. Black deckhands had a far different situation than the officers. See *Yazoo City Herald*, 17 September 1886, for a report of deckhands attempting to organize and maintain a strike against the boats. The deckhands in Vicksburg asked for wages of $60 per month, but violence broke out between the strikers and scabs, and the strike was unsuccessful.

3. *Vicksburg Daily Herald*, 21 July 1880, in Carroll Papers.

4. Newspaper clippings in Carroll Papers.

5. Twain, *Life on the Mississippi*, 214.

6. U.S. Tenth Census, 1880, Manuscript Population Schedules, Vicksburg, Warren County, Mississippi.

7. Ibid.

8. U.S. Seventh Census, 1850, Manuscript Population Schedule, Yazoo City, Yazoo County, Mississippi; Marriage Records, Yazoo County, Yazoo County Courthouse, Yazoo City, Mississippi; U.S. Tenth Census, 1880, Manuscript Population Schedules, Vicksburg, Warren County, Mississippi; advertisements in the *Vicksburg Daily Herald*, 1878, 1881.

9. Yazoo County Marriage Records; Lizzie Craig and her son signed as witnesses to S. H. Parisot's Will.

10. Compiled from U.S. Census, Manuscript Population Schedules, 1850–80, Vicksburg.

11. U.S. Tenth Census, 1880, Vicksburg; Warren County Marriage Records.

12. WPA, "Source Materials for Mississippi History," Yazoo County, 42–43; *Yazoo Sentinel*, 7 September 1882.

13. Compiled from Deed Records in Yazoo and Warren counties, especially Yazoo County, Deed Records, Book AF, pp. 29–33, 195–97, Book X, pp. 376–77; Warren County, Deed Records, Book PP, pp. 4–5, Book 54, p. 52.

14. The best summary of Parisot's Yazoo River lands may be found in his mortgage to Samuel L. Wooldridge, 4 January 1884, in Yazoo County Deed Records, Book AF, pp. 29–33.

15. A good description of Parisot's Silver Creek holdings may be found in his deed to Edmund H. Wooldridge, 16 February 1886, in Yazoo County, Deed Records, Book AI, pp. 272–74; L. A. Campbell, et ux per H. C. McCabe, trustee, deed to S. H. Parisot, 17 March 1884, in Yazoo County, Deed Records, Book AF, pp. 195–97.

16. S. H. Parisot, deed of trust to George P. La Barre, 17 March 1884, in Yazoo County, Deed Records, Book AF, pp. 197–99.

17. S. H. Parisot, Mortgage to Samuel L. Wooldridge, 4 January 1884, ibid., Book AF, pp. 29–33.

18. *New Orleans Daily Picayune*, 8 December 1884.

19. United States Circuit Court, Jackson, Mississippi, U.S. Chancery Court, 1878–1910, General Court Docket Number 1, pp. 441, 442, 479, 517, Record Group 21, National Archives Branch, Atlanta; hereinafter cited as U.S. Circuit Court, Jackson, Docket. According to the archivist at the National Archives, Atlanta Archives Regional Branch, the extensive litigation involving Parisot was "not shipped to us from Jackson" (Charles Reeves to Harry P. Owens, 7 February 1984, in the author's possession). A diligent search of the Federal district court in Jackson, Mississippi, failed to reveal the case files. The county records, two incomplete case files of two relatively minor cases and four pages of closely written docket records, are all that remain.

20. *New Orleans Times-Democrat*, 7 December 1884; *New Orleans Daily Picayune*, 8 December 1884; *Yazoo Valley Flag*, 13 December 1884.

21. *John J. Adams and Company* v. *S. H. Parisot*, Case No. 323, Record Group 21, B 029/020 C 045, National Archives, Atlanta Regional Archives Branch, was filed 10 February 1882 and seems to have been adjudicated in favor of the defendant. *Union National Bank of New Orleans, Louisiana*, v. *S. H. Parisot*, Case No. 2950, ibid., B 029/02 F 092, filed 25 May 1883, involved $1,236.24 in a cotton futures contract and was judged for the plaintiff. Other actions joining the Kentucky bank included the Fayette National Bank, the National Exchange Bank of Lexington, Kentucky, the Second National Bank of Louisville, Kentucky, the J. Amsden and Company, the Citizens Bank of Midway, and S. L. Wooldridge; all noted in U.S. Circuit Court, Jackson, Docket, pp. 441, 517. The deeds transferring the various plantations were as follows: S. H. Parisot, per Silas Pittman Special Commissioner, deed to Edmund H. Wooldridge, 16 February 1886, Yazoo County Deed Records, Book AI, pp. 272–74; E. H. Wooldridge, deed to Samuel L. Wooldridge, 16 February 1886, ibid., 274–76; George S. Irving by decrees, 2 December 1886 and 3 May 1887, deed to Samuel L. Wooldridge, 3 May 1887, ibid., Book AK, pp. 52–54.

22. The pertinent deeds of trust and title deeds in the Yazoo County Deed Records are found in Book AK, pp. 51–59, 69–73, and Book AL, 185–87.

23. Ibid., Book AL, pp. 186–87; ibid., Book BC, pp. 170–71; Wooldridge to Irving, agreement, ibid., Book AK, pp. 72–73; and Mary A. Kinkead, deed of trust to S. L. Wooldridge, 13 January 1887, ibid., 69–72.

24. Undated newspaper clippings, Scrapbook of Annie Kinkead Dent, in possession of Bruce (Mrs. James K.) Dent, Kinkead Plantation Office, Yazoo City, Mississippi; *Yazoo City Herald*, 28 September 1888.

25. See Marriage Records, Yazoo County, 1892, Yazoo County Courthouse, Yazoo City, Mississippi; Yazoo County Deed Records, Book AY, p. 570, 8 September 1898; Mary A. Kinkead, Will, filed 9 October 1930, Yazoo County Will, Book D, p. 137, Yazoo County Courthouse, Yazoo City, Mississippi; Mrs. Bruce Dent, her sons, and Amanda Dent Bailey and her sons are the heirs of the late James K. Dent, Jr., and John Dent respectively, and represent the third and fourth generations associated with P. Line Home.

26. Yazoo County Deed Records, Book AF, pp. 90–93, 195–96.

27. S. H. Parisot, deed of trust to George P. La Barre, trustee, 17 March 1884, ibid., Book AF, pp. 197–99.

28. George S. Irving, deed to W. A. Campbell, 29 December 1885, ibid., Book AG, p. 670.

29. S. H. Parisot per Silas Pittman, Special Commissioner, deed to Edmund H. Wooldridge, 16 February 1886, ibid., Book AI, pp. 272–74; Edmund H. Wooldridge, deed to Samuel L. Wooldridge, 16 February 1886, ibid., 274–76.

30. Samuel L. Wooldridge, deed to George S. Irving, ibid., Book AI, pp. 276–78; George S. Irving, deed of trust to E. H. Wooldridge, trustee, S. L. Wooldridge, ibid., 278–80; for deed of release, see ibid., Book AL, p. 716. A search through the Abstract of Titles, Yazoo County, Books 10 and 11, indicated that Irving and his heirs held most if not all of the land until 1913.

31. Abstract of Titles, Yazoo County, Book 11, Office of the Chancery Clerk; Yazoo County Courthouse, Yazoo City, Mississippi, recorded that Irving executed a lien on his property to G. S. Irving Grocery and Provision Company.

32. Undated newspaper clipping, Annie K. Dent Scrapbook.

33. Compiled from *Annual Reports, Chief of Engineers*, 1886, 1887.

34. Contracts and schedules in Carroll Papers; U.S. Congress, House of Representatives, *Offers for Carrying the Mails*, House Executive Document 226, 47th Cong., 1st sess. p. 1859; U.S. Congress, House of Representatives, *Contracts for Carrying the Mails*, House Executive Document 266, 48th Cong., 2d sess., p. 251. Stops on the Yazoo River were at Fox Landing, Haynes' Bluff, Satartia, Yazoo City, Belle Prairie, Chew's Landing, Gum Grove, Roseneath, Palmetto Home, Belzoni, Devolante, Idlewild, Head of Honey Island, Sheppardstown, Sidon, Roebuck, and Greenwood.

35. Compiled from river news columns in *Yazoo Valley Flag, Yazoo City Herald,* and *Vicksburg Herald,* 1886; for praise of the P. Line, see *Yazoo Sentinel,* 7 January 1886, in Carroll Papers.

36. "Enrollment Certificates," *Alert,* no. 105708, *Alice,* no. 10611, *Beta,* no. 3033, RG 41, NA; *Yazoo City Herald,* September 1883–December 1885; *Yazoo Valley Flag,* 16 December 1880.

37. Charter of Incorporation of the Sunflower River Packet Company, 12 November 1886, in Corporate Records Division, Secretary of State Office, Jackson, Mississippi; the company advertised as the Vicksburg, Sunflower and Yazoo Packet Company; "Enrollment Certificates," *Addie E. Faison,* no. 106505, *Crown Point,* no. 126330, *Josie D. Harkins,* no. 76712, and *Headlight,* no. 95405, RG 41, NA; *Yazoo City Herald,* 5 August 1889, reported that P. Line boats stopped running in the Sunflower River.

38. U.S. Ninth Census, 1870, Manuscript Population Schedules, Yazoo County, p. 227; "Enrollment Certificates," *Lake City,* no. 140812, RG 41, NA; *Yazoo City Herald,* 14 December 1883, 24 February 1888; *Yazoo Valley Flag,* 29 May 1886.

39. "Enrollment Certificates," *Ike Bonham,* no. 100231, RG 41, NA; *Yazoo City Herald,* 19 March, September–October 1886, 6 May 1887. Several years later, the *New Evergreen* was appropriately painted green (ibid., 14 April 1890).

40. Summarized from *Annual Report, Chief of Engineers,* 1885–1895.

41. Ibid., 1889.

42. *Yazoo City Herald,* 1 April, 6 May 1887. One of the earliest known references to W. D. Pugh as "commodore" appeared in ibid., 12 November 1886.

43. Ibid., 9, 16, 23 September, 7 October 1887; *Annual Report, Chief of Engineers,* 1887–89.

44. "Enrollment Certificates," *R. L. Cobb*, no. 110614, 1 October 1887, and 25 August 1888, RG 41, NA; *Yazoo City Herald*, 23 September, 7 October 1887.

45. Charter of Incorporation of the Yazoo and Tallahatchie Transportation Company, 10 August 1888, Corporate Records Division, Secretary of State Office, Jackson, Mississippi. Captain Carroll retained a newspaper clipping which reported that the company had capital stock of $185,000, but a blue line was neatly drawn through the sentence (Carroll Papers).

46. *Yazoo City Herald*, 4 January 1889.

47. Ibid., 3 August 1888, 26 July, 2 August 1889; "Enrollment Certificates," *John F. Allen*, no. 76545, and *Mountain Girl*, no. 91347, RG 41, NA.

48. See below, Chapter 8, for accounts of steamboat accidents.

49. *Yazoo City Herald*, 23 August 1889. Parisot's term as president expired on 4 September 1890. Pugh Line boats were the *Ike Bonham*, *John F. Allen*, *Lake City*, *Mountain Girl*, and *New Evergreen*; Parisot's boats were the *Birdie Bailey*, *Blanks Cornwell*, *Katie Robbins*, and *R. L. Cobb*. See also "Enrollment Certificates," *Addie E. Faison*, no. 106505, dated February 1891, RG 41, NA.

50. *Yazoo City Herald*, 17 October 1890, reported F. M. Andrews as president, T. M. Smedes as vice-president, D. B. Rundle as secretary, and D. Mayer as treasurer; members of the Board of Directors were E. C. Carroll, Oscar E. Mayer, J. B. Mattingly, R. F. Beck, C. M. Cain, W. D. Pugh, J. J. Hays, and Henry Marx.

Chapter 8

1. Hunter, *Steamboats*, 167–80; Charles H. Fitch, "Report on Marine Engines and Steam Vessels in the United States Merchant Service," in U.S. Department of the Interior, *Report on Power and Machinery Employed in Manufactures* (Washington, D.C.: Department of the Interior, Census Office, 1888), 43, 59–60, 82–97; Henry Hall, "Report on the Ship-Building Industry of the United States," in U.S. Congress, House of Representatives, Miscellaneous Document 42, pt. 8, 47th Cong., 2d sess., 130, 174–95.

2. Ibid., 174–95.

3. Known sidewheel steamboats were the *Alice*, *Blue Wing*, *Belle Yazoo*, *Calumet*, *Countess*, *De Smet*, *Era No. 8*, *Home*, *Hope*, *Idaho*, *Issaquena*, *Lucy Keirn*, *Marcello*, *Myrtle*, *Plain City*, *Selma*, *Sully*, and *Warren Belle*.

4. "Enrollment Certificates," *Lucy Keirn*, no number, RG 41, NA; Ledger, pp. 114–15, Downs Collection; Tippett, lost 1871, vol. 2, p. 5; the "barge" *Lucy Keirn* was included in the sale of the P. Line, see "Memorandum of Agreement," 17 July 1880, *Tobin v. Parisot*, 10414.

5. *Yazoo Valley Flag*, 12 January 1884.

6. Ibid., 22 March 1884.

7. "Enrollment Certificates," *De Smet*, no. 6744, dated 26 October 1885, RG 41, NA. The *De Smet* burned 12 June 1886 on the White River near Newport, Arkansas (Way, *Way's Packet Directory*, 125–26).

8. Way, *Way's Packet Directory*, 216; "The Late Capt. Portwood Got a Start on the Tallahatchie, A Yazoo Tributary," *Waterways Journal*, 31 December 1960, p. 9.

9. "Enrollment Certificates," *Alice*, no. 106011, RG 41, NA; *Yazoo City Herald*, 24 December 1886, 22 February 1889.

10. Way, *Way's Packet Directory*, 74, 120; "Enrollment Certificates,"

Dime, no. 6790, RG 41, NA; Hall, "Ship-Building," 230–32, describes canal boat construction; *Vicksburg Daily Times*, 18 April 1873; *Vicksburg Daily Herald*, 24 December 1868.

11. *Vicksburg Daily Herald*, 9, 21 October 1868; Way, *Way's Packet Directory*, 458.

12. "Enrollment Certificates," *Tributary*, no. 145285, RG 41, NA; *Yazoo City Herald*, 1885–86.

13. "Enrollment Certificates," *J. B. O'Brian*, no. 76049, RG 41, NA, recorded measurements of 70.8 x 15.2 x 7 feet for this iron-hull towboat; *Josephine Lovinza*, no. 105974, with measurements of 113.6 x 22.2 x 3.7 feet. Annual trips on the rivers were reported in the *Annual Report, Chief of Engineers*, 1893–98.

14. "Enrollment Certificates," *Des Arc*, no. 157312, *Maggie*, no. 92616, *Fifteen*, no. 120959, *Blanks Cornwell*, no. 3363, *Hibernia*, no. 95636, RG 41, NA.

15. One steamer measured less than 50 feet long; twelve measured 50 to 74 feet; forty-four measured 75 to 99 feet; forty-three measured 100 to 124 feet; thirty-seven measured 125 to 149 feet; seventeen measured 150 to 174 feet; three measured 175 to 200 feet; and three measured 200 feet or more.

16. "Enrollment Certificates," *Golden Era*, no. 85695, dated 16 January 1885, RG 41, NA; *Yazoo City Herald*, 2 October, 16 November 1883, 16 April 1886; a verse printed in the *Yazoo City Herald*, 23 July 1886, praised the steamer and the P. Line.

17. "Enrollment Certificates," *Lake City*, no. 140812, RG 41, NA; *Yazoo Valley Flag*, 19 January 1889; *Yazoo City Herald*, 23 November 1888.

18. "Enrollment Certificates," *Maggie*, no. 92616, RG 41, NA; round trips were compiled from *Annual Reports, Chief of Engineers*, 1895–1903.

19. "Enrollment Certificates," *L.L.B.*, no. 141096, RG 41, NA; *Annual Report, Chief of Engineers, 1896, 1897.*

20. The eleven P. Line sternwheelers longer than 150 feet were the *Cherokee, City of Yazoo, E. C. Carroll, F. Barksdale, Gus Fowler, Hallette, John M. Chambers, Phil Armour, Rees Pritchard, S. H. Parisot*, and *Yazoo Valley.*

21. The six competing boats measuring longer than 150 feet were the *Big Horn, Carrie Converse, Emma No. 2, Hard Cash, Lottawanna*, and *Seminole.*

22. The noncompany boats at the turn of the century were the *American, Elk, Henry Sheldon, Mabel Cameaux, Ruth*, and *Wash. Honshell.*

23. "Enrollment Certificates," *Yazoo Valley*, no. 27611, RG 41, NA, reporting measurements of 180 x 36 x 5.5 feet; *Louisville Courier-Journal*, 1 October 1876; undated newspaper clippings in Carroll Papers. When the *Yazoo Valley* burned on the Red River in 1887, nine years after leaving the Yazoo River, the *Yazoo City Herald*, 11 March 1887, and the *Yazoo Valley Flag*, 12 March 1887, reported the accident.

24. "Enrollment Certificates," *City of Yazoo*, no. 125759 (200 x 49 x 6.2 feet), *S. H. Parisot*, no number (225 x 40.5 x 7 feet), *Cherokee*, no. 125173 (210.2 x 38.8 x 6.6 feet), RG 41, NA; *Louisville Courier-Journal*, 27 September 1879; *New Orleans Daily Picayune*, 30 October 1882; undated newspaper clippings, Carroll Papers.

25. "Enrollment Certificates," *F. Barksdale*, no. 120600 (155 x 30.5 x 5.4 feet), RG 41, NA. She was built at Jeffersonville, Indiana, in 1884, and reached the Yazoo River in November 1884.

26. "My Favorite" were published in the *Yazoo Sentinel*, 17 March 1887; a copy may be found in Carroll Papers.

27. "Enrollment Certificates," *Hallette*, no. 95928, RG 41, NA. Way, *Way's Packet Directory*, 205–6, reported that she was built in 1887 at Jeffersonville, Indiana, for the New Orleans–Red River trade; she was first reported on the Yazoo River in 1902; *Annual Reports, Chief of Engineers*, 1902–4.

28. "Enrollment Certificates," *Sallie Carney*, no. 115460, RG 41, NA; *Yazoo City Herald*, 18 July 1884, 25 December 1885.

29. "Enrollment Certificates," *Yazonia*, no. 27662, RG 41, NA; *Annual Report, Chief of Engineers*, 1895–99.

30. "Enrollment Certificates," *Birdie Bailey*, no. 3338, RG 41, NA; *Yazoo City Herald*, 19, 26 November 1886, 28 January 1887, 28 September 1888; *Annual Report, Chief of Engineers*, 1893–97.

31. "Enrollment Certificates," *Leflore*, no. 140327, *Carrie Hogan*, no. 125619, RG 41, NA; *Yazoo City Herald*, 23 November 1877; *Yazoo Valley Flag*, 10 March 1881. Parisot named both the *Belle Yazoo* and the *Carrie Hogan* in honor of Carrie McKee Hogan, wife of Eugene M. Hogan of Satartia and daughter of John McKee of Satartia, who was a New Orleans cotton factor; see DeCell and Prichard, *Yazoo*, 364.

32. "Enrollment Certificates," *Katie Robbins*, no. 14430, RG 41, NA; *Yazoo City Herald*, 19 March 1886, 6 May, 10 June, 23 December 1887; "My Favorite," in newspaper clipping in Carroll Papers.

33. "Enrollment Certificates," *Blanks Cornwell*, no. 3363, RG 41, NA; *Yazoo City Herald*, 8 February 1889, 7 February 1896; Fishbaugh, *From Paddle Wheels to Propellers*, 203; Jessie M. Davis to Captain Donald T. Wright, 18 April 1957, Yazoo River Letter File, *Waterways Journal* Office, St. Louis, Missouri. *Annual Report, Chief of Engineers*, 1893–96; and Way, *Way's Packet Directory*, 55, report the spelling as *Cornwall*, but the Enrollment Certificates and Annie Kinkead Dent spelled her name *Cornwell*.

34. *Yazoo City Herald*, 11 July 1884; *Vicksburg Daily Times*, 11, 12 September 1868; *Yazoo City Herald*, 20, 27 August 1886, 10 June 1887.

35. *Yazoo City Herald*, 1, 22 August, 4 September, 11 July 1884.

36. Ibid., 28 June 1895, 11 November 1898, 7, 21 May 1886; *Yazoo Valley Flag*, 22 February, 15 March 1878; *Yazoo City Herald*, 25 June 1886.

37. William Stokes, "The Excursion," *Yazoo Valley Flag*, 12 January 1884.

38. *Vicksburg Daily Times*, 14 February 1868; *Yazoo City Herald*, 19 August 1898, 9 July, 8 August 1888.

39. *Vicksburg Daily Times*, 17 August 1874; *New Orleans Daily Picayune*, 29 September 1883; WPA, "Source Material for Mississippi History," Tallahatchie County, n.p.

40. WPA, "Source Materials for Mississippi History," Humphreys County n.p.; *Vicksburg Daily Times*, 15 December 1868; *Yazoo City Herald*, 25 January 1889; "Enrollment Certificates," *Electric*, no. 136414 (77.6 x 20 x 2.8 feet), RG 41, NA, and the *Annual Report, Chief of Engineers*, 1897–99, record the *Electric* as steam powered, which contradicts Captain Frederick Way's assertion that showboats were never self-propelled; see *Way's Packet Directory*, "Preface," n.p.

41. WPA, "Source Materials for Mississippi History," Humphreys County, n.p.

42. Ibid., Tallahatchie County, n.p.

43. *Vicksburg Daily Whig*, 28 March 1842; *Yazoo City Whig*, 1 March 1844.

44. *Yazoo Valley Flag*, 15 February 1878, 8 September 1881; *Yazoo City Herald*, 7 March 1890.

45. Way, *Way's Packet Directory*, 458, reported the *Trade Palace* as 154 x 29.5 x 5 feet; *Vicksburg Daily Herald*, 9 October 1868.

46. *Vicksburg Daily Times*, 5 September, 1 November 1871; the *B. H. Hunt*, measuring 80 x 20 x 4 feet, in *Vicksburg Daily Herald*, 13 April 1873; "Enrollment Certificates," *C. P. Huntington*, no number, *Ed Foster*, no. 135328 (100 x 26.5 x 4 feet), *George Baker*, no. 85468, *Arkansas City*, no. 105622, RG 41, NA; *Yazoo City Herald*, 7 October 1887; *Yazoo Valley Flag*, 2 July, 4 December 1879.

47. For the *Alpha*, see *Vicksburg Daily Times*, 3 August 1874; "Enrollment Certificates," *Beta*, no. 3033, RG 41, NA; *Yazoo Valley Flag*, 8 February 1878; for the *Gamma*, see *Yazoo City Herald*, 23 November 1888, 15 November 1889; *Annual Report, Chief of Engineers*, 1894.

48. Hall, "Ship-Building," 192–93; *Yazoo Valley Flag*, 16 August 1878, 19 February 1879, 21 October 1880, 22 February, 13 December 1878, 15 May, 8 April 1879, 19 May 1881; "Enrollment Certificates," *Granger*, no number, RG 41, NA; Way, *Way's Packet Directory*, 197, 450.

49. *Yazoo City Herald*, 31 January 1890, 10 December 1897; "Enrollment Certificates," *Rover*, no. 111021, *C. H. Woods*, no. 126923, RG 41, NA; *Annual Report, Chief of Engineers*, 1898–1901; Way, *Way's Packet Directory*, 66.

Chapter 9

1. WPA, "Source Materials for Mississippi History," Humphreys County, 2.

2. Quoted in Gary B. Mills, *Of Men and Rivers: The Story of the Vicksburg District* (Vicksburg: U.S. Army, Corps of Engineers District, 1978), 89.

3. *Yazoo City Herald*, 3 March 1888.

4. Ibid., 6 August 1886; *Yazoo Valley Flag*, 9 February 1882.

5. Undated newspaper clipping, Carroll Papers.

6. *Vicksburg Daily Times*, 14, 16 December 1871, 4 June 1873, 4 March 1875; *Yazoo City Herald*, 22 October 1886, 2 September, 21, 28 October, 23 December 1877, 4 March 1875.

7. *Vicksburg Daily Times*, 4 November 1866, 5 February 1868, 21, 25 January 1875; Way, *Way's Packet Directory*, 290.

8. *Yazoo Valley Flag*, 2 November 1882; *Yazoo City Herald*, 13 November 1885, 14 October 1887, 26 September, 5 October, 24 February, 23 November 1888.

9. *Yazoo City Herald*, 7 February 1896.

10. Ibid., 31 January, 7 February 1896; "Enrollment Certificates," *Blanks Cornwell*, no. 3363, RG 41, NA; Davis to Wright, 18 April 1957, *Waterways Journal*, Yazoo File.

11. *Yazoo Sentinel*, 5, 12 March 1903; *Yazoo City Herald*, 6 March 1903.

12. Hunter, *Steamboats*, 275–77, n. 14.

13. *Vicksburg Daily Herald*, 14 October 1868; *Yazoo Valley Flag*, 4 November 1880; *Yazoo City Herald*, 1 August 1890, 16 March 1888; "Enrollment Certificates," *R. L. Cobb*, no. 110614, RG 41, NA.

14. *Yazoo City Herald*, 22 April 1887; Lytle and Holdcamper, *Merchant Steam Vessels*, 254; Ledger, pp. 88–89, Downs Collection.

15. *Yazoo City Herald*, 24 January 1890.

16. For the *Novelty*, see *Annual Report, Chief of Engineers*, 1899; *S. H. Parisot*, see above, Chapter 5, and *New Orleans Daily Picayune*, 19 Novem-

ber 1883; the *Thomas Powell* was reported in the *Vicksburg Daily Times*, 20 October 1871; for the *C. P. Huntington*, see Tippett Papers, lost 1877, vol. 3, p. 2; "Enrollment Certificates," *Hibernia*, no. 95636, RG 41, NA, and *Yazoo City Herald*, 3 November 1899; *Silverthorn*, see *Yazoo City Herald*, 23 April 1886; the *Ella Belle* was recorded in Ledger, pp. 58–59, Downs Collection; the *Bill Nigh* was reported in the *Yazoo City Herald*, 31 January 1890; *Annual Report, Chief of Engineers*, 1899, recorded the loss of the *Yazonia*; and the *Sallie Carney* was reported in *Yazoo City Herald*, 22 December 1885, and the *Yazoo Valley Flag*, 26 December 1885.

17. Newspaper clipping, Carroll Papers.

18. "Enrollment Certificates," *F. Barksdale*, no. 120600, RG 41, NA; *Yazoo City Herald*, 4, 11 January 1888.

19. "Enrollment Certificates," *Carrie Hogan*, no. 125619, RG 41, NA; *Yazoo Valley Flag*, 10 March 1881.

20. *Yazoo Valley Flag*, 7 June 1878; *Vicksburg Daily Times*, 15 March 1875; *Yazoo City Herald*, 19 March 1886, 8 June 1888.

21. *Vicksburg Daily Times*, 20 October 1866, reported that the two boats would salvage the wrecks of the *Cairo, De Kalb, Petrel, Livingston, Van Dorn, General Polk, Edward J. Gay, Mobile, Star of the West, Thirty-Fifth Parallel, Republic, Magnolia, Magenta, J. F. Pargoud, Prince of Wales, Peytona, Natchez, Scotland, Golden Age, R. J. Lackland, John Walsh, Mary E. Keene, Acadia, Ferd Kennett, Hartford City, Cotton Plant, H. D. Mears, Argo,* and *Emma Bett.* See also *Vicksburg Daily Herald*, 16, 22 October 1868.

22. Way, "Wrecks of Thirty Packets on Yazoo May Serve in Future Scrap Drive," 9–12; Willie Morris, *North Toward Home,* (Oxford, Miss.: Yoknapatawpha Press, 1982), 3–151 passim, and Willie Morris, *Good Old Boy: A Delta Boyhood,* Oxford, Miss.: Yoknapatawpha Press, 1980), 10–11, 44, refers to the mystique of the Yazoo River, Civil War incidents along the waterway, steamboats, and boat wrecks. Leathers to Congressman Benjamin Butterworth, 4 January 1889, and copy of Senate Bill 1074, 1 June 1894, "A Bill for the Relief of T. P. Leathers," Leathers Family Papers; *Vicksburg Daily Herald*, 19 November 1868.

23. *Annual Report, Chief of Engineers*, 1878, 678; ibid., 1873, 483–84; "An Act Making Appropriations for Rivers and Harbors," *Statutes at Large*, vol. 17, chap. 416, sec. 2.

24. *Congressional Globe*, 22 February 1873, p. 1643.

25. Ibid., 1649; *Statutes at Large*, vol. 18, chap. 233, sec. 1.

26. Benyaurd to A. A. Humphrey, Chief of Engineers, 31 July 1873, Letters Received, File Box 39, Office of the Chief of Engineers, RG 77, NA.; *Annual Report, Chief of Engineers*, 1873, 485; ibid., 1874, 364–65, reported bids to remove the wrecks of the *Acadia, R. J. Lackland, Golden Age, Clyde* (an antebellum wreck), *Petrel, Van Dorn, Ivy, Polk,* and *Idaho.*

27. Report of Joseph Burney, 29 June 1874, *Annual Report, Chief of Engineers*, 1874, 365–67.

28. *Annual Report, Chief of Engineers*, 1876, 594–95; ibid., 1878, 626–29.

29. Report of W. H. H. Benyaurd, 30 June 1875, ibid., 1875, 522. The 1875 Yazoo River map was destroyed in the 1960s, but it had been microfilmed and designated as Map Y-1-1 in the microfilm collection of the Vicksburg District Office.

30. Abel C. Tuttle, *Complete Directory of the City of Vicksburg . . .* (Vicksburg: Rogers & Groome Steam Book and Job Printers, 1877), 18–24; Tuttle, *Business Directory of Vicksburg . . . 1879*, 80–92.

31. *Yazoo City Herald,* 22 April 1887.

32. *Annual Report, Chief of Engineers,* 1879, 967, 984–85.

33. Annual appropriations were compiled from ibid., 2554–55; ibid., 1921, 1155–62; ibid., 1926, 992–96. Appropriations for the waterways were as follows: Yazoo River, 1873–1926: $642,278.51; Big Sunflower River, 1879–1926: $832,890.15; Tallahatchie and Coldwater rivers, 1879–1924; $342,878.78; Tchula Lake, 1881–94: $48,969.15; Steele's Bayou, 1884–92: $24,049.81; Yalobusha River, 1881–86: $11,000; Bear Creek, 1910–13: $5,432.78, for a total expenditure on the waterways of $1,907,499.18.

34. *Annual Report, Chief of Engineers,* 1916, 25–30.

35. Mills, *Of Men and Rivers,* 89–91.

Chapter 10

1. Robert L. Brandfon, *Cotton Kingdom of the New South: A History of the Yazoo Mississippi Delta from Reconstruction to the Twentieth Century* (Cambridge, Mass.: Harvard University Press, 1967), 67.

2. John Hebron Moore, *The Emergence of the Cotton Kingdom in the Old Southwest: Mississippi, 1770–1860* (Baton Rouge: Louisiana State University Press, 1988), chaps. 1–6, provides an excellent summary of agricultural settlement patterns in Mississippi; Brandfon, *Cotton Kingdom,* 264.

3. *Yazoo Valley Flag,* 5 November 1887; *Yazoo City Herald,* 7 September 1888; *Annual Report, Chief of Engineers,* 1897–1901.

4. Brandfon, *Cotton Kingdom,* 65–90, provides a good summary of railroad expansion in the Delta.

5. The commercial statistics published in the *Annual Report of the Chief of Engineers,* 1879–1929, are summarized in Appendix D, below. The first report from the Yazoo River system was published in 1879, and the number of cotton bales was based on information provided by Captain E. C. Carroll. The Corps of Engineers began reporting cottonseed tonnage the next year, and they continued to publish statistics on these two commodities for the next eleven years. They adopted a new form in 1890, and the *Annual Reports,* 1890–1919, recorded the tons of cotton, cottonseed, hides and skins, livestock, lumber, staves, provisions, grain, and "miscellaneous" freight shipped aboard boats and their barges for each waterway in the Yazoo system. These reports also recorded the annual tonnage of logs that were rafted, towed, or barged on each stream. A new form adopted in 1920 provided more sophisticated information but limited the comparative validity of specific commodities except for cotton, cottonseed, lumber, staves, and rafted logs.

6. *Annual Report, Chief of Engineers,* 1890–1917; see Appendix D.

7. *Annual Report, Chief of Engineers,* 1890–1928.

8. Ibid.

9. Ibid.

10. Ibid.

11. Ibid., 1920–1935.

12. Compiled from the *Annual Report, Chief of Engineers,* 1892. The P. Line boats were *Addie E. Faison, Birdie Bailey, Blanks Cornwell, Hibernia, Ike Bonham, John F. Allen,* and *Lake City.*

13. Compiled from *Annual Report, Chief of Engineers,* 1890–96.

14. "Enrollment Certificates," *Ferd R.,* no. 120922, and *E. A. Pharr,* no number, RG 41, NA. The *Ferd R.* measured 70 x 16 x 2 feet in 1892, and when rebuilt she measured 93.8 x 16.2 x 3 feet. The *E. A. Pharr* was 90 x 29.9 x 4.2 feet.

15. "Enrollment Certificates," *General Miles*, no. 85567; *Fifteen*, no. 120959, measured 103 x 18 x 3 feet; *Maggie*, no. 92616, measured 85 x 19 x 3.5 feet, RG 41, NA; *Yazoo City Herald* advertisements and river news columns, 1894–96.

16. *Yazoo City Herald*, 16 July, 20 August 1897; Charter of Incorporation of the Yazoo City Transportation Company, approved September 9, 189[7], in Corporate Division, Secretary of State of Mississippi, Jackson, Mississippi.

17. *Yazoo City Herald*, 20 August 1897; Charter of Incorporation of the Greenwood Transportation Company, approved August 9, 1897, and Charter of Incorporation of the Vicksburg and Yazoo River Packet Company, approved December 22, 1897, Corporate Division, Secretary of State of Mississippi, Jackson, Mississippi. Gus Meissonnier was a director for both the Yazoo City and the Greenwood companies, while Joseph J. Powers served as a director on the Vicksburg company and as a director for the Mulholland Line on the Mississippi River trade. Captain Pugh held stock in the Yazoo City company and later in the Vicksburg company. By 1903 he also owned the Pugh Transportation Company, which ran between Vicksburg and Greenville on the Mississippi. Pugh's boats were variously with one company or the other. See *Vicksburg American* advertisements 1902–3.

18. WPA "Source Materials for Mississippi History," Humphreys County, n.d., n.p., contains the story of Steve Castleman's experience.

19. *Yazoo City Herald*, 20 May 1888; *Annual Report, Chief of Engineers*, 1900–1924.

20. *Vicksburg American*, 26 May, 7 December 1902, 6, 9 January, 11 May 1903.

21. Ibid., 5, 17 December 1902, 28 January 1903; Mills, *Of Men and Rivers*, 89–92; *Annual Report, Chief of Engineers*, 1903.

22. *Vicksburg American*, 5 December 1902; "Enrollment Certificates," *American*, no. 107729, RG 41, NA; *Annual Report, Chief of Engineers*, 1903.

23. *Vicksburg American*, 28 April, 2, 8 May 1903.

24. Compiled from *Annual Report, Chief of Engineers*, 1902–9.

25. Ibid., 1902–34.

26. Ibid., 1890, 1894, 1900, 1905.

27. Ibid., 1910, 1916, 1920, 1925, 1928.

28. Sherman H. Parisot, Will, dated 3 December 1917 and filed 15 January, Will Book C, Warren County, pp. 219–20, Warren County Courthouse, Vicksburg, Mississippi; *Vicksburg Daily Herald*, 30 December 1917.

29. From AKD, "My Favorite," *Yazoo Sentinel*, 17 March 1887.

Bibliography

Primary Sources

U.S. GOVERNMENT UNPUBLISHED DOCUMENTS

Atlanta, Georgia. National Archives. Atlanta Regional Archives Branch. *John J. Adams and Company* v. *S. H. Parisot.* Case No. 323, B 029/020 C 045, 10 February 1882, Record Group 21.
————. *Union National Bank of New Orleans, Louisiana* v. *S. H. Parisot.* Case No. 2950, B 029/02 F 092, 25 May 1883, Record Group 21.
————. United States Circuit Court, Jackson, Mississippi. U.S. Chancery Court, 1878–1910. General Court Docket Number 1, Record Group 21.
Fort Worth, Texas. National Archives. Fort Worth Regional Archives Branch. *John Tobin et al* v. *S. H. Parisot.* Case No. 10228. United States Fifth Circuit Court, Eastern District of Louisiana. General Case Files, 1836–1911, Record Group 21.
————. *John Tobin et al* v. *S. H. Parisot,* Case No. 10414. United States Fifth Circuit Court, Eastern District of Louisiana. General Case Files, 1836–1911, Record Group 21.
Washington, D. C. National Archives. "Enrollment Certificates." Bureau of Marine Inspection and Navigation. Record Group 41.
————. "New Orleans Inspection Certificates, 1854–1855." Bureau of Marine Inspection and Navigation. Record Group 41.
————. "Log of the U. S. S. *Forest Rose.*" Old Army and Navy Records. Record Group 45.
————. "Letters Received." Records of the Chief of Engineers. Record Group 77.
————. "Yazoo River Claims Papers, February 1863–April 1864." Records of the Field Offices, Mississippi, Treasury Department. Record Group 365.
————. "Papers Pertaining to Vessels of, or Involved with the Confederate States of America." War Department Collection of Confederate Records. Record Group 109 (also Microcopy M 909).

MAPS

Atlas to Accompany the Official Records of the Union and Confederate Armies. Washington, D.C.: Government Printing Office, 1891–1895.

Vicksburg, Mississippi. United States Army, Corps of Engineers. Vicksburg District Office. "Yazoo River Map, 1875." Microcopy Map Y-1-1.

————. "Sketch of Tallahatchie and Yazoo Rivers from Sharkey's Landing to Vicksburg [ca. 1879]." Microcopy Map Y-1-3.

————. "Map of Tchula Lake and Vicinity, 1882." Microcopy Map Y-1-5.

————. "Basin of the Yazoo River and Its Tributaries, 1881, 'The Willard Map.' " Microcopy Map Y-1-6.

————. "Sketch Map of the Yazoo River, Mississippi, and a Portion of the Tallahatchie River, 1924." Microcopy Map Y-1-11.

Washington, D.C. National Archives. "Map of Greenwood and Vicinity, 1863." Office of the Chief of Engineers. Cartographic Division, Record Group 77.

————. "Map of Yazoo Pass Partly from U.S. Land Survey, 1863."

————. "Map of Yazoo River Drainage Basin, n.d."

————. "Map Showing Site of Proposed Crossing of the Yazoo River, State of Mississippi, by the Georgia Pacific Railway, 1887."

U.S. GOVERNMENT PUBLISHED DOCUMENTS

U. S. Congress. Congressional Globe, 42d Cong., 2d sess., 15 April 1872, p. 2454.

————. 43d Cong., 3d sess., 22 February, 1 March 1873, pp. 1643, 2056.

————. Department of War. Annual Report of the Chief of Engineers, 1875–1938.

————. House of Representatives. Contracts for Carrying the Mails. House Executive Document 266, 48th Cong., 2d sess.

————. Offers for Carrying the Mails. House Executive Document 226. 47th Cong., 1st sess.

————. "Report on the Ship-Building Industry of the United States." Report prepared by Henry Hall. House Miscellaneous Document 42, Pt. 8. 47th Cong., 2d sess.

U.S. Department of the Interior. "Report on the Marine Engines and Steam Vessels in the United States Marine Service." Report prepared by Charles H. Fitch, in Report on Power and Machinery Employed in Manufactures. Washington, D.C. Department of the Interior, Census Office, 1888.

The War of the Rebellion: A Compilation of the Official Records of the Union and Confederate Armies. Ser. 1. 128 vols. Washington, D.C.: Government Printing Office, 1880–1901.

Official Records of the Union and Confederate Navies in the War of the Rebellion. Ser. 1, 27 vols. Washington, D.C.: Government Printing Office, 1894–1917.

Official Records of the Union and Confederate Navies in the War of the Rebellion. Ser. 2, 3 vols. Washington, D.C.: Government Printing Office, 1921–1923.

STATE AND COUNTY RECORDS

Corporate Charters

Baton Rouge, Louisiana. Office of the Secretary of State of Louisiana. Corporate Records Division. Amendment to the Charter of the Mississippi and Yazoo River Packet Company, Delta, Louisiana.

Jackson, Mississippi. Office of the Secretary of State, State of Mississippi. Corporate Records Division. Charter of Incorporation of the Greenwood Transportation Company.

_____. Charter of Incorporation of the Sunflower River Packet Company.

_____. Charter of Incorporation of the Vicksburg and Yazoo River Packet Company.

_____. Charter of Incorporation of the Yazoo and Tallahatchie Transportation Company.

_____. Charter of Incorporation of the Yazoo City Transportation Company.

_____. Charter of Incorporation of the Yazoo River Merchants and Planters Transportation Company.

Tallulah, Louisiana. Madison Parish Courthouse. Office of the Clerk of the Court. Corporate Charter of the Mississippi and Yazoo River Packet Company.

U.S. Census, Manuscript Population Schedules

Jackson, Mississippi. Mississippi Department of Archives and History. Warren County, Fifth Census, 1830; Sixth Census, 1840; Seventh Census, 1850; Eighth Census, 1860; Ninth Census, 1870; Tenth Census, 1880. Yazoo County, Fifth Census, 1830; Sixth Census, 1840; Seventh Census, 1850; Eighth Census, 1860; Ninth Census, 1870; Tenth Census, 1880.

Other Documents

_____. Mississippi Department of Archives and History. Works Progress Administration, Federal Writers Project. "Source Material for Mississippi History, Humphreys County, Mississippi." Typescript. Ca. 1936.

_____. "Source Material for Mississippi History, Tallahatchie County, Mississippi." Typescript. Ca. 1936.

_____. "Source Material for Mississippi History, Yazoo County, Mississippi." Typescript. Ca. 1936.

Mississippi. *Laws of the State of Mississippi Passed at the Regular Session of the Legislature Held at the City of Jackson, 3 January 1882–9 March 1882.* Jackson: J.L. Brown, State Printers, 1882.

Vicksburg, Mississippi. Warren County Courthouse. Office of the Clerk of the Chancery Court. Deed Records, Books PP and 54.

_____. Warren County Marriage Records.

_____. Warren County Wills, Book C.

Yazoo City, Mississippi. Yazoo County Courthouse. Office of the Clerk of the Chancery Court. Abstract of Titles, Books 10 and 11.

_____. Deed Records, Books 4, AF, AG, AI, AK, AL, AY, BC, and X.

_____. Yazoo County Marriage Records.

_____. Yazoo County Wills, Book D.

CONTEMPORARY ACCOUNTS

Brown, Isaac N. "The Confederate Gun-Boat *Arkansas.*" In Robert U. Johnson and Clarence C. Buel, eds., *Battles and Leaders of the Civil War.* 4 vols. New York: Century Company, 1887–88.

Carroll, E.C. Captain E.C. Carroll Papers. Old Court House Museum, Vicksburg, Mississippi.

Carney, Kate S. Diary of Kate S. Carney. Southern Historical Collection. University of North Carolina, Chapel Hill, North Carolina.

Christ Episcopal Church, Parish Records, Vicksburg, Mississippi.

Dent, Annie Kinkead. Scrapbook of Annie Kinkead Dent. In the possession of Mrs. Bruce Dent, Kinkead Plantation Office, Yazoo City, Mississippi.

Downs, Rees V. The Rees V. Downs Collection. Memphis Room, Memphis and Shelby County Public Library and Information Center, Memphis, Tennessee.

Fike, Claude E., ed. "Diary of James Oliver Hazard Perry Sessions of Robeka [sic.?] Plantation on the Yazoo." *Journal of Mississippi History* 39 (August 1977): 239–54.

Gift, George W. "The Story of the *Arkansas*." *Southern Historical Society Papers* 12 (January–May 1884): 48–54, 115–19, 163–70.

Grant, Ulysses S. *Personal Memoirs of U. S. Grant.* 2 vols. New York: C. L. Webster, 1885–86.

Johnson, John F. Personal Papers of John F. Johnson. In the possession of John W. Brannon, Oxford, Mississippi.

Leathers, Thomas P. The Leathers Family Papers. Department of Archives and Manuscripts, Louisiana State University Library, Baton Rouge, Louisiana.

————. Thomas P. Leathers Papers. Mississippi Department of Archives and History, Jackson, Mississippi.

Porter, David D. *Incidents and Anecdotes of the Civil War.* New York: D. Appleton and Company, 1885.

Quaife, M. M. *Absalom Grimes: Confederate Mail Runner.* New Haven: Yale University Press, 1926.

Read, Charles W. "Reminiscences of the Confederate States Navy." *Southern Historical Society Papers* 1 (May 1876): 331–62.

Sherman, William T. *Memoirs of General William T. Sherman.* 2 vols. New York: D. Appleton and Company, 1875.

Tippett, William H. The William H. Tippett Collection. 3 vols.; mimeographed. Memphis Room, Memphis and Shelby County Public Library and Information Center, Memphis, Tennessee.

Tunnard, W. H. *A Southern Record: The History of the Third Regiment of Louisiana Infantry.* Baton Rouge, 1866; Facsimilie ed. with Preface and Notes by Edwin C. Bearss, Dayton, Ohio: Morningside Bookshop, 1970.

Tuttle, Abel C. *Business Directory of Vicksburg, Jackson, Meridian . . . . Landings, Distances, Etc. Yazoo and Tallahatchie Rivers, Tchula Lake . . . .* Vicksburg: Rogers & Groome Book and Job Printers, 1879.

Tuttle, A[bel] C. *Complete Directory of the City of Vicksburg. . . .* Vicksburg: Rogers & Groome Steam Book and Job Printers, 1877.

Twain, Mark. *Life on the Mississippi.* New York: Heritage Press, 1944.

Wilson, J. B. *Handbook of Yazoo County, Mississippi.* N.p., 1884.

Waterways Journal. Yazoo River Letter File. *Waterways Journal* Office, St. Louis, Missouri.

Wooldridge, F. L. The F. L. Wooldridge Collection. Memphis Room, The Memphis and Shelby County Public Library and Information Center, Memphis, Tennessee.

NEWSPAPERS

Ariel (Natchez, Mississippi)
Courier de la Louisiana (New Orleans)
Greenwood (Mississippi) *Oriental*
Greenwood (Mississippi) *Reporter*
Louisville (Kentucky) *Courier-Journal*
Natchez (Mississippi)
New Orleans Daily Picayne
New Orleans Times-Democrat
St. Louis Post-Dispatch
St. Louis Times
Vicksburg American
Vicksburg Daily Herald
Vicksburg Daily Register
Vicksburg Daily Times
Vicksburg Daily Times and Republican
Vicksburg Evening Post
Vicksburg Herald
Vicksburg Register
Vicksburg Sentinel
Vicksburg Tri-Weekly Sentinel
Vicksburg Tri-Weekly Whig
Vicksburg Weekly Whig
Vicksburg Whig
Yazoo Banner (Yazoo City, Mississippi)
Yazoo City Daily Herald
Yazoo City Herald
Yazoo City Herald-Democrat
Yazoo City Whig
Yazoo Democrat
Yazoo Sentinel (Vicksburg, Mississippi)
Yazoo Valley Flag (Greenwood, Mississippi)

Secondary Sources

Bearss, Edwin C. *Decision in Mississippi.* Jackson: Mississippi Commission on the War Between the States, 1962.

Bettersworth, John K., ed. *Mississippi in the Confederacy: As They Saw It.* Baton Rouge: Louisiana State University Press, 1961.

Brandfon, Robert L. *Cotton Kingdom of the New South: A History of the Yazoo Mississippi Delta From Reconstruction to the Twentieth Century.* Cambridge, Mass.: Harvard University Press, 1967.

Carmer, Carl. *Stars Fell on Alabama.* American Century Series. New York: Hill and Wang, 1961.

Coulter, E. Merton.*The Confederate States of America, 1861–1865.* Baton Rouge: Louisiana State University Press, 1950.

Curry, Jane. *The River's in My Blood: Riverboat Pilots Tell Their Story.* Lincoln: University of Nebraska Press, 1983.

DeCell, Harriet. "The Yazoo River." In Richard A. Bartlett, ed., *Rolling Rivers: An Encyclopedia of America's Rivers.* New York: McGraw-Hill, 1984.

DeCell, Harriet, and JoAnne Prichard. *Yazoo: Its Legends and Legacies.* Yazoo City, Miss.: Yazoo Delta Press, 1976.

DeRosier, Arthur H., Jr. *The Removal of the Choctaw Indians.* New York: Harper Torchbooks, 1972.

Fishbaugh, Charles Preston. *From Paddle Wheels to Propellers.* Indianapolis: Indiana Historical Society, 1970.

Foote, Shelby. *The Civil War: A Narrative.* 3 vols. New York: Random House, 1958–74.

Getchell, Charles M., Jr. "Defender of Inland Waters: The Military Career of Isaac Newton Brown, Commander, Confederate States Navy, 1861–1865." Master of Arts Thesis. University of Mississippi, 1978.

Gosnell, H. Allen. *Guns on the Western Waters: The Story of River Gunboats in the Civil War.* Baton Rouge: Louisiana State University Press, 1949.

Hunter, Louis C. *Steamboats on the Western Rivers: An Economic and Cultural History.* Cambridge, Mass.: Harvard University Press, 1949.

Klingberg, Frank W. *The Southern Claims Commission.* Berkeley: University of California Press, 1955.

"The Late Captain Portwood Got a Start on the Tallahatchie, A Yazoo Tributary." *Waterways Journal.* 31 December 1960: 1.

Lytle, William M., and Forrest R. Holdcamper. *Merchant Steam Vessels of the United States, 1807–1868,* "The Lytle List." Mystic, Conn.: Steamship Historical Society of America, Publication 6, 1952.

Mills, Gary B. *Of Men and Rivers: The Story of the Vicksburg District.* Vicksburg: U.S. Army, Corps of Engineers District, 1978.

Moore, John Hebron. *Agriculture in Antebellum Mississippi.* New York: Bookman Associates, 1958.

———. *Andrew Brown and Cypress Lumbering in the Old Southwest.* Baton Rouge: Louisiana State University Press, 1967.

———. *The Emergence of the Cotton Kingdom in the Old Southwest: Mississippi, 1770–1860.* Baton Rouge: Louisiana State University Press, 1988.

Morris, Willie. *Good Old Boy: A Delta Boyhood.* Oxford, Miss.: Yoknapatawpha Press, Inc., 1980.

———. *North Toward Home.* Oxford, Mississippi. Yoknapatawpha Press, Inc., 1982.

Owens, Harry P. "An Assessment of Historic Period Cultural Resources along the Yazoo River between River Miles 75.6 and 273.0 Including Tchula Lake and Honey Island, Mississippi." University, Miss.: Center for Archaeological Research, University of Mississippi, 1979.

———. "Steamboat Landings on the Yazoo and Tallahatchie Rivers, (1875–1882)." *Journal of Mississippi History* 47 (November 1985): 266–283.

Potter, David M. *The South in the Sectional Conflict.* Baton Rouge: Louisiana State University Press, 1968.

Powell, Lawrence N., and Michael S. Wayne. "Self-Interest and the Decline of Confederate Nationalism." in Owens, Harry P., and James J. Cooke, eds. *The Old South in the Crucible of War.* Jackson: University Press of Mississippi, 1983.

Roark, James L. *Masters without Slaves: Southern Planters in the Civil War and Reconstruction.* New York: Norton, 1977.

Scharf, J. Thomas. *History of the Confederate States Navy from Its Organization to the Surrender of its Last Vessel.* New York: Rogers & Sherwood, 1887.

Smith, Frank E. *The Yazoo River.* New York: Rinehart & Company, 1954.
Still, William N. *Iron Afloat: The Story of the Confederate Ironclads.* Nashville: Vanderbilt University Press, 1971.
Way, Frederick, Jr. *Way's Packet Directory, 1848–1893.* Athens, Ohio: Ohio University Press, 1983.
——————. "Wrecks of Thirty Packets on the Yazoo May Serve in Future Scrap Drives." *Waterways Journal,* 28 December 1963, pp. 9–12.
Wynn, Jack T. "Cultural Resources Survey of Rocky Bayou Project, Yazoo County, Mississippi, Conducted for Vicksburg District, Corps of Engineers." Starkville, Miss.: Archaeological Research, 1980.

Index

Acadia (sidewheel steamboat), 42, 57, 59, 61, 62, 65, 66, 216 n. 35, 218 n. 39, 219 n. 51, 232 n. 21, 232 n. 26

Addie E. Faison (sternwheel steamboat), 109, 113, 134–35, 233 n. 12

Aden, Lula, 166

Admiral Schley (steam propeller boat), 163

Afton (sidewheel steamboat), 24, 34–35, 211 n. 4

Afton, Jr. (sidewheel steamboat), 33

Albert Gallatin (sidewheel steamboat), 18

Alcorn, James Lusk, 139, 219 n. 3

Alert (sternwheel steamboat), 78, 79, 94, 109, 118, 124

Alex Scott (steamboat), 22

Alice (sidewheel steamboat), 94, 109, 117, 228 n. 3

Alice Maria (sidewheel steamboat), 33

Alonzo Child (sidewheel steamboat), 42, 50, 51, 52, 63, 67

Alpha (sternwheel steamboat), 128

American (sternwheel steamboat), 161, 162, 229 n. 22

Amy (gasoline boat), 163

Andrews, F. M., 109, 113, 158, 159–60, 228 n. 50

Anna (sidewheel steamboat), 35

Argo (sternwheel steamboat), 24, 32, 36, 42, 46, 64, 215 n. 20, 218 n. 39, 218 n. 40, 232 n. 21

Argosey (steamboat), 214 n. 6, 218 n. 40

Arkansas (steam propeller boat), 43, 44, 45, 47, 48, 49, 52, 57

Arkansas City (steam propeller boat), 128

Arkansas River, 16, 21, 23, 38, 39

Articles of Agreement (1877), 77–78, 79, 81–82, 91, 93, 97

Ashland City (sternwheel steamboat), 123, 161

Atalanta (sternwheel steamboat), 29

Auter, John, 109

B. H. Hurt (trading boat), 128

Badger State (sidewheel steamboat), 21

Barksdale, Fountain, 25, 109

Barksdale, Josephine Parisot, 25

Baron de Kalb (Union ironclad boat), 63, 65, 66

Battle of Champions' Hill (1863), 49

Battle of Memphis (1862), 39, 44

Bear Creek, 79, 233 n. 33

Beck, Frank, Jr., 74, 77, 82, 84, 89, 90, 92, 224 n. 31

Beck, R. F., 228 n. 50

Bell, John, 80

Belle (circus boat), 126

Belle of Ouachita (sidewheel steamboat), 29

Belle Yazoo (sidewheel steamboat), 74, 116, 132, 220 n. 15, 228 n. 3, 230 n. 31

Belmont (sidewheel steamboat), 23

Belzoni, Miss., 7, 17, 26, 58, 94, 110, 112, 122, 124, 126, 149, 150, 159, 160, 161, 164

Ben Lee (sternwheel steamboat), 31, 212 n. 32

Ben McCulloch (sternwheel steamboat), 38, 42, 47, 54, 64, 65, 218 n. 39, 219 n. 59
Benedict, Joseph, 67
Benedict, W. S., 91
Bennett, Caleb P., 12, 22
Bently, Jacob, 22
Benyaurd, William Henry Harrison, 139, 140, 141
Beta (sternwheel steamboat), 109, 123–24, 128, 132, 133
Big Black (sidewheel steamboat), 18
Big Black River, 49, 52
Big Horn (sternwheel steamboat), 73, 229 n. 21
Big Sunflower (sternwheel steamboat), 74, 78, 125
Big Sunflower River, 5, 11, 17, 26, 46, 48, 69, 74, 103, 107, 119, 121, 141, 142, 148, 233 n. 33
Bill Nigh (sternwheel sawmill steamboat), 129, 136
Birdie Bailey (sternwheel steamboat), 109, 111, 122, 132, 134–35, 136, 149, 228 n. 49, 233 n. 12
Bixby, Horace E., 162
Black Bayou, 59, 212 n. 21
Blackburn, Joseph, 69
Blanks Cornwell (sternwheel steamboat), 111, 123, 124, 133–34, 149, 228 n. 49, 233 n. 12
Blue Wing (sidewheel steamboat), 72, 116, 228 n. 3
Bluella (sternwheel steamboat), 75, 118
Bluff City (sidewheel steamboat), 34, 213 n. 38
Bocaletti, Charley, 80, 85–86, 127, 128, 136
Bogue Phalia, 5, 42, 54, 59, 60, 61, 62, 148
Booker, Charley, 127
Bookout, Benjamin, 140
Bookout, George W., 75, 109, 125, 133, 140
Bowman, Robert, 72
Brandywine (sidewheel steamboat), 7
Bride (sidewheel steamboat), 21
Brooks, John, 55, 219 n. 56
Brown, George W., 63

Brown, Isaac N., 45, 47, 48, 53, 56, 57, 58, 60, 61, 62–63, 64–65, 67, 216 n. 13
Brown, J. C., 11, 23, 27, 29, 34
Bruinsburg, Miss., 4, 62
Buchanan, Captain, 138
Bunker Hill (sidewheel steamboat), 18
Burney, Joseph, 139–40
Butler, E. S., 35

C. H. Woods (sternwheel steamboat), 129
C. P. Huntington (sternwheel steamboat), 80, 85, 127, 128, 136
Cain, C. M., 228 n. 50
Cairo (Union ironclad boat), 51, 53, 66, 232 n. 21
Caldwell, J. V., 32
Calumet (sidewheel steamboat), 72, 73–74, 102, 116, 123, 127, 138, 228 n. 3
Campbell, Leonidas A., 81, 82, 84, 91, 103, 106, 222 n. 1
Campbell, W. A., 106
Campbell, William, 91
Campbellsville Landing, 107, 112, 150, 160, 161
Cannon, John W., 35, 70, 71, 76, 77, 78, 82, 90, 91, 120
Capitol (sidewheel steamboat), 39, 47, 49, 51, 52, 67, 140
Carondolet (Union ironclad boat), 48
Carras, George W., 21, 26
Carrie Converse (sternwheel steamboat), 229 n. 21
Carrie Hogan (sternwheel steamboat), 78, 82, 122, 137, 230 n. 31
Carrie Williams (steam propeller boat), 117
Carroll, Charles C., Jr., 84, 222 n. 2, 224 n. 31
Carroll, Ed C., 78, 80, 82, 84–85, 86, 87–88, 89, 91, 92, 93, 97, 101, 102, 111, 112, 113, 122, 125, 133, 161, 222 n. 2, 224 n. 31, 225 n. 45, 228 n. 45, 228 n. 50, 233 n. 5
Carroll, Ellen Wilson, 102
Carter, Ed C., 46–47, 56–57, 67, 219 n. 56

Castleman, Steve, 160
Chalmers, James R., 65
Champion, R. E., 72
Charles H. Tompkins (sternwheel steamboat), 86, 223 n. 10
Charles Rebstock (sternwheel steamboat), 94, 124
Charm (sidewheel steamboat), 36, 37, 49, 52, 215 n. 29
Cherokee (sternwheel steamboat), 96, 97, 103, 119, 120, 229 n. 20
Chickasaw Bayou, 34, 44, 51, 53
Chickasaw Indians, 7
Choctaw Indians, 3, 7
Choctaw Line, 95, 98
Cincinnati, Ohio, 10, 11, 14, 18, 27, 43, 79, 139
City of Greenwood (sternwheel steamboat), 150
City of Yazoo (sternwheel steamboat), 78–79, 81, 82, 89, 93, 94, 95, 97, 119, 120, 229 n. 20
Civil District Court of Orleans Parish, 91
Civil War and steamboats, 29, 35, 36, 37, 38–39, 42–68, 69; Confederate Yazoo Fleet, 38, 39, 42, 44, 51–52, 66–67, 69; Confederate River Defense Fleet, 43–45
Clara S. (sternwheel steamboat), 95, 224 n. 37
Clarksdale, Miss., 141, 148, 149
Cleopatra (sidewheel steamboat), 7
Cleveland, Grover, 43
Clyde (steamboat), 232 n. 26
Coldwater River, 5, 7, 18, 55, 141, 142, 150, 155, 233 n. 33
Col. T. H. Judson (sidewheel steamboat), 21, 35
Columbus, Ohio, 72
Compromise (sidewheel steamboat), 22
Confederate Navy Yard, 45, 62, 63, 65
Corkery, William F., 57, 65, 219 n. 56
Cotton Plant (sidewheel steamboat), 32, 36
Cotton Plant (sidewheel steamboat, formerly *Flora Temple*), 42, 46, 54, 56, 218 n. 39, 219 n. 51, 232 n. 21

Cotton Plant (59-ton sidewheel steamboat), 32, 36, 42, 46, 64
Countess (sidewheel steamboat), 73, 74, 116, 228 n. 3
Craig, Emily Barksdale, 101
Craig, James, 110
Craig, Lizzie Barksdale, 101
Craig, Robert, 101
Craig, Thomas, 101
Craig, W. A., 110
Craig, Willie C., 160
Creole (sidewheel steamboat), 23, 30
Crown Point (sternwheel steamboat), 109
Crump, Richard P., 21–22
Culver, W. B., 3

D. O. Fogel (steamboat), 112
D. S. Stacy (sidewheel steamboat), 21
Dart (steam propeller boat), 75, 117
David Stinson (sternwheel steamboat), 80, 82
Davis, Charles, 38, 39
Davis, Jefferson, 43
De Haven, David, 42, 50, 63
De Kalb (steamboat), 232 n. 21
De Smet (sidewheel steamboat), 78, 82, 85, 88, 92, 93, 94, 95, 97, 99, 116–17, 119, 124–25, 127, 132, 134, 149, 228 n. 3, 228 n. 7
Deer Creek, 5, 11, 17, 36, 54, 55, 59, 60, 73, 75, 117, 118, 137, 150
Deer Creek (sternwheel steamboat), 78, 82, 94, 118, 127
Deer Creek Slackwater Navigation Company, 72
Delia No. 2 (steamboat), 133
Delta, La., 84, 111
Dent, Annie Kinkead, 102, 106, 120, 123, 133–34, 136, 166
Dent, Charles, 101, 102
Dent, Frank, 101
Dent, James K., 101, 102, 106, 117, 120, 133, 134
Dent, John, 102
Dent, John L., 25, 29, 35, 74, 101, 102, 165
Dent, Joseph, 101, 102
Dent, Mary A., 25, 102
Dent, Milton P., 23, 25, 27, 28,

29–30, 35, 46, 49, 71, 73, 74, 77, 101, 102, 116, 118, 165, 220 n. 17
Des Arc (sternwheel steamboat), 118
Dew Drop (sidewheel steamboat), 14–15, 27–30, 31, 32, 35, 37, 42, 46, 54, 60, 61, 62, 64, 67, 71, 82, 215 n. 29, 218 n. 39, 218 n. 40
Dime (steam propeller boat), 117
Dixie (sidewheel steamboat), 29–30, 35, 42, 46, 49, 52, 71, 215 n. 29
Dolphin (gasoline boat), 163
Dove (sternwheel steamboat), 11, 15
Dye, Andrew Jackson, 65, 66

E. A. Pharr (sternwheel steamboat), 159, 233 n. 14
E. C. Carroll, Jr. (sternwheel steamboat), 78, 82, 86, 94, 134, 229 n. 20
Eads, James B., 138
Economist (sternwheel steamboat), 71, 75
Ed Foster (sternwheel steamboat), 128
Ed Richardson (steamboat), 85, 94
Eddie (sternwheel steamboat), 72, 118
Edward J. Gay (sidewheel steamboat), 43, 55, 218 n. 39, 219 n. 51, 219 n. 56, 219 n. 58, 232 n. 21
Electric (sternwheel steam showboat), 126, 230 n. 40
Elk (sternwheel steamboat), 162, 229 n. 22
Ella Belle (sternwheel steamboat), 136
Ellet, Alfred W., 39, 45, 47–48
Emma (sternwheel steamboat), 75, 221 n. 19
Emma No. 2 (sternwheel steamboat), 229 n. 21
Emma Bett (sternwheel steamboat), 36, 42, 46, 54, 59, 61–62, 64, 218 n. 39, 232 n. 21
Enterprise (sidewheel steamboat), 18, 30
Era No. 8 (sidewheel steamboat), 73, 116, 228 n. 3
Era No. 10 (sternwheel steamboat), 95, 224 n. 37
Erin (sidewheel steamboat), 18

Eva Alma (sternwheel steam towboat), 129

F. Barksdale (sternwheel steamboat), 106, 109, 111, 112, 120, 136–37, 212 n. 21, 229 n. 20, 229 n. 25
Fair Play (sidewheel steamboat), 24, 36, 46, 47, 49, 52, 67, 215 n. 20
Fairfield (steam propeller boat), 117
Fairplay (sternwheel steamboat), 78
Faison, G. W., 109
Farmers' Union, 86, 223 n. 12
Farragut, David G., 38, 39, 42, 44
Favorite (steam propeller boat), 73, 117
Federal Writers Project, Works Progress Administration, 4
Ferd Kennett (sidewheel steamboat), 42–43, 55, 57, 218 n. 39, 219 n. 51, 219 n. 58, 232 n. 21
Ferd R. (sternwheel steamboat), 159, 233 n. 14
Ferguson, Samuel W., 59
Fetherston, Winfield S., 59
Fifteen (sternwheel steamboat), 118, 159, 161
First National Bank, Lexington, Ky., 104, 105, 106, 107
Fish Lake, 102–03, 124
Floweree, C. C., 82, 84, 97, 101, 102, 222 n. 1, 224 n. 31
Floweree, Jennie Wilson, 102
Foote, Shelby, 39
Forest Rose (sternwheel steam gunboat), 63, 64
Fort Adams (steamboat), 4, 25
Fort Pemberton, 55–56, 58, 60, 61, 216 n. 8
Foster, Stephen, 22
Frank Beck, Jr. (sternwheel steamboat), 74, 75, 137, 220 n. 17
Frank Pargoud (steamboat), 71, 74, 76, 77
Franklin Pierce (steamboat), 34
Freedman's Bureau Landing, 9, 134
Freestone (sternwheel steamboat), 66, 69, 70

Gamma (sternwheel steamboat), 128, 158
Garvin's Ferry, 62, 141

General Clark (steamboat), 47, 48,
  214 n. 6
General Earl Van Dorn
  (Confederate sidewheel steam
  gunboat), 39, 44, 45, 47, 48, 70
General Miles (sternwheel
  steamboat), 158, 159
General Polk (sidewheel
  steamboat), 43, 44, 45, 47, 48, 232
  n. 21, 232 n. 26
General Quitman (steamboat), 70
General R. H. Stokes (sidewheel
  steamboat), 11, 12, 23, 211 n. 4
George, W. C., 159
George Baker (sternwheel
  steamboat), 128
Georgia Pacific, 149
Gladiator (sidewheel steamboat), 33
Glendora, Miss., 121, 136
Glendy Burke (sidewheel
  steamboat), 22
Golden Age (sidewheel steamboat),
  61, 63, 67, 232 n. 21, 232 n. 26
Golden Era (sternwheel steamboat),
  94, 108, 111, 119, 127, 133
Gorgas, Josiah, 70
Granger (sawmill sternwheel
  steamboat), 129
Grant, U. S., 51, 53, 59, 62, 68, 139
Green, Duff, 84–85
Green Sharkey's Gate. *See*
  Sharkey's Landing
Greenville, Miss., 16, 61, 69, 148
Greenwood, Miss., 5, 8, 11, 14, 17,
  18, 21, 27, 28, 30, 33, 34, 42, 44,
  45, 47, 49, 54, 55, 56, 60, 63, 64,
  65, 66, 73, 75, 76, 81, 82, 85, 86,
  87, 93, 94, 97, 98, 108, 110, 117,
  119, 121, 123, 126, 129, 136, 137,
  148, 149, 150, 158, 159, 162, 164,
  212 n. 21, 219 n. 51
Greenwood Transportation
  Company, 159, 160, 161, 234 n. 17
Grenada (sidewheel steamboat),
  21–22, 34
Grenada, Miss., 5, 17, 18, 23, 34, 51,
  54, 65, 147
Gus Fowler (sternwheel steamboat),
  229 n. 20
Gwartney, Michael, 21

H. D. Mears (sidewheel steamboat),
  62, 64, 218 n. 34, 218 n. 39, 232 n.
  21
Hale, Ira, 128
Hall, Henry, "Report on the Ship-
  Building Industry of the United
  States," 129
Hallette (sternwheel steamboat),
  121, 162, 229 n. 20, 230 n. 27
Hannibal (sidewheel steamboat), 18
Hannan's Bluff, Miss., 3. *See also*
  Yazoo City, Miss.
Hard Cash (sternwheel steamboat),
  95, 97, 119, 224 n. 37, 229 n. 21
Hard Times (sidewheel steamboat),
  23
Harry, Milt R., 117
Harry Bluff (sidewheel steamboat),
  18
Hartford City (sidewheel
  steamboat), 42, 47, 50, 218 n. 39,
  219 n. 51, 232 n. 21
Hatchie Eagle (sidewheel
  steamboat), 31
Haynes' Bluff, 26, 49, 50, 51, 53, 54,
  55, 59, 60, 62, 63
Hays, J. J., 228 n. 50
Headlight (sternwheel steamboat),
  88, 92, 109
Hearvason, Captain, 65
Helen McGregor (steamboat), 4
Helen Meade (sternwheel steam
  towboat), 111, 135
Hendricks, Joseph M., 34
Henry Sheldon (sternwheel
  steamboat), 229 n. 22
Herron, Francis J., 65
Hester (gasoline boat), 163
Hibernia (sternwheel steamboat),
  118, 136, 161, 233 n. 12
Hiern, Mary, 35
Hill, Robert, 105
Holly Springs, Miss., 51, 147
Holmes, Richard, 67
Home (sidewheel steamboat), 23,
  36, 78, 79, 82, 117, 211 n. 4, 212 n.
  21, 228 n. 3
Honey Island, 5, 63, 80, 132
Hope (sidewheel steamboat), 36, 37,
  50, 54, 61, 64, 71, 72, 73, 74, 78,
  95, 116, 215 n. 29, 218 n. 39, 218
  n. 46, 219 n. 51, 228 n. 3
Howard, James, 26

Howard, John C., 89
Howard Ship Yards, 42, 76, 79, 89, 119, 123, 127
Howell, W. M., 126
Hunter, Carrie, 72
Hunter, G. M., 72
Huntington, Collis P., 148

Idaho (sidewheel steamboat), 69, 70, 135, 138, 228 n. 3, 232 n. 21
Ike Bonham (sternwheel steamboat), 109, 110, 111, 112, 137, 228 n. 49, 233 n. 12
Illinois Central Railroad, 147–48, 149
Ingersol, W. K., 224 n. 31
Irving, George S., 105–06, 107, 112, 161
Issaquena (sidewheel steamboat), 124, 228 n. 3
Ivy (sidewheel steamboat), 43, 44, 62, 218 n. 38, 232 n. 26

J. B. O'Brian (steam propeller boat), 118
J. F. Pargoud (sidewheel steamboat), 56, 62, 65, 70, 216 n. 8, 218 n. 39, 219 n. 51, 219 n. 58, 232 n. 21
J. M. Sharp (sidewheel steamboat), 24, 31, 36, 42, 46, 59, 64, 65–66, 218 n. 39, 218 n. 40
J. M. White (steamboat), 71, 85, 92, 94
Jackson, Andrew, 7
Jackson, Miss., 28, 147, 148
James Jacobs (sidewheel steamboat), 34
Jeff Davis (sidewheel steamboat), 23, 29, 34
Jeffersonville, Ind., 26, 42, 76, 89, 122
Joan of Arc (sidewheel steamboat), 29
Joe (steam propeller boat), 158
John F. Allen (sternwheel steamboat), 112, 228 n. 49, 233 n. 12
John M. Chambers (sternwheel steamboat), 78, 229 n. 20
John Strader (sidewheel steamboat), 23, 211 n. 4

John Walsh (sidewheel steamboat), 42, 56, 63, 67, 216 n. 8, 232 n. 21
John Wesley (sidewheel steamboat), 24, 26
Johnson, Frank, 36
Johnson, Marcy, 109
Johnston, John, 73
Johnston, Joseph E., 64, 65
Jones, R. T., 65
Josephine Lovinza (steam propeller boat), 118
Josephine Spengler (sternwheel steamboat), 86, 134
Josie D. Harkins (sternwheel steamboat), 109, 113, 135
Julia (sidewheel steamboat), 20–21

Kate (steam propeller boat), 72
Kate Dixon (sternwheel steamboat), 79
Katie Robbins (sternwheel steamboat), 109, 111, 112, 113, 122–23, 124, 127, 133, 135–36, 228 n. 49
Kentucky (steamboat), 32
Kenwood (sidewheel steam gunboat), 65
Keoto (sternwheel steamboat), 72, 118
King, Henry, 75
King, John, 75
Kinkead, Mary Ann, 103, 105, 106, 125, 162
Kinkead, Richard, 81, 88, 96, 102, 103, 120
Kinman, R., 31
Klein, C. M., 224 n. 31
Kuroki (gasoline boat), 163

L. L. B. (sternwheel steamboat), 119
Lacon (sidewheel steamboat), 23
Lafourche (steamboat), 37
Lake Centennial, 100, 142, 161, 162
Lake City (sternwheel steamboat), 109–10, 111, 112, 118, 128, 130, 133, 228 n. 49, 233 n. 12
Lake Dick, 94, 125
Lake George, 42, 45, 48, 64
Lake Washington (sidewheel steamboat), 111
Lamkin, David, 101
Lamkin, Martha, 101

Lancaster (sidewheel steamboat), 47–48

Landrum, Harry, 67

Laurel (sidewheel steamboat), 23

Lawrence (steamboat), 4

Leathers, Bowling S., 79

Leathers, Thomas P., 12, 43, 57, 58, 67, 70, 71, 76, 77, 78, 79, 82, 90, 91–92, 93, 94, 95, 96, 97, 98, 103, 104, 108, 117, 119, 120, 124, 138, 140, 142, 152, 216 n. 13, 219 n. 5, 225 n. 45

Leathers, Mrs. Thomas P., 76

Ledbetter, Ellison, 28

Ledbetter, Thomas G., 24, 31, 71, 82, 85, 92, 141, 213 n. 38, 214 n. 4

Lee, Stephen D., 60, 61

Leflore (sternwheel steamboat), 78, 82, 87, 94, 122, 133

Levie, I. R., 125

Lewis Whitman (sidewheel steamboat), 22, 24, 26, 101, 211 n. 4

Liddell, J. M., Jr., 86–87, 92, 93, 98, 105

Lincoln, Abraham, 43

Linden (sternwheel steamboat), 63, 64

Lioness (Union boat), 48

Little P. (sternwheel steamboat), 78

Little Sunflower River, 5, 26, 34, 46

Little Tallahatchie River, 5, 23, 53, 54

Liverpool Landing, 33, 45, 47, 48, 49, 51, 52, 57, 62, 63

Livingston (sidewheel steamboat), 43–44, 45, 47, 48, 232 n. 21

Lizzie (sternwheel steamboat), 133

Loring, William W., 54, 55–56, 58, 59–60, 61

Lottawanna (sternwheel steamboat), 75, 132, 229 n. 21

Louisville, Ky., 10, 12, 20–21, 27, 50, 67, 74, 76, 89, 116, 120

Louisville Courier-Journal, 79, 81

Louisville, New Orleans and Texas Railroad, 148–49

Lucy Keirn (sidewheel steamboat), 74, 76, 82, 116, 212 n. 21, 220 n. 16, 228 n. 3

Lucy Long (sternwheel steamboat), 30

Lumberman (sternwheel sawmill steamboat), 129

Lynch, William F., 45, 49, 51

Mabel Cameaux (sternwheel steamboat), 229 n. 22

McCullogh, Joe, 162

McElroy, Ed, 135

McElroy, Thomas, 66

McKee, George C., 138, 139

McKown, J. D., 138

McVay, A., 89, 90

Magenta (sidewheel steamboat), 43, 57, 58, 61, 62, 65, 67, 218 n. 39, 219 n. 51, 219 n. 58, 232 n. 21

Maggie (sternwheel steamboat), 118, 134, 150, 159, 161

Magnolia (sidewheel steamboat), 43, 46, 57, 58, 61, 65, 218 n. 39, 219 n. 51, 219 n. 58, 232 n. 21

Maid of Osage (sidewheel steamboat), 30

Major Aubrey (sidewheel steamboat), 21

Mammoth Cave (sidewheel steamboat), 22, 31, 34

Manchester, Miss., 3, 7, 16, 25, 33. *See also* Yazoo City, Miss.

Mann, Charles, 128

Marcello (sidewheel steamboat), 228 n. 3

Marine Railway Company, 27

Marmora (sternwheel steamboat), 66

Martin Walt (steamboat), 71

Marx, Henry, 228 n. 50

Mary E. Keene (sidewheel steamboat), 37, 43, 46, 57, 58, 61, 62, 65, 218 n. 39, 219 n. 56, 219 n. 58, 232 n. 21

Mary T. (steam propeller boat), 32, 37

Mattingly, J. B., 228 n. 50

May (gasoline boat), 163

Mayer, D., 228 n. 50

Mayer, Oscar E., 228 n. 50

Meissonnier, Gus, 159, 160, 234 n. 17

Memorandum of Agreement (1880 sale of P. Line), 82, 83, 222 n. 42

Memphis, Tenn., 12, 14, 16, 21, 22,

31, 37, 38, 39, 42, 43, 45, 57, 117, 147, 148

Memphis and Vicksburg Line, 148

Merchants and Planters Packet Company, 162

Metzler, Christine, 72, 165

Metzler, Thomas, 71, 72, 73, 74, 75, 77, 116, 118, 134, 165, 220 n. 17

Mike Davis (sternwheel steamboat), 79–80

Milliken, Lewis, 65

Milliken's Bend, Miss., 21, 46, 49, 52

Mississippi & Yazoo River Packet Company. *See* P. Line

Mississippi and Yazoo River Packet Company (1880), 84, 111, 224 n. 43. *See also* Yazoo and Tallahatchie Transportation Company

Mississippi Central Railroad, 147

Mississippi Delta, 5

Mississippi River, 5, 10, 11, 12, 13, 14, 15, 16, 18–19, 21, 29, 30, 31, 32, 38, 39, 43, 45, 46, 48, 49, 55, 58, 61, 62, 64, 69, 73, 76, 81–82, 87, 90, 91, 93, 95, 96, 98, 100, 103, 114, 115, 136, 137, 141, 142, 148, 158, 161, 162, 163, 164, 165, 212 n. 21, 234 n. 17; steamboat "trades" on, 16, 17

Mississippi Valley and Ship Island Railroad, 148

Missouri (sidewheel steamboat), 3, 4

Missouri River, 42, 85

Mobile, Ala., 21, 22, 24, 35, 127, 212 n. 32

Mobile (sidewheel steamboat), 44, 47, 49, 57, 63, 232 n. 21

Monarch (sidewheel steam ramboat), 47–48

Montgomery, Ed, 43, 70

Montgomery, James E., 39

Moon Lake, 5, 55

Moore, William, 23, 36

"Mosquito fleet," 17–19, 20

Mountain Girl (sternwheel steamboat), 112, 228 n. 49

Mulholland, Charles D., 111

Mulholland Line, 234 n. 17

Murray, Thomas, 101

Muscle No. 2 (sidewheel steamboat), 34

Myrtle (sidewheel steamboat), 73, 125, 133, 134, 228 n. 3

Naomi (sternwheel steamboat), 72, 118

Natchez, "Under the Hill," Miss., 3

Natchez, Miss., 16, 30, 120, 136, 158

Natchez (steamboats with same name), 12, 37, 38, 43, 57, 58, 70, 71, 76, 77, 79, 82, 85, 94, 95, 97, 138, 212 n. 21, 232 n. 21

Nellie Thomas (steamboat), 75

New Albany, Ind., 10, 24, 27, 43

New Evergreen (sternwheel steamboat), 106, 109, 110, 125, 127, 227 n. 39, 228 n. 49

New Idea (sternwheel steam showboat), 126, 158

New National (sidewheel steam gunboat), 65

New Orleans, La., 3, 10, 12, 14, 16, 17, 20, 21, 22, 23, 24, 25, 29, 30, 31, 35, 36, 37, 38, 42, 43, 44, 57, 70, 71, 73, 75, 76, 77, 78, 79, 81, 87, 89–90, 91, 92, 93, 94, 95, 97, 123, 124, 126, 158, 160, 211 n. 4

New Orleans and Bayou Sara Mail Company, 42

New Orleans and Bend Packet Company, 89, 92

New Orleans and Vicksburg Packet Company. *See* Pool Line

New Orleans Picayune, 37–38, 81, 90, 93, 97

New Orleans Wrecking and Salvage Company, 139

Newsboy (sternwheel steamboat), 72

Novelty (sternwheel steamboat), 136

O. G. Wagoner (sternwheel steamboat), 140

Ohio River, 10, 12, 23, 27, 85, 114, 115

Orange (sawmill steamboat), 129

Oriole (Union gunboat), 69–70

Oronoko (sidewheel steamboat), 18

Owen, Elias K., 66

Oxbows, Miss., 23, 132, 134

P. C. Wallis (sidewheel steamboat), 21

P. Line, 25, 71, 72, 74–76, 77–78, 79, 80, 81, 82, 83, 84, 85, 86–87, 88–89, 90, 91, 92–93, 94, 95, 96, 97–98, 99, 100, 101–02, 103, 107, 108–09, 110, 111, 112–13, 114, 116, 117, 118, 120, 121, 122, 125, 132, 133, 134, 135, 136, 137, 140, 141, 145, 148, 149, 152, 155, 158, 159, 160, 161, 165, 166, 229 n. 20; and mail contracts, 108, 117, 118, 227 n. 34, 228 n. 49

Pare, Charles, 101, 102, 220 n. 17

Pare, Sarah Dent, 102

Parisot, Amandus Augustus, 25–26, 81

Parisot, Franklin, 25

Parisot, Henry, 25

Parisot, Mary S. Lamkin, 76, 80, 83, 101, 102–03, 105, 111, 135, 166

Parisot, Sherman H., 9, 14, 24, 25–30, 35, 37, 44, 46, 49, 60, 64, 67, 70, 71–72, 73–76, 77–78, 79, 80–82, 83, 84, 85, 86, 88–89, 90, 91–92, 93, 94, 95, 96, 97, 98, 99–100, 101, 102–03, 109, 110, 111, 112, 113, 116, 117, 118, 119, 120, 122, 123, 124, 125, 132, 133, 134, 135, 136, 137, 138, 140, 141, 142, 145, 152, 155, 158, 160, 161, 162, 165, 166, 213 n. 38, 214 n. 4, 220 n. 9, 224 n. 31, 228 n. 49; land holdings of, 81, 88, 98, 102, 103, 104, 105, 106, 107–08, 109; his P. Line Home, 81, 88, 100, 102, 103, 105, 106, 120, 125, 162; farming ventures, 103–04; financial difficulties, 103–05, 106–07, 108, 226 n. 21

Parisot Line. *See* P. Line

Parmale, Andrew Jackson, 29

Parrisott, John M., 25

Patrick Henry (sidewheel steamboat), 18

Paul Jones (sidewheel steamboat), 49, 52, 71, 215 n. 29

Paul Pry (sternwheel steamboat), 11

Pemberton, John C., 59, 60, 61

Pepper, D. G., 117

Petrel (sternwheel steam gunboat), 63, 66, 69, 232 n. 21, 232 n. 26

Pettus, Edmund W., 61, 62

Peytona (sidewheel steamboat), 50, 60, 62, 65, 67, 218 n. 39, 219 n. 51, 219 n. 58, 232 n. 21

Phelps, Stephen L., 48

Phil Armour (sternwheel steamboat), 229 n. 20

Pinkney, Robert F., 44, 45, 48

Pitkin, W., 97

Pittman, W. B., 106

Pittsburgh, Pa., 10, 80

Plain City (sidewheel steamboat), 73, 116, 134, 228 n. 3

Planter (sidewheel steamboat), 35

Pleasants, F. P., 12, 31

Plummer, Franklin E., 25

Poland (sternwheel steamboat), 69, 135

Polk, Leonidas, 39

Pool Line, 71, 77–78, 82, 90, 91, 92, 93, 94, 95, 96, 97–98, 118

Porter, David D., 59

Powell, A. O., 18

Powell, B. F., 22, 24, 36

Powell, G. F., 128

Powell, J. D., 128

Power, Dyas, 22

Powers, Joseph J., 160, 234 n. 17

Prairie Bird (sidewheel steam gunboat), 66

Prince (sidewheel steamboat), 35

Prince of Wales (sidewheel steamboat), 37, 43, 56, 65, 218 n. 39, 219 n. 51, 232 n. 21

Pugh, William D., 109, 110–11, 112, 113, 121, 128, 130, 133, 134, 159, 160, 161, 162, 228 n. 50, 234 n. 17

Pugh Line, 109, 110, 111, 112, 113, 228 n. 49

Pugh Transportation Company, 234 n. 17

Quachita River, 21, 22

Quakemeyer, George, 109, 117, 160

Queen of the West (Union ramboat), 48

Quinby, Isaac, 60

Quiver River, 5, 42, 54, 62, 64, 65, 71

R. J. Lackland (sidewheel

steamboat), 42, 62, 63, 67, 232 n.
21, 232 n. 26
R. L. Cobb (sternwheel steamboat),
111, 132, 135, 228 n. 49
Railroads. *See* Steamboats: and
railroads
Ramay, W. F., 159
Ranger (sternwheel steamboat), 27,
28, 29
Raynolds, William F., 138
Read, Charles W., 47
Red River, 16, 23, 35, 38, 49, 52, 70,
73, 85, 215 n. 29
Reed, Thomas B., 51, 53, 55
Rees Pritchard (sternwheel
steamboat), 125, 161, 162, 229 n.
20
Reindeer (sidewheel steamboat), 7
Reives, John C., 36, 37, 49
Republic (sidewheel steamboat), 42,
63, 218 n. 38, 232 n. 21
Rescue (sternwheel steamboat), 161
Rice, Ruth, 126
Richardson, Ed, 80, 94
Richardson, Lee, 162
Richardson & May, cotton factors,
94, 104, 105
Richmond, Va., 50, 67
Richmond (sidewheel steamboat),
11
Roach, Benjamin, 53
Rob't E. Lee (steamboat), 43, 70, 71,
76, 77, 212 n. 21
Roebuck (sidewheel steamboat), 23,
27, 28
Rolling Fork, Miss., 59, 61, 133, 148
Roma Wheeler (sternwheel
steamboat), 72, 73, 118
Rover (sternwheel steamboat), 127,
129
Rundle, David B., 80, 84, 93, 111,
113, 228 n. 50
Ruth (sternwheel steamboat), 229
n. 22

S. H. Parisot (sternwheel
steamboat), 89–90, 91, 92, 93, 94,
95, 96, 103, 119, 120, 136, 229 n.
20
S. H. Parisot & Co., 103–04, 106,
108

S. H. Parisot & L. A. Campbell,
Cotton Factors, 81, 88, 101, 104
S. S. Prentiss (sidewheel steamboat),
14, 26–27, 30
St. James (sidewheel steamboat),
31–32
St. Louis, Mo., 4, 16, 69, 76, 84, 138,
162
St. Mary (sidewheel steamboat), 38,
44, 56, 57, 58, 61, 65, 66
Sallie Carney (sternwheel
steamboat), 94, 121, 122, 123, 124,
136
Sallie Robinson (sidewheel
steamboat), 22
Salvor Wrecking Company, 138
Sampson (Union boat), 48
Sannoner, J. H., 122
Sarah (sidewheel steamboat), 23,
32, 211 n. 4
Satartia, Miss., 11, 17, 26, 34, 37,
125, 132, 162
Sawyer, Philetus, 138
Scotland (sidewheel steamboat), 42,
63, 67, 232 n. 21
Scudder, John A., 84
Searles, S. J., 162
Seddon, James, 70
Selma, Ala., 50, 63, 70
Selma (sidewheel steamboat), 75,
228 n. 3
Seminole (sternwheel steamboat),
79, 229 n. 21
Service boats, 116, 118, 127–29, 130
Sharkey's Landing, 17, 97, 124, 164,
212 n. 21
Shawnee (sternwheel steamboat),
129
Sherman, William T., 51, 53, 59, 71,
218 n. 40
Shirley, James, 3, 4
Shirley, John T., 63
Showboats. *See* Steamboats: shows
on
Shreveport, La., 35, 79
Sidewheel steamboats, 9–10, 11,
13–14, 18–19, 39, 115, 116, 210 n.
14; guards of, 13, 115
Signal (sternwheel steam gunboat),
63, 65
Silver Creek, 103, 104, 105, 106, 107,

Silverthorn (sternwheel steamboat), 94, 96, 136

Smedes, T. M., 228 n. 50

Smith, F. G., 57

Smith, George H., 82, 84, 101

Smith, Mose, 135

Smith, Murray F., 82, 83, 84, 86, 88–89, 91, 93, 100, 101, 222 n. 1, 224 n. 31

Smith, Richard, 125

Smith, Thomas R., 64

Smith, Watson, 55, 56

Snyder's Bluff, 45–46, 49, 50, 51, 52, 53, 57, 58, 59, 60, 61, 62, 63

Southworth's Bar, 63, 67, 132

Spencer, A. Nye, 84

Sportsman (steamboat), 11

Star of the West (sidewheel steamboat), 38, 44, 56, 140, 216 n. 8, 232 n. 21

Steam propeller boats, 115, 117–18; as towboats, 118, 145, 158–59, 161

Steamboat landings, 8–9, 16

Steamboatmen, 99, 100, 101; lives of officers, 99; black deckhands, 100, 225 n. 2

Steamboats: builders of, 10, 12; physical specifications of, 10–11, 12–14, 15–16, 39, 42, 114–16, 210 n. 14; operating expenses on, 30; cargo carried, 31–32; and storms, 32; and low water, 33; wrecks, 33–35, 68, 69, 112, 122, 131, 132, 133, 134, 137–38, 141, 159; and railroads, 110, 145, 146, 147–49, 159, 164, 165; excursion trips on, 123–25; alcoholic beverages on, 125–26; shows on, 126–27, 158; and underwater obstructions, 131–34, 138–40; collisions of, 134–36; fires and boiler explosions on, 134, 136–37; passengers on, 149–50; freight services on, 150, 152, 154–55, 158, 163–64, 233 n. 5; and gasoline powered boats, 163, 164

Steele, Frederick, 60–61

Steele's Bayou, 5, 44, 46, 50, 55, 58, 59, 60, 136, 142, 150, 233 n. 33

Stella (sidewheel steamboat), 13

Sternwheel steamboats, 9, 10, 11, 12, 20, 39, 42, 115, 116, 118–23, 210 n. 14; "hog chains" of, 10, 20, 115; as towboats, 12, 19, 116, 158–59, 161

Stevens, George, 137

Stokes, William, 116, 124–25

Stout, Louisa H., 91

Strathmore (landing), 8, 9

Straszer, Justin, 140

Sturdivent, Ben W., 117

Submarine No. 11, 138, 232 n. 21

Submarine No. 12, 138, 232 n. 21

Sully (sidewheel steamboat), 73, 228 n. 3

Sunflower (steamboat), 82, 88

Sunflower Belle (sternwheel steamboat), 78

Sunflower River, 22, 24, 32, 36, 42, 45, 46, 50, 51, 53, 54, 55, 59, 60, 61, 62, 63, 64, 65, 66, 71, 72, 73, 75, 77, 79, 94, 107, 108, 109, 112, 117, 118, 122, 128, 132–33, 135, 136, 141, 142, 143, 148, 150, 155, 158, 159, 160, 161, 162, 163, 164, 218 n. 39, 218 n. 40

Sunflower River Packet Company, 107, 108, 109, 111, 113, 158

Susie B (sternwheel steamboat), 92

T. B. Butts (gasoline boat), 163

T. P. Leathers (sidewheel steamboat), 11, 12, 22

Tallahatchie (two steamboats with same name), 24, 31, 78, 82, 132

Tallahatchie River, 4, 5, 7, 8, 9, 17, 18, 21, 23, 24, 26, 29, 30, 32, 36, 42, 53, 55, 56, 57, 58, 60, 65, 73, 74, 75, 77, 79, 86, 87, 94, 97, 110, 117, 119, 121, 124, 126, 128, 129, 131, 132, 134, 136, 137, 140, 141, 142, 143, 148, 150, 155, 158, 161, 164, 221 n. 19, 233 n. 33

Talma (sidewheel steamboat), 3, 7

Tanner, J. J., 125

Tchula, Miss., 11, 17, 81, 82, 148

Tchula Lake, 5, 18, 27, 34, 42, 54, 57, 63, 64, 65, 112, 117, 133, 135, 137, 142, 143, 150, 159, 233 n. 33

Texana (sidewheel steamboat), 34

Thirty-Fifth Parallel (sidewheel steamboat), 46–47, 56–57, 67, 219 n. 56, 232 n. 21

Thomas B. Florence (sternwheel sawmill steamboat), 129
Thomas Powell (sternwheel steamboat), 71, 136
Thompson, Harper, 134
Thompson, Maggie Kinkead, 134
Tillatoba, Miss., 11, 17
Timmie Baker (sternwheel steamboat), 86, 132
Tobin, John W., 62, 70–71, 74, 75, 77, 78, 82, 90, 91, 92, 94, 95, 96, 117, 120
Tobin, Mary F., 91
Towboats (gasoline powered), 155, 158–59, 161. *See also* Sternwheel steamboats; Steam propeller boats
Trade Palace (steam propeller boat), 117, 127
Trader (sternwheel steamboat), 127–28
Treaty of Dancing Rabbit Creek (1830), 7
Treaty of Doaks Stand (1820), 7
Treaty of Fort Adams (1801), 7
Tributary (steam propeller boat), 108, 117, 118
Tunnard, Will H., 59, 60
Turnage, Mrs. Molly, 106
Tuttle, Abel C., *Complete Directory of the City of Vicksburg,* 140–41
Twain, Mark, 42, 99, 100
Tyler (sidewheel steam gunboat), 48

U. S. Aid (sternwheel steamboat), 34
Uncle Billie (sternwheel steamboat), 158
Underwriters Wrecking Company, 139
Unicorn (sidewheel steamboat), 31, 34
United States Army Corps of Engineers, 131, 136, 138, 139–40, 141, 142–43, 149, 150, 155, 158, 161, 163, 164, 233 n. 5
United States Circuit Court, Jackson, Mississippi, 104, 107
United States Fifth Circuit Court, 90, 91, 96, 97

United States Supreme Court, 96–97

Van Dorn, Earl, 47, 51, 53
Van Dorn (steamboat), 232 n. 21, 232 n. 26
Veteran (sidewheel steamboat), 33
Vicksburg (sternwheel steamboat), 34, 70, 75
Vicksburg, Miss., 5, 11, 12, 16, 17, 18, 21, 22, 23, 24, 25, 26, 27, 28, 29, 30, 31, 32, 33, 34, 35, 36, 37, 38, 39, 43, 44, 45, 46, 47, 48, 49, 51, 53, 54, 59, 60, 62, 64, 70–71, 73, 74, 75, 76, 77, 79, 80, 85, 86, 87, 90, 91, 92, 93, 94, 95, 96, 97, 98, 100–01, 102, 103, 107, 108, 109, 110, 111, 112, 117, 118, 120, 121, 123, 124, 125, 126, 133, 136, 137, 138, 139, 140, 142, 148, 149, 150, 152, 155, 158, 159, 160, 161, 162, 164
Vicksburg and Yazoo River Packet Company, 160, 234 n. 17
Vicksburg Whig, 11, 14, 27, 28, 32
Volant (sidewheel steamboat), 23, 25, 34

W. N. Sherman (sidewheel steamboat), 34, 213 n. 38
W. P. Swiney (sidewheel steamboat), 11–12, 31, 211 n. 4
Wabash Valley (sidewheel steamboat), 30
Wagoner (sternwheel steamboat), 34
Waite, Morrison R., 96–97
Walker, John G., 62, 63, 64, 65
Wallace, John S., 22, 23–24, 29, 34–35, 36
Wallis, P. C., 14
Walter Scott (sidewheel steamboat), 3, 7
Warren (sternwheel steamboat), 162
Warren Belle (sidewheel steamboat), 228 n. 3
Wash. Honshell (sternwheel steamboat), 229 n. 22
Waters, F. A., 29
Way, Frederick, Jr., 99
Wells, Charles V., 35
Whemhoff, Henry, 119
White, D. C., 109, 123, 128, 133, 159

White River, 11, 38
Whitehead, Irene C., 106
White's Bar, 132, 133
Wichita (sternwheel steamboat), 161, 162
Wiley, Joshua, 24, 27, 31, 36, 46, 49, 64, 71, 132, 136, 215 n. 20
Willard, Joseph L., 131, 142
William Garvin (steamboat), 27
Wilson, Charles G., 102
Wilson, John W., 101, 102
Wilson, John W., Jr., 102
Wilson, Margaret Dent, 102
Wilson, Victor, 102
Wimberly, A. T., 128
Wooldridge, Edmund H., 107
Wooldridge, Samuel L., 104, 105, 106, 107
Woolfolk, Richard H., 89

Yalobusha Line, 51, 53, 54
Yalobusha River, 5, 17, 18, 21, 34, 42, 51, 53, 55, 56, 65, 66, 73, 86, 94, 132, 142, 143, 147, 148, 233 n. 33
Yazonia (sternwheel steamboat), 99, 121–22, 125, 127, 136, 159
Yazoo (sidewheel steamboat), 13, 24, 36, 39, 49, 52
Yazoo (sternwheel steamboat), 74, 78, 125
Yazoo & Mississippi Valley Railroad, 149
Yazoo and Tallahatchie Transportation Company, 111, 113, 160, 228 n. 45, 228 n. 50
Yazoo City, Miss., 3, 5, 7, 8, 11, 12, 14, 17, 18, 19, 20, 21, 22, 24, 26, 27, 28, 29, 30, 31, 32, 34, 36, 37, 42, 44, 45, 46, 47, 54, 57, 61, 62, 63, 64, 65, 66, 69, 75, 76, 78, 79, 81, 82, 86, 88, 93, 94, 95, 96, 101, 103, 109, 110, 111, 112, 113, 117, 119, 121, 122, 123, 124, 126, 132, 133, 148, 149, 150, 152, 158, 159, 161, 162, 164, 218 n. 46, 219 n. 51

Yazoo City (sidewheel steamboat), 89
Yazoo City Herald, 81, 125, 133, 135
Yazoo City Transportation Company, 160–61, 163, 234 n. 17
Yazoo Competition Line, 75
Yazoo Cotton Oil Company, 128
Yazoo Delta, 4, 5–6, 16, 48, 60; sale of land in, 7–8; development of steamboat landing sites in, 8–9
Yazoo Democrat, 14, 22, 26, 28
Yazoo Diversion Canal, 161–62
Yazoo Pass, 5, 44, 55, 60
Yazoo Pass Expedition, 58, 60
Yazoo River, 3–5, 7, 8, 9, 10, 11, 12, 13, 14, 15, 16, 19, 21, 31, 34, 35, 37, 38, 39, 42, 43, 44, 45, 46, 47, 48, 49, 50, 51, 53, 55, 56, 57, 58, 59, 60, 61, 62, 63–64, 65, 66, 68, 69, 70, 71, 86, 89, 92, 100, 108, 124, 129, 135, 136, 138, 139, 140, 141, 142–43, 148, 158, 159, 161, 162, 163, 216 n. 8, 218 n. 39, 233 n. 33; steamboat trade on, 16–18, 20–23, 30–33, 37, 38, 69, 70, 72–73, 74–76, 77–78, 79–80, 81, 82, 85, 87, 88, 90, 91, 92, 93, 94, 95, 96, 97, 98, 107, 110, 112, 114, 117, 118–19, 120, 121, 127, 134, 143–44, 145, 146, 150, 155, 160, 161, 165–66, 211 n. 4, 215 n. 29; dangers of, 131–32, 133; and Rivers and Harbors Bill, 138–40; 1875 map of, 140, 141
Yazoo River Merchants and Planters Transportation Company, 86, 88, 134, 223 n. 11
Yazoo River Packet Company, 74. *See also* P. Line
Yazoo Sentinel, 102
Yazoo Valley (sternwheel steamboat), 76–77, 78, 82, 116, 119–20, 124, 125, 137, 149, 229 n. 20, 229 n. 23
Yazoo Valley Flag, 80, 86–87, 92, 93, 105
Young, John, 101
Young, Thomas F., 101, 141